Ad

I'm not sure how some ... business and profitability to something sinful, but it couldn't be further from the truth. God is creative, and He has given us the ability to create so that we may prosper. After all, it takes resources to responsibly care for yourself and your family, let alone feed the hungry and clothe the naked. In this book, Kevin Cullis shares what the Bible really says about doing business, making money and making it all work for God's glory.

Joel Comm, New York Times Best-Selling Author

"What a wonderful book Kevin has written! We are like that from which we come. We come from a Creator and therefore we create. God has given each of us gifts. The intersection of the thing you're most passionate about and the thing you're gifted and best at is usually where your greatest earning potential resides because that's typically where you can create the most value for people. This is no accident - it's a principle and in the nature of the design. God created the world based on principles and when we live in alignment with His principles, life just seems to work better. Some call this wisdom. And wisdom works whether in biz or your personal life. Kevin's book lays out a clear understanding of this and is a blessing for everyone in business."

Kevin Knebl, CMEC - Int'l Speaker/Author/Trainer
and Executive Coach

Kevin Cullis asks the question that Christian business owners should be asking, "How would Jesus do business?" The answers are found in this well-researched, meticulously-organized, biblically-grounded work that teaches the principles for success -- God's way. Surprised that Jesus would have answers to modern business problems? While much is made of the Jesus' public ministry, Cullis reminds us that He spent most of his earthly life as a craftsman and businessman. In fact over 80 percent of the parables relate to the marketplace. Not only should this be on the desk of every entrepreneur, it should also be on the desk of every pastor

David Rupert
Business communicator, teacher, and coach
Community Editor, the High Calling

Kevin Cullis shares his realizations and insights into Judeo-Christian business principles which have stood the test of time for thousands of years. I share his wonderment as to why someone hasn't written this book before! Kevin artfully lays the foundation starting with the credentials of the biblical authors and builds layers and complexities of tools and tips for winning results in our businesses, which are our life work.

Tim R. Brown
CEO, Plan B Dynamics
Castle Rock, CO

From tap dancing through business principles to igniting your fire for success, the essential elements of operating a business and putting your God-given talents to work are in this book. You'll catch yourself looking back to apply the information better. You'll learn to appreciate Biblical concepts more. You'll develop a greater understanding of success, and why you have a duty to yourself, your family, and your clients to BE SUCCESSFUL in business. This is required reading for every business owner.

Jan Verhoeff
CEO, Denver Web Studio

HWJDB How Would Jesus Do Business? is a book that contains many wonderful surprises. Each page is filled not just with worthwhile-to-read sentences, but the truth of the "Word of God" is interwoven in a unique way, that is available to the reader in a format that's easy to understand and visually pleasing to the eye. One golden nugget that I took as "my truth" is Kevin's explanation that "doing good" is when you serve another human being, elevating their situation, which is honorable and right and good from God's perspective and which in turn gives the "do-gooder" a reward that will last throughout eternity. Do good!

Wolfgang Kovacek
The CEO's New Best Friend
Los Angelos, CA

My brother from another mother, Kevin Cullis, has written another outstanding book for those considering, starting, or have already started their own business. While other books require that you search for their individual gold nuggets to take away and use, Kevin has provided a golden vein throughout his book of high quality Bible information, inspiration, and insights. God uniquely created each of us to fulfill His plan using our individual talents, so you and I are no accidents. Let go and let God! Kevin has been faithful to God's Word for business. And when you're faithful with the talents God has created you with and called you to perform, you'll receive bountiful blessings for your efforts! God is faithful!

Beatrice Bruno, The Drill Sergeant of LifeAuthor of, "How To Get Over Yourself" Series and "The Baby Chronicles"

I find that many Christians have an unstable relationship with money and the very concept of business. Some don't realize that a successful business is God's way of offering blessings! Instead of believing in the lies that the evil one tries to impose upon us, we need to be looking at what the bible says about business. We need to ask: how would Jesus do business? This is where Kevin's brilliant book comes in. His book brings a whole new way to perceive money and business; in a biblical way and a Godly way! This book helped me gain a whole new perspective on what I have to offer to the world through my business and how God sees me as a business woman! There is a reason why God intended for some of us to do business; for His glory!

Claudia Elms

Congratulations! Finally a book from someone, Kevin Cullis, without "alphabet soup" behind their name that gets to the heart of the heart. For a long time I have been coaching young entrepreneurs that they must be prepared to produce something rather than talking about something, and that their values must be consistent with their value. Kevin hits key areas (some between the lines) for entrepreneurs to be successful… a cohesive team, service to others, ethics, using Godly principles and life's lessons, just to name a few. Kevin has constructed a road map in his book on how success is achieved where the reward for their labor is not what they receive but what they become by it. Kevin's book is a must read for aspiring entrepreneurs.

Rick Ward
President/CEO, Rick Ward Consulting, LLC
Parker, CO

HWJDB

How Would Jesus Do Business?

Bible Secrets for Startups and Entrepreneurs

Kevin Cullis

Denver, CO

Title: HWJDB How Would Jesus Do Business?
Subtitle: Bible Secrets for Startups and Entrepreneurs

Disclaimer and Terms of Use: No information contained in this book should be considered as financial, tax, or legal advice. Your reliance upon information and content obtained by you at or through this publication is solely at your own risk. The author assumes no liability or responsibility for damage or injury to you, other persons, or property arising from any use of any product, information, idea, or instruction contained in the content or services provided to you through this book. Reliance upon information contained in this material is solely at the reader's own risk.

20160403

TX
ISBN-13: 978-1-5075826-19
ISBN-10: 1-5075826-17

I would like to thank my favorite Jewish business mentor, Jewish friend, and most importantly, my Lord and Savior, Jesus Christ, because He was able to articulate through His Word why people are in business for God.

John 15:13-15 Greater love has no one than this, that one lay down his life for his friends. You are My friends if you do what I command you. No longer do I call you slaves, for the slave does not know what his master is doing; but I have called you friends, for all things that I have heard from My Father I have made known to you.

Table of Contents

Introduction

Mark 8:36 For what does it profit a man to gain the whole world, and forfeit his soul?

I was not prepared for what I encountered. In October, 2013 I volunteered to help an organization sell its products at a local convention event. I always keep my eyes and ears open when I'm out and about to connect with others that are like minded and to find potential connections. Before the event started, I went in search for bottled water and met Jimmy Graham.[1] We both headed to get our water and on the way, gave our elevator speeches. He learned I served in the USAF during the first Gulf War I and I learned that he was a former Navy SEAL.

Navy SEAL?

I had researched about mental toughness in the Navy SEALs and other Special Forces to compare them to my experience with both entrepreneurs and Veterans. I had revised my first book[2] to reflect that mental toughness is the start of an entrepreneur's mindset. Meeting Jimmy I thought that maybe, just maybe, with my introduction to Jimmy I might be able to see if what I read about SEALs was true (Yep, everything is true). Besides, Navy SEALs are that difficult to find, and, because they're the "quiet professionals," they don't seek nor need the limelight. Meeting a former Navy SEAL in real life is more difficult than finding an animal on the endangered species list (they graduate less than 200 SEALs every year). There was a mutually beneficial reason I was hoping to grow a friendship with Jimmy going forward. And since our meeting, it has become a double

---

1 dutytoact.com

2 *How to Start a Business: Mac Version* by Kevin Cullis

blessing: we're of the brotherhood of Christ, first, and the brotherhood of the military, second (Additionally, a portion of ALL book sale profits will be donated to the navysealfoundation.org to continue supporting our service and family members in their time of need).

Jimmy and I collected our water and continued our discussion, eventually deciding to meet later to see how we could help one another. What started out as a one-time meeting over coffee turned into more frequent, longer, and more detailed discussions around our businesses. Our discussions also expanded to include how to help Christian men and ultimately, how helping men could help the broader Christian community. Our talks coalesced around both work and business issues and we've observed various stumbling blocks that were in our Christian paths, even if there were good intentions involved. The Christian state of affairs are less than positive and not near as productive for those needing help, nor as helpful doing God's purpose.

"Scripture has 500 verses on prayer, less than 500 verses on faith, but over 2,000 verses on the subject of money."[3] But something else became apparent. These 2,000 verses, and our weaknesses about the Bible, were not just about money. The themes were business, commerce, and business relationships, too. Neither Jimmy or I were alone in our perceptions within the Church. Jeffrey Van Duze was asked if he had any questions during a job interview for dean of the Seattle Pacific University business school. He replied, "'Well, you're a Christian business school; what difference does that make?' That question prompted us to do a big literature review [on business and theology], but hardly anything had been written."[4]

Judeo-Christian culture and communities. While God created Adam and Eve, the Bible tells the good, the bad, and the ugly, and codifies Man's behaviors and shows how sinful Man is. Through Noah, Abraham, Isaac and then Jacob, these were God's chosen. Later Jacob, as an individual, became a family and then a tribe and ultimately his family grew into a Jewish nation (Gen 49:16, 28) named Israel (Gen 32:28). Prime responsibility of each of God's chosen: *sharing of God and His message with your family, tribe, community, nation, and the rest of the world.*

Since Jesus was from Israel and Jewish, any conversation regarding Him, His life, and His business needs some background information. It should include the Torah and the Jewish community, God, and how to

---

3 bible.org See *Financial Faithfulness* by J. Hampton Keathley III

4 faithandleadership.com See *Jeffrey Van Duzer: Another way of doing business*

conduct life and business. Next, since Jesus was the "chief corner stone" (Acts 4:11) bringing both the Jews and Gentiles together, we must explore the same issues with the Body of Christ and Christian community. Being the chief cornerstone, Jesus reveals the Jewish and Christian similarities (salvation, love, faith, hope, etc.). He also showed the differences (the *Body of Christ* versus the *nation of Israel*, etc.), and are brought together in unity around a common theme of action: Serving God first and then your neighbor as yourself.

The discussion subjects Jimmy and I talked about were many, and they all have caused various levels of consternation, disagreement, and many arguments within the Judeo-Christian community. No matter the discussed subject, one issue that the Judeo-Christian Communities rarely, if ever, has delved into or learned to a good degree.

Jesus balanced His life as a Jewish general contractor businessman!

"Wait a minute, I thought Jesus was a carpenter?!" most Christians might say. But Jesus' neighbors asked, "Isn't this the carpenter (Greek τέκτων tektōn)?" (Mark 6:3; Matt. 13:55). The Greek word tektōn (where we get our word technology from) has been represented as "carpenter," but was more than that. Here is Strong's G5045 usage: a worker in wood, a carpenter, joiner, builder; a ship's carpenter or builder; any craftsman, or workman; the art of poetry, maker of songs; a planner, contriver, plotter; an author. Jesus was a builder, a craftsman. His first career, before His Ministry began at age 30, comes even more into focus when you see that *around 85 percent of Jesus' parables contained some "business" setting or topic.*[5] Additionally, many of the Greek words used in the parables were business terms. So it strongly indicates Jesus was an astute businessman and understood many industries and their details. (See Luke 14:25-35, specifically verse 28).

Why are Christians tap dancing around business?

So why has the Christian community not actively engaged this aspect of Jesus' life? Jesus started His ministry at age 30 *only after* He apprenticed under Joseph starting around age 12 and worked in His earthly construction vocation for nearly two decades! This intentional or not "dance of ignorance" indicates that Christians may or may not be fully productive or fulfilling their full potential for God. Have we ignored or neglected the very

---

5 tifwe.org See *Examining Jesus's inclusion of work roles in His parables* by Klaus Issler

experiential work and business foundation of Jesus' ministry? Or has Satan strategically misled us into believing a Christian's work, career, or business is bad? Here's the premise.

Jesus ran a successful Jewish business following Jewish law as God outlined it!

While Jesus was the Son of God, His nearly two decades of business experience should be a significant issue for all Christians. Also significant: Jesus fulfilled completely the Jewish law as God outlined it to be, not how Man saw it. There was *no fault or failure* in His application of Jewish law in His business, His transactions, His income, and His customer service.

> Matt 5:17 Do not think that I came to abolish the Law or the Prophets; *I did not come to abolish but to fulfill.* [emphasis added]

Jesus's comments, actions, and efforts were counter to what the Pharisees and the Sadducees were doing. His comments mean *God is for wealth or money*. God created money and wealth, no matter the amount, for our use by solving problems or elevating a person's situation. Doesn't God want *the best 10 percent or more of our earned wealth for Himself* while we decide how to be good stewards with the other 90 percent?

Money, wealth, and prosperity are inanimate tools to be used by man to work in an economy. Since these are the basic ideas, Jesus' commentary was *fighting against the specific Jewish denominational teachings that went against what God said* and what He wanted from them.

> Matt 16:11-12 "How is it that you do not understand that I did not speak to you concerning bread? But *beware of the leaven [yeast] of the Pharisees and Sadducees.*" Then they understood that He did not say to beware of the leaven of bread, *but of the teaching of the Pharisees and Sadducees.* [emphasis added]

What was (and is) Jesus so against in these teachings?

> Mark 7:8-9 "*Neglecting the commandment of God, you hold to the tradition of men.*" He was also saying to them, "You are *experts at setting aside*

the commandment of God in order to keep your tradition." [emphasis added]

Mark 7:9 of the Amplified Bible says, "And He said to them, You have a fine way of rejecting [thus thwarting and nullifying and doing away with] the commandment of God in order to keep your tradition (your own human regulations)!" Erroneous Judeo-Christian edicts and habits apply equally toward the spiritual and the physical side, and most important to this study, they apply to work, startups, entrepreneurs, and businesses in general. Improvements and advances in technology have helped man externally, but man's internal sinful soul and struggle will never change.

So that brings up some rather serious issues about who Jesus supported in His community then and today: Where is the positive role model of Jesus as a Jewish businessman for the Christian entrepreneur? What are the Christian business stumbling blocks in this unique aspect of Jesus' life? Jesus points out that it is not wealth or business that are the issues, He and others in the Old Testament were honorably successful in all aspects. Money, work, nor business is the root of evil, but it is the *love of wealth/ money that is the root of all evil* (i.e. greed, Pro 28:22, 1 Tim 6:10). Does that mean we as Christians are to avoid money? Work? Business? No, more than likely we're to learn how to handle money, work, and business in the right and honorable way. God's way.

Teaching about money, business, and business relationships in the Jewish community is more common than in the Christian community as a legitimate part of an honorable life. In fact, in the Hebrew language there is no word for "winning money," but only "earning money."[6] This significance is that all money should be earned and presupposes that you have provided a needed product or service in exchange for earned money. When an oil change, eye exam, or groceries are delivered, there's a vital exchange of money for a product or service.

Christians, however, have been hindered by both various theological, work, business, and wealth bias issues. Seminaries are partly to blame training pastors, ministers, and clergy that are ill-prepared for marketplace issues. Mark Green of London Institute for Contemporary Christianity says, churches see their primary mission as, "to recruit the people of God to use some of their leisure time to join the missionary initiatives of church-paid workers."[7] Ken Eldred's book *The Integrated Life: Experience the*

---

6 *Business Secrets from the Bible* by Rabbi Lapin, pg 97-100

7 patheos.com See *Challenges and Crises in Seminary and University Education*

Powerful Advantage of Integrating Your Faith and Work shows that the Church needs to do more with the Sunday-Monday gap of living your faith beyond the church doorstep. John Knapp's book *How the Church Fails Businesspeople* extends the application of faith-to-business conversation and how to integrate one's Christian faith and talent with the secular and business world. George Barna, a foremost researcher of modern Christianity in the country, recently spoke about a two-year research project studying why modern-day pastors and churches are so silent regarding political issues, including those which affect businesses.

> *"What we're finding is that when we ask them about all the key issues of the day, [90 percent of them are] telling us, Yes, the Bible speaks to every one of these issues. Then we ask them: Well, are you teaching your people what the Bible says about those issues?--and the numbers drop...to less than 10 percent of pastors who say they will speak to it."*[8]

Politics affect businesses, so entrepreneurs need to be involved. It's not just politics, but today's Christian clergy, pastors, even lay people often show benign neglect, or even outright hostility, toward the marketplace and business in general.[9] Regarding work and the marketplace, "Our surveys reveal that 90-97 percent of Christians have never heard a sermon relating biblical principles to their work life," Sherman writes.[10] He says that being a USAF fighter pilot, he hung around the flight room with the other fighter jocks, no different than a business break room or other company or industry hangouts. A Type A personality fighter pilot or Special Forces military member is driven to succeed, but inherent with this "pushing the envelope" of one's personal capabilities comes a harshness and bravado that is always present. That is, until the military chaplain walks into the room, then the bravado gets sucked right out of the air.

A chaplain entering the fighter pilot world is about as awkward as the fighter pilot walking into the chapel. Fighter pilot Top Gun heroes are in stark contrast to the heroes in ministry laboring "on the street" to spread the gospel worldwide, start ministries, or grow churches. And this attitude shows in how the church views work and business.

---

8 chuckbaldwinlive.com See *New Research: Pastors Deliberately Keeping Flock in the Dark*

9 christianitytoday.com See *Scripture and The Wall Street Journal*

10 *Your Work Matters to God* by Doug Sherman

> *[When there is] "an unspoken word that says workplace believers are second class citizens spiritually by the words and actions [of others],...we commission missionaries in public services without ever commissioning workplace believers as having equal importance,...and we equate ministry with their activity in the local church, we are saying the rest of the week at work is not ministry."*[11]

While Jesus taught in the synagogue, consider this. In the New Testament, of Jesus' 132 public appearances, 122 were in the marketplace. Of 52 parables Jesus told, 45 had a workplace context. Of 40 miracles in the book of Acts, 39 were in the marketplace.[12] That is where most of Jesus' ministry took place. Jesus spent most of His life learning the Torah and being in business before going into His Ministry, shouldn't Christians learn and use His business life as a model for their ministry and career? Shouldn't pastors and ministers need this training, then apply it to a new focus of a major "9-5 Window of Work" ministry? Better yet, how about those that do shift work versus the typical "9-5 professional" career? The time is now for a *conversation and a conversion* to this new information that Christians must have to further the cause for Christ.

But it's not all "doom and gloom" regarding Christians at work or in business, the path is shifting towards a more "groom and bloom" because of an uptick in recent years in the number of pastors who say they preach on work. But since "most church-goers still doubt the significance of their work to God," more work is needed. A 2014 study[13] found three responses that give insights into what church-goers see at church regarding their work:

1. "I love the work I do" (42% agree)
2. "I can clearly see how the work that I am doing is serving God or higher purpose" (30% agree)

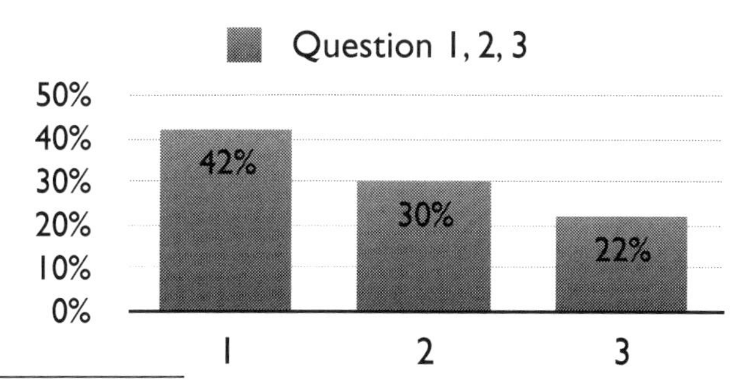

11 intheworkplace.com See *What Is Workplace Ministry?* by Os Hillman

12 *marketplaceleaders.org* See the article, *Jesus was a workplace minister*

13 centerforfaithandwork.com See *Is the Gap Between Pulpit & Pew Narrowing?*

3. "I believe that the work I am doing is just as important as the work of a pastor or priest." (22% agree)

God and the Bible: source and authority for business

When discussing the bible and business together, there should be few differences between both Jewish[14] and Christian thoughts about work and entrepreneurship, sadly there are, but shouldn't be. So it is with the differences between Apple and Microsoft, both are IT companies and both employ humans to do their work, but both have differences.

For the purposes of this book, the New American Standard Bible (NASB) text will be used in quoting Bible verses so that things are consistent. However, the Amplified Bible will be used on occasion to dig deeper into the Bible's meanings. I'll use the generic term Man/man when discussing the sexes and is in no way a disparagement toward working or business women; it keeps the writing simple.

This book will be by no means an exhaustive research on entrepreneurship in the Bible from a Judeo-Christian perspective, but is meant to be a general overview into the work and business that Man is required to perform. Men and women are required to work to stay alive, earn their keep, and to be productive in a society.

There are three reasons why we are looking at Judeo-Christian views. First, because God chose Israel and the Jews to be His people. Second, God "wrote" both of the Jewish and Christian texts, and third, Jesus was a Jew. Since Jesus brought together both the Jew and Gentile, understanding both sides of the Judeo-Christian perspectives of life, liberty, and the pursuit of happiness as an entrepreneur becomes important. How one views and interprets the Bible and how God works determines how one sees both one's calling and life's work under His will. It also determines how we connect as a vibrant community of businesses and customers.

Theology, work, and business. Theology is the study of the nature of God and religious belief. Doctrine is a belief or set of beliefs held and taught by a church or synagogue. Errors are just that: errors in one's beliefs. The Bible provides a study in human nature and behaviors, both the good and the bad, the heavenly and the evil. We'll start from the Bible for this perspective to address startups, entrepreneurship, and business.

Since Jesus was Jewish, we'll start with Jewish views of business and their views of business and life that Jesus fulfilled in His business dealings.

---

14 jewishencyclopedia.com

Finally, we'll look at some of the Christian views of business within the Christian community.

It was not until I was nearly done with this book that I realized that writing my first book *How to Start a Business: Mac Version* gave me the basic knowledge to tackle this new project. God's plans sometimes feel like driving on a winding rural road at night and only being able to see as far as the headlights can shine. God has the plans; we do the work, He causes the increase and growth!

Lastly, this book is not an attempt to elevate business above spirituality. It is to learn how one's spirituality becomes the source and inspiration for one's business and work. It also gives one the opportunity to spread the gospel of Jesus Christ, grow His Kingdom, and of serving our neighbors for His sake. This book has a sequence that builds upon the previous portion, just as in erecting a building. If you have difficulty, you may reference the previous chapter or section and see how your foundation is constructed.

In essence:

> *This book is more about providing a "toolbox" of information and insights for startups and businesses in determining God's plan for you and your business and work and your neighbor, and less about having a "fine dining experience" of reading biblical content.*

Your eternal salvation - it's the thought that counts

Eternal Truth: Eternal Life. Starting a business by yourself is an endeavor that requires talents and tenacity, but when God is on your side, the process, support, and progress is much greater than without Him. So let's start at the very beginning.

How does an individual receive eternal life has a rather simple answer, sometimes people think it is too simple, but that's the point. When you explain the salvation message so a child can understand, then the message is simple enough. So here's the story.

> Luke 23:39-43 *One of the criminals* who were hanged there was hurling abuse at Him, saying, "Are You not the Christ? Save Yourself and us!" But the other answered, and rebuking him said, "Do *you not even fear God,* since you are under the same sentence of condemnation? And we indeed are suffering justly, for we are

> receiving what we deserve for our deeds; but *this man has done nothing wrong*." And he was saying, "Jesus, *remember me* when You come in Your kingdom!" And He said to him, "Truly I say to you, *today you shall be with Me* in Paradise." [emphasis added]

This is the perfect example and picture of the salvation message. Two individuals were "condemned" to die for their criminal actions and behaviors. But notice that neither of the robbers can do anything from where they are. They're hanging on a cross; they will die a slow and painful death, and they can't change this path or what is about to happen to them.

Then, with both of them hanging on a cross with Jesus, one of the robbers *sees Jesus for who He really is* (the Son of God coming to die for a sinful world) and *who he is* (a sinful man).

The robber had one thought before he spoke: "Remember me!"

Jesus, the Son of God, intimately knows our thoughts.

The robber's thoughts reached Jesus.

Immediately Jesus seals the robber's fate for all eternity with Him.

Because we are expressive individuals, the robber made his thought into a simple request, "Jesus, remember me when You come in Your kingdom."

The robber's thought sealed his fate with Jesus and he was bound for Paradise. Jesus comfortingly replies, "Truly I say to you, today you shall be with Me in Paradise."

It is that simple.

The one thought, "I believe in Jesus," and you're saved for all eternity.

The simplicity of eternal life is just one thought.

It is also in one verse.

> John 3:16 For God so loved the world, that He gave His only begotten Son, that *whoever believes in Him shall not perish, but have eternal life*. [emphasis added]

A simple act of faith, belief. That's all it took and all it takes.

The Holy Spirit convicts every person of their sinfulness and in the need for the saving work of Jesus Christ. There is only *one sin* which God will never forgive. It is the sin of unbelief, i.e. failing to listen to the Holy Spirit convicting you of the need to believe in Jesus as Savior. It is unbelief that is unforgivable; *every other sin* has been, is, and will be, forgiven.

> John 16:8 And He, when He comes, will *convict the world concerning sin and righteousness and judgment*; [emphasis added]

The conviction by the Holy Spirit of one's sinfulness…

> John 16:8-9 And He, when He comes, *will convict the world concerning sin and righteousness and judgment; concerning sin,* because they do not believe in Me; [emphasis added]

…is coupled with the need for Jesus redemption, comfort, and relief that God loves you unconditionally.

> Rom 5:8 But *God demonstrates His own love toward us*, in that while *we were yet sinners,* Christ died for us. [emphasis added]

But what else can we gather from the book of Luke regarding the robbers and receiving salvation from God? Neither of the thieves could get circumcised (to become Jewish), join a local synagogue, give money, get baptized, do mission work or perform any number of various Jewish (or today's Christian) expected duties or actions. All they could do was hang on their respective crosses and prepare to die.

But let's get a full picture of these two robbers from two other verses.

> Matt 27:44 *The robbers* who had been crucified with Him *were also insulting Him with the same words.* [emphasis added]

Notice, the *robbers*, plural, were insulting Jesus Christ while all three of them were hanging on the cross. The word "insulting" in Greek means "to reproach, upbraid, revile." To "reproach" means to "address (someone) in such a way as to express disapproval or disappointment." To "upbraid" means to "find fault, scold." To "revile" means to "criticize in an abusive or angrily insulting manner." So in other words, both thieves were not saying nice words to Jesus. And the next verse.

Mark 15:32 "Let this Christ, the King of Israel, now come down from the cross, so that we may see and believe!" *Those who were crucified with Him were also insulting Him.* [emphasis added]

The two thieves were part of the mob mentality. *Both robbers* were insulting and cursing Him. But at some point, and we don't know when, in Luke's version one of the robbers has a change of heart.

Reading the other verses we have a better picture. Both were insulting Jesus, and one has a change of heart. It boils down to just one word for the thief, and applies for *every individual in the world.*

Believe!

That's it. John 3:16 above says it simply enough. When you see the two robbers being crucified together with Jesus, on their very own "deathbed" hanging on a cross, gaining eternal life could not have been any easier. The perfect illustration to eternal life: one thief believes, one thief does not.

Believe!

Faith alone in Christ alone. Faith + nothing else. God is fair, His path to salvation has not changed. He's unchangeable. If you see this story and Jesus says this is salvation, then this process applies equally for everyone else in the world. There are no other "roads" or "avenues" for gaining eternal life. To add anything more to salvation is to add to what God's Essence and His Word says.

Eph 2:8-9 For *by grace you have been saved through faith*; and that not of yourselves, it is *the gift of God*; not as a *result of works, so that no one may boast.* [emphasis added]

Positional Truth: Eternal Security. The instant you believe, you are eternally secure and have eternal life because the Bible says so (and in multiple places regarding the same topic), just as Jesus said it. But here is the strongest verse.

Heb 13:5 Make sure that your character is free from the love of money, being content with what you have; for He Himself has said, "I WILL NEVER DESERT YOU, NOR WILL I EVER FORSAKE YOU," [Josh 1:5]

What is interesting about this verse is reading it in the Amplified Bible because the Greek verse has three negatives in it (which you don't get in English). "Let your character or moral disposition be free from the love of money [including greed, avarice, lust, and craving for earthly possessions] and be satisfied with your present [circumstances and with what you have]; for He [God] Himself has said, I will not in any way fail you nor give you up nor leave you without support. [I will] not, [I will] not, [I will] not in any degree leave you helpless nor forsake you nor let [you] down (relax My hold on you)! [Assuredly not!]."

What a statement made by God regarding you, your salvation, and your life and business. He has complete control over your eternal and physical life, you can trust Him to take care of you, no matter what. Regardless of what any man may say, you're eternally secure no matter what you do here on earth.

Once saved, always saved.

You cannot please God with your efforts in your life and your business until you connect with Him on a personal level, following His direction and will using your efforts. All of your efforts, even being in business, will be worthless until you're saved, however all is not lost, God will still use your unsaved past for His future work from you.

> Heb 11:6 And *without faith it is impossible to please Him*, for he who comes to God must believe that He is and that *He is a rewarder of those who seek Him.* [emphasis added]

Because *Jesus saves*, you can trust and rely upon Him and the Holy Spirit's power and guidance for your eternal salvation and to keep you *in Him.* For those that might tell you that you can lose your salvation, their view of salvation *relies upon some form of effort or work on your part.* No matter how small an effort is, salvation is no longer 100 percent grace of what Jesus Christ provides when *any work or effort* shows up in one's salvation. It is no longer grace.

Experiential Truth: Eternal Rewards. Once you're eternally saved, your focus now is on growing in the knowledge of Jesus Christ and in doing good works. Learn to *know what is good,* so you can accurately tell what good works are, then *do good.*

> Eph 2:8-10 For *by grace you have been saved through faith*; and that *not of yourselves*, it is the *gift of God; not as a result of works*, so that *no one may boast.* For *we are His workmanship*, created in Christ Jesus *for good works*, which *God prepared beforehand* so that *we would walk in them.* [emphasis added]

You can trust Him, eternally, securely, now that you're saved. The grace of God says you do good after salvation because you *received* salvation, never because you *earned* salvation. Now that your eternal life is secure at the moment you decide, you're to work toward heavenly rewards based on God's purpose for our life, using both your physical talents and your spiritual gift, in love.

> 1 Cor 3:11-14 For no man can *lay a foundation other than the one which is laid, which is Jesus Christ.* Now if any man builds on the foundation with gold, silver, precious stones, wood, hay, straw, *each man's work will become evident;* for the day will show it because it is to be revealed with fire, and the fire itself will test the quality of each man's work. If *any man's work which he has built on it remains, he will receive a reward.* [emphasis added]

All works that glorify God will be eternally rewarded for all to see, all human works that glorify us will be burned up (See Chapter six below for a more detailed discussion of this issue).

Here is how it looks in a practical view.

Positional: Salvation	**Experiential: Christian Walk**
"Believer in Christ"	"Follower of Christ"
Faith + Nothing	Faith + Works
Eph 2:8-9 For **by grace you have been saved through faith;** and that not of yourselves, it is the gift of God; **not as a result of works,** so that no one may boast.	James 2:17 Even so **faith, if it has no works, is dead,** being by itself.

Sin less versus sinless. Being eternally secure with the positional truth of salvation means you're still a sinner, but now eternally bound for heaven. Of prime importance is that now as a child of God, you may *sin less*, as you learn to live as God (Father, Son, and Holy Spirit) want you, you sin less over time, but you never are *sinless*, i.e. you never sin again. If you consider yourself sinless, you're no longer a *child of God*, but you become a *brat of God*, subject to His discipline (Heb 12:5-11) of your life. Sinless perfection is not what God intends, but He emphasizes us to sin less over time.

Your Christian walk and life in a nutshell is this statement.

> *God created you for worship, to create work, to serve others, to prosper, and to share.*

Won't you believe in Jesus right now? He loves you; He died for you, He loves you, He wants YOU, we all want YOU, to become a part of His forever family. He loves you and will take you just as you are. Right now.

It takes one act. Your one thought counts.

Believe right now.

This one thought counts for eternity. Believe!

This book's premise and hope

At a conference at Princeton Theological Seminary gathered a number of Fortune 500-type corporations, they were accompanied by ministers, priests, and rabbis from their churches and synagogues.

> *"One thing stood out boldly. The business leaders were largely innocent of biblical ethics as well as the daily doings of congregation and denomination, and religious leaders were largely innocent of modern economics, as well as the daily doings of a business."*[15]

Zinbarg's book *Faith, Morals, and Money* came out in 2005, it seems like the issue has not gone away and has been around for a long time. His comment seems to be traced to changes in our educational history over 100 years ago.

> *When the great universities moved the study of economics from their religious departments to their science departments, they were actually driving a wedge*

15 *Faith, Morals, and Money*, by Edward Zinbarg, pg 172

> *between the profoundly uplifting activity of business and the moral arguments and spiritual dimensions that underpin the validity of economics.*[16]

I am editing this book in the November 2014, and I had a conversation with my wife about her real estate business. She discussed an interaction between her and a colleague, how the colleague had a neighbor, a mother, and her baby, and both died during the birth. My wife's colleague was upset about the situation: How could a loving God allow something so precious, a mother and her child, die? We talked about it, and I helped my wife see what she could do, but this was not the end of our conversation, it was just the beginning.

My wife was also upset; she felt that her real estate job was not "as worthy" compared with someone like me, mentoring others in their business or a pastor following their "calling." I told her nonsense! Serving others with one's talents is honorable, but then this issue is what I had encountered in my research. Then the day after our talk, I connected via LinkedIn (in the group *Faith Driven Business*) with Eric, a geologist, who wrote me and commented about the ideas in this book and said:

> *At times I think I am weird because the Lord has been leading me on an interesting path. Some talk of the second reformation, but it seems [we need] a total makeover. We cannot expect 1% of the body of Christ to accomplish the task our master has entrusted in our hands. All hands have to get on deck for us to impact our communities in a meaningful way. It has to go beyond the walls of the local church.*

I was shocked. Not at my wife's comment about her not being worthy working in real estate or Eric feeling "weird." We as a community seem to be exhibiting what is in James 2:1, "My brethren, do not hold your faith in our glorious Lord Jesus Christ with *an attitude of personal favoritism* [emphasis added]." This favoritism shows up by the "heroes" we hold up, pastors, worship leaders, etc., and seem to lessen the efforts of those who work "in the trenches" outside the church. Some are considered or consider themselves "less" because they were not "called to the ministry," when in fact, God called each of us to *full time ministry* with each of our unique ministries. We work to *serve someone else, not to be subservient* (love your neighbor *as* yourself), by using all of our skills and talents in what God has called us to do. Our heroes are not just the Navy SEALs or a pastor, but it's

---

16 *Thou Shall Prosper*, by Rabbi Lapin, pg 163

also a single mom or dad taking care of their family, the garbage collector, someone suffering burnout, or the forgotten homeless.

Work = Worship. Work (Hebrew עָבַד `abad) in Hebrew means both to work and to worship. *Work as in worship:* Exodus 8:1 – "Thus saith the LORD, Let my people go, that they may serve me." And "My Father is always at his work to this very day, and I, too, am working" (John 5:17). *Work as in labor:* Exodus 34:21 – Moses renewing the covenant with God says, "You shall work six days, but on the seventh day you shall rest."[17] When we are productive at work as God designed us serving Him and others. We're worshiping God with our talents and gifts serving Him and others.

My hope. My hope is fourfold:

1. **Change the path of Christian culture.** The focus of this book is to change our Christian culture for the better, to get on track what we're to do on this earth in the marketplace.

2. **Pastors need to add more content.** Pastors, do not buy my book and preach from it. Rather tell your whole congregation to buy one. Then, having kicked off this new business ministry, now dig into the Bible and *add more content* from the ideas laid out here. We lack good Christian business content in the Church. Pastors need to be "equipping the saints for the work of service, to the building up of the body of Christ." We need to equip fellow believers with information, principles, and tools from the Bible, but let believers do the work as God leads them, because *business is the mission* in the marketplace.

3. **Multiply and duplicate the change.** Congregations, buy this book, read it and discuss it. Then partner up with your church leadership and congregation and let God lead you and how to apply everyone's unique talents and gift towards His goals and will as a team.

4. **Businesses change how you do business.** Do not fit people into your job description box, but find out what each person's unique and many talents and abilities are. Use them in such a way that it maximizes their talents, spiritual gift, and skills in your organization. Not per your organizational chart, but organized by who they are toward your business goals. It means changing the process of how your Human Resources views each person. Imagine when your whole organization has everyone firing on all cylinders instead of half, imagine how much more productive your organization will be.

---

17 aholyexperience.com See *Avodah: The One Act of Work and Worship*

Until the day God calls us home to be with Him, we all have more learning and work to do, so let's get cracking!

Faith without works is dead, or in business lingo, ideas are a dime a dozen, it's all about execution.

Execute!

1 Biblical foundation for business

Gen 1:1 In the beginning, God created…

During one of my many conversations with Jimmy regarding struggling with our businesses, I was struck by a thought. As one who has process improvement skills, you look for the root of a problem to solve, not a symptom or an assumption to solve, so you don't waste resources. My thought: if we were all struggling with various business issues, was there a hint of a larger problem? How much or little did our parents teach us about money and business? I asked Jimmy, "What did your father teach you about money?" He replied, "Nothing." Tim, also in the group's conversation, said, "Well, I got a little more, all my dad said was, 'Save your money!' and that was it." Two other gentlemen in the group also said they, too, got very little "training" from their parents and had learned it all on their own. While money was the topic at hand, further questions revealed that we were all not alone when it came to the lack of learning about money, work, and especially business. Did others have similar experiences growing up? How is one prepared, or not, to earn a living? Or start a business, if at all?

I was in the final stages of writing my first book *How to Start a Business: Mac Version* when I attended a CIPA[18] book publishing conference in Denver. I wanted to learn what came next after writing it and what it takes to have a best selling book. I learned it was not just about the book by itself, but it also included market research, book sales, and the business side of books, i.e. how to make a profit as an author.

18 cipacatalog.com

Tama Kieves[19] was their luncheon keynote, and she discussed her life growing up. She told of one afternoon running into her Brooklyn Jewish home after school, and with bubbly excitement said to her mother, "I know what I want to be when I grow up!"

"What?" her mother asked.

"I want to be a writer!" she said a certain youthful clarity in her voice. Over time, however, she was ultimately persuaded to pursue something different. She dutifully and tenaciously applied herself and graduated with honors from Harvard Law School and then joined a prestigious corporate law firm. Thereafter, she started seeing a therapist.

"What seems to be the problem?" asked the therapist.

"I don't like what I do!"

After listening to her story, he asked: "What do you want to do?"

"I just want to write!"

"Well, go and do that?" the therapist finally summarized.

So, she did. That's the short of it, but you get the idea.

Kieves left one of Denver's largest elite corporate law firms to write and eventually became the bestselling author of *This Time I Dance! Creating the Work You Love.* Today Kieves helps others discover and soar in their life's work.

During the Q&A part of her keynote, I asked her a rather geeky question: "What kind of analog or digital tools do you use?"

Long pause.

My smile quickly vanished. I had caught her off guard, so now I was caught a little off guard.

"What?!" she asked somewhat mystified.

Somewhat taken aback and thinking fast, I repeated my question, "Well, … what analog or digital tools do you use in your writing?"

She looked bewildered. Our exchange was not going well.

I quickly added, "I mean, do you use mostly pen and paper or do you use a computer, and what computer programs do you use for your writing? Or, what other methods do you use to help you write?" As a struggling writer myself, I wanted to know what she uses to help her with her writing that might help me out.

"Oh, OK, I got it now. Because at first *I didn't have a clue* as to what you asked me," she said. She proceeded to tell me that she writes with pen and paper because she has to feel the pen and paper in her hands when she writes. Talking with her later at her vendor table she had to ask her husband

---

19 tamakieves.com

what computer software she used. By the tone of her questions to him, she rarely used them, if at all.

In a recent email reintroduction after our only encounter, I reminded her of my question and that she may not have remembered me. She answered back, "I DO remember you! And even your question…which threw me then and would throw me now!"

Kieves finally found and trusted her internal "voice" or "calling," not following someone else's, after many years of strong, disciplined, and sadly some misguided efforts in getting her law degree from Harvard. Many of us search out what we're supposed to do, frustrated that we have not found the right fit for who we are and where we belong in life. Imagine if Kieves had taken those years of disciplined Harvard efforts and applied them to her correct path and what she is born to do, how much further would she have gotten in life? It's a matter of finding your right "groove" (remember, God *never lets bad things go to waste*, "all things work together for good," Rom 8:28).

For example, the creative bunch and entrepreneurs, more so than others, use different methods, habits, and processes to get their ideas out of their heads and into the marketplace. Writers are no different, and they're not a strictly "nine to five" bunch.[20] C.S. Lewis, author of *Mere Christianity*, *The Chronicles of Narnia*, and *The Screwtape Letters,* talked about what motivated his writing and some of his habits:

> *"I would choose always to breakfast at exactly eight and to be at my desk by nine, there to read or write till one. If a cup of good tea or coffee could be brought me about eleven, so much the better. A step or so out of doors for a pint of beer would not do quite so well; for a man does not want to drink alone and if you meet a friend in the taproom the break is likely to be extended beyond its ten minutes. At one precisely lunch should be on the table; and by two at the latest I would be on the road. Walking and talking are two very great pleasures, but it is a mistake to combine them. The return from the walk, and the arrival of tea, should be exactly coincident, and not later than a quarter past four. Tea should be taken in solitude, as I took it as Bookham on those (happily numerous) occasions when Mrs. Kirkpatrick was out; the Knock himself disdained this meal. For eating and reading are two pleasures that combine admirably. Of course not all books are suitable for mealtime reading. At five a man should be at work again, and at it till seven. Then, at the evening meal and after, comes the time for talk, or, failing that, for lighter*

20 jamesclear.com/daily-routines-writers

reading; and unless you are making a night of it with your cronies (and at Bookham I had none) there is no reason why you should ever be in bed later than eleven."[21]

Ernest Hemingway, author of *The Old Man and the Sea*, *The Sun Also Rises*, and *A Farewell to Arms* talked of his writing routine:

"When I am working on a book or a story I write every morning as soon after first light as possible. There is no one to disturb you and it is cool or cold and you come to your work and warm as you write."

Benjamin Franklin's father pointed out his lack of "elegance of expression," so he taught himself to write more elegantly and expressively. Franklin wrote *Poor Richard's Almanac*, *The Art of Virtue*, and *The Way To Wealth* and made mental notes about his writing:

Ben Franklin knew the benefits of working long hours, as well as being known among his peers as being a person who worked long hours. This work ethic was essential for growing his printing business. He also had a routine of asking himself questions during the day. Ben Franklin asked himself each morning (at 5 am), "What good shall I do today?" every night before bed (around 10 pm), "What good have I done today?"[22]

Every individual has a personal approach to how they work. Some can be rather odd at times, but one can pull examples from these famous authors and apply some of their better habits to one's life. This personal approach is not just for writers. Learning from others will make you better, or as another well-known person says.

Learn to do common things uncommonly well; we must always keep in mind that anything that helps fill the dinner pail is valuable. — George Washington Carver

Each of us has completely different talents, gifts, and processes, but all of us need to be productive. Learning from God and others will make us

---

21 dailyroutines.typepad.com See *C. S. Lewis*

22 creativethinking.net See *Weird habits and rituals of famous historical figures*

HWJDB F

Love

better individuals and we need to take our God-giver use them to serve others.

Entrepreneurs, more than others, are people th. strike out on their own as God has designed us each to It is His model that we will explore in the following pages.

"Some see private enterprise as a predatory target to be shot, others as a be milked, but few are those who see it as a sturdy horse pulling the wag
— Winston Churchill

Before you build a house, you have to have a plan, and then you have to build on a strong foundation. Once the foundation is in, you add other floors, erect walls, and roof, then begin adding interior plumbing, HVAC, and the rest of the "infrastructure." After the outside, you work on the inside. Next it's a matter of adding the furniture, picture frames, and filling the fridge with food and drink. The house is complete. Now it's on to the exterior and landscaping, and it's now a home for the family.

What if the foundation of the house is either designed incorrectly or poorly installed? The house would be potentially dangerous to the family requiring extensive repairs to avoid the whole house needing to be demolished and rebuilt from the ground up. Not a pretty sight and it would be costly for any customer or builder to have to redo, but it was preventable.

Jesus talks about a strong and a weak foundation.

Luke 6:47-49 "Everyone who *comes to Me* and *hears My words* and *acts on [does] them*, I will show you whom he is like: he is like a man building a house, who dug [dug and went] deep and *laid a foundation on the rock*; and when a flood occurred, the torrent [river] burst against that house and could not shake it, because it had been well built. But the one who has heard and *has not acted accordingly*, is like a man who *built a house on the ground without any foundation*; and the torrent [river] burst against it and immediately it collapsed, and *the ruin of that house was great.*" [emphasis added]

That is the perspective this book will explore. If you've always wanted to know the basics of what the Bible says about business, this is the place to start. You'll understand the foundational issues about starting and running a business from God's perspective, not the secular world.

your neighbor AS yourself, not FOR yourself

"Jesus lived a Jewish life," a knowledgeable person might say to you.

"Undeniable," would be your reply.

"Jesus was a carpenter/builder," they'd say, getting more detailed.

"No questions there," would be your comeback.

"Jesus ran a successful Jewish business for nearly two decades!" they could reply, smiling as they waited for your reaction.

"What? Hold on there!" you'd say in astonishment. "That's not a subject that I have been taught or learned in church. Well, maybe I might have heard about it, but I didn't give it much thought. I mean, I'm mostly concerned with the 'higher issues' of eternal life, spirituality, and God Himself to be too concerned with such earthly issues," as you begin contemplating this new thought.

Jesus was grounded in the Jewish Torah regarding His life and His ministry. But it seems there is one often overlooked aspect of Jesus' life by the Christian community: running His business as God intended it.

In the Gospels, Jesus was tested by certain Jewish denominations and individuals, some hostile, some not, but not all Jews approached Him with the same line of trapping questions. Here is one such example that gives us a glimpse into His thinking regarding this line of questioning.

> Matt 22:34-40 But when the Pharisees heard that *Jesus had silenced* the Sadducees, they gathered themselves together. One of them, a lawyer, asked Him a question, *testing* Him, "Teacher, which is the *great* commandment in the Law?" And He said to him, " 'YOU SHALL LOVE THE LORD YOUR GOD WITH ALL YOUR HEART, AND WITH ALL YOUR SOUL, AND WITH ALL YOUR MIND.' [Deu 6:5] This is the great and foremost commandment. The second *is like it*, 'YOU SHALL LOVE YOUR NEIGHBOR AS YOURSELF.' [Lev 19:18]. On these two commandments *depend* the whole Law and the Prophets."[emphasis added]

Love that is dependent upon some outside factor such as money, status, titles, etc. is temporary. Once the outside factor no longer exerts its influence, the love vanishes. However, love that is genuine and from the inside, intrinsic to each person, lasts and imparts durability.

In Thayer's Greek Lexicon[23], the lawyer's question to "test" (Greek πειράζω, peirazō) Jesus was used with a good and not a malicious intent, as if to trip him up. But Jesus cuts through the pettifogging hair-splitting to the heart of the question, defining the word "great" (Greek μέγας, megas). Thayer's defines "great" as "to be highly esteemed for their importance." The lawyer wanted to rank by importance the commandments.

The word "like" means "like," but has additional comments by Thayer's, "like i.e. corresponding or equivalent to, the same as, in authority." The Amplified Bible says, "And a second *is like it*, [emphasis added]," so the second commandment could be said to be near equal in authority as the first commandment.

The word "depend" (Greek κρεμάννυμι kremannymi) in the Greek is present tense, passive voice, indicative mood.[24] It is a fact that all the Law and the Prophets depend on these two verses. This word occurs six times it describes hanging like hanging on a cross, this verse is different. Thayer's says this word means "to be suspended, hang on." Thayer further says, "where the meaning is, all of the Law and Prophets (i.e. the teaching of the OT on morality) is summed up in these two precepts." The Amplified Bible says in verse 40, "These two commandments sum up and upon them depend all the Law and the Prophets."

As, for, and instead of yourself. Love is a mutual concern about the relationship between you and God and you and your neighbor, which could include a spouse, your children, a pastor or rabbi, even a foreigner that visits your country. When you love your neighbor *as* yourself, you see your neighbor as an equal partner in an economic transaction, not someone to be ripped off just for the sake of the love of money. But let's take a deeper dive into this word *as* that Jesus used in His discussion about love.

- You < Neighbor. Love your neighbor *instead of* yourself, you're *self-sacrificing*, loving yourself *less than* your neighbor, i.e. subservient. It's an unequal partnership; a lose/win situation, you lose, they win.
- You = Neighbor. Love your neighbor *as* yourself, you're loving your neighbor equally. It is about *serving* your neighbor as an *equal* partner in a win/win situation, i.e. you're a servant.
- You > Neighbor. Love your neighbor *for* yourself, you're being *self-serving*, loving yourself *greater than* you love your neighbor, i.e. superior. It's an unequal partnership; a win/lose situation, you win, they lose.

---

23 blueletterbible.org Reference *Thayer's Greek Lexicon* of the word

24 blueletterbible.org See *Understanding How Greek Verbs Work*

Business is about *mutual-gain* where there is equality of opportunity, not *self-gain* where one receives the greater value of the transaction. An *equal partnership is never about equal outcomes or results.* A neurosurgeon should not get the same pay as a plumber, nor an architect the same pay as a cashier in a retail establishment. An *unequal partnership* occurs when a business or a customer has a win/lose situation, and either the business wins and the customer loses or the customer wins and the business loses. That is why love is so important in a business relationship.

> *Life is relationships; the rest is just details. This is the greatest truth. Everything in life that truly matters can be boiled down to relationships.*[25]

Love sees another human being as an equal partner whether that person is a business or a customer, and a partner is one that is not to be taken advantage.

So when reading Jewish commentary about the 613 commandments, each of the commandments are equal in their sacredness, equal in their binding to us, and equally the Word of God. When you couple this comment with the comment by Jesus, it shows the other 611 commandments *hang on, connect to, or precede from* these two commandments. In other words, if you know and start from these two commandments, you understand how the other 611 commandments instruct our relationships with God and our neighbor, including one's business.

The ten commandments, sayings, or matters

Most people understand that the Ten Commandments were given by God, "Then God spoke all these words" over 3,000 years ago to Moses and the Jews and not given by anyone else, king or government. In Hebrew and Jewish rabbinical texts, the familiar phrase "Ten Commandments"[26] is more accurately translated as the "Ten Sayings," Statements, Declarations, Words, Matters,[27] or even the Ten Things.[28] While these Ten Sayings are a start, Judaism sees not just the Ten Commandments but includes and considers the *broader inclusiveness of all 613 commandments.*

---

25 *The DNA of Relationships*, by Dr. Gary Smalley, pg 3

26 pragеruniversity.com See *The Ten Commandments: Introduction*

27 bfainternational.com See *Ten Matters That Still Matter*

28 jewfaq.org/10.htm See *Aseret ha-Dibrot: The "Ten Commandments"*

For instance, the ninth commandment says, "you shall not bear a false witness." Lev 19:16 says, "you shall not go about as a slanderer." Prov 20:19 writes, "do not associate with a gossip." You see the combined results of speech in Prov 18:21, "Death and life are in the power of the tongue, And those who love it will eat its fruit." It also means acquiring the skill using good words in bad situations. These concepts and connections will start a business conversation.

The ten sayings are and their context:

1. **Believe in God** Ex. 20:2 "I am the LORD your God…" Enough said.

2. **Prohibition of Idol Worship** Ex. 20:3-6 "You *shall have no* other gods before Me…" Don't worship other gods and don't use an idol as an intermediary between God and you.

3. **Prohibition of Oaths** Ex. 20:7 "You *shall not* take the name of the Lord your God in vain …" Your word and your reputation are your bond. This prohibition include perjury, breaking, or delaying the performance of vows or promises, and unnecessary oaths. Words are powerful. This prohibition is not just limited to one's *language*, but it encompasses one's *life* and how one lives it for God, oneself, and others. Both one's language and life should be congruent, authentic.

4. **Observance of Times that are Sacred** Ex. 20:8-11 "*Remember* the sabbath day…" It encompasses all commandments related to the Sabbath, holidays, or other times sacred to God. It's about having down time to listen to what God wants you to do for the next six days.

5. **Respect for Parents** Ex. 20:12 "*Honor* your father and your mother…" is the sound foundation for starting and continued learning to be a good human being.

6. **Prohibition of Murder** Ex. 20:13, "You *shall not* murder." It is a prohibition against the *desire to kill*, to go on the offensive, versus the *desire to protect*, being defensive. The definition of murder is, "unlawful premeditated killing of one human being by another." No weapon is defined (gun, knife, poison, biological weapons, etc.), just the results of the offensive act. God allows you to defend yourself, and others against criminal people, organizations, or governments.

7. **Prohibition of Adultery** Ex. 20:14, saying, "You *shall not* commit adultery" is about respecting the sanctity of marriage. (Prov 6:25-26; Matt 5:28; Rom 1:24; Eph 5:3)

8. **Prohibition of Theft** Ex. 20:15 "You *shall not* steal." While most consider robbery as a primary form of theft, it also includes theft by deception or unethical practices. It includes *respecting property rights* and not

just limited to physical property. Stealing includes non-material property such as intellectual property, trust, dignity, reputation,[29] as well as not wasting resources, including natural resources. (Prov 11:1, 16:8, 21:6, 22:16; Jer 17:11; Mal 3:8)

9. **Prohibition of Perjury** Ex. 20:16 "You *shall not* bear false witness against your neighbor." Giving "false evidence" about your neighbor is the best translation. Words are powerful. But *false evidence* also applies asking for help from a business, using up their resources, with no intention of buying from them but buy online to "get it cheaper." Someone tells a member of the opposite sex that "they love them" when they don't, false evidence!

10. **Prohibition of Coveting** Ex. 20:17 "You *shall not* covet your neighbor's house…*or anything that belongs to your neighbor.*" There are three categories of expression—thought, speech and deed. In Jewish tradition, controlling one's actions is the simplest level of self-control. Speech is a little harder. One's thoughts are at the most intimate and personal level of a person and are the hardest of all to control. This commandment differs from the first nine, and virtually all 613 commandments, because it focuses on one's *thoughts* while the rest focus on *behaviors,* and because coveting leads to the others. This prohibition is not about desiring a 1971 Oldsmobile 442, but it's desiring *your neighbor's* 1971 Oldsmobile 442, because it belongs to them. You're prohibited from desiring *what belongs to someone else* and covers someone's time, tools, and treasures. How many times have you heard someone say, "I'd like to pick your brain" about your expertise and they do not want to pay you or pay you very little for what you know?

How the Ten Commandments/Sayings are used shows intent.

When law and morality contradict each other, the citizen has the cruel alternative of either losing his moral sense or losing his respect for the law.[30]

God tells us why He gave these laws to the Jews.

> Deu 11:26-28 See, I am setting before you today a blessing and a curse: *the blessing, if you listen to the commandments of the LORD your God*, which I am commanding you today; and *the curse, if you do not listen to the commandments of the LORD your God*, but turn aside from

29 prageru.com See *Do Not Steal*

30 *The Law* by Frederic Bastiat, pg 7

> the way which I am commanding you today, by following other gods which you have not known. [emphasis added]

When individuals follow the commandments/sayings/categories, they will be blessed and not cursed, "they'll be prosperous and have success." It's about how one behaves toward God, to oneself, and then to others.

> Josh 1:8 This book of the law shall not depart from your mouth, but you *shall meditate* on it day and night, so that *you may* be careful to do according to all that is written in it; for then *you will make your way prosperous*, and then you *will have success.* [emphasis added]

The sequence is important: the first "you shall" is followed by "you may," and finally with "you will." The command phrase "you shall" is coupled with "not depart" and "meditate on it day and night", which means to constantly think and talk about it. The use of "you may" encourages you to decide and do what is right, but it's still your choice. The results of making good decisions? "Then you will" be "prosperous" and have "success" based on your efforts. It is telling us that your *future results* come from your *current good thinking, good decisions, and good actions.*

> 1 Sam 15:22 Samuel said, "Has the LORD as much delight in burnt offerings and sacrifices, As in obeying the voice of the LORD? Behold, *to obey is better than sacrifice, And to heed than the fat of rams.*" [emphasis added]

To do good is better than to do bad and then seek forgiveness. While some people think that no one is watching their life, in reality, someone is.

> 1 Sam 16:7 But the LORD said to Samuel, "Do not look at his appearance or at the height of his stature, because I have rejected him; for *God sees not as man sees, for man looks at the outward appearance, but the LORD looks at the heart.*" [emphasis added]

God sees what is in a man's heart while men look outwardly to determine their motivation. Watching outward behaviors and actions over time, and that will give some indications as to what their intent is.

The Ten Commandments are not a fence to confine us, but a guardrail to protect us, and to ignore them is to our peril.

Ex 12:49 The [Literally: One law] *same law shall apply* [Literally: be] to the native as to the stranger [Literally: sojourner] who sojourns among you. [emphasis added]

These are the Ten Commandments, not Jewish Ten Commandments; they apply equally to everyone, and Thomas Jefferson writes.

Have you ever found in history one single example of a Nation thoroughly corrupted, that was afterwards restored to virtue, and without virtue, there can be no political liberty?[31]

To be a prosperous business, society, and nation, it starts with God.

31 *The Adams-Jefferson Letters* Edited by Lester Cappon, pg 550

2 God, the Bible, wisdom, and wealth

Deut 8:18 But you shall remember the LORD your God, for it is He who is giving you power to make wealth

Like in the last chapter, the discussions Jimmy and I had circled around and moved to the outer fringes of the subjects of money, work, and business. We began discussing a subject that was a bit more difficult, not complicated, but that even at our ages, few of us had had a good foundation concerning it. The subjects: earning money and producing wealth. While nearly all Christians I know have discussed money, sadly it was in the context of being poor and the parable of the window's mite, not having enough. Earning more is in the forefront of all of our efforts, but rarely is wealth discussed. Jimmy and I no longer see wealth as a bad thing; wealth is good.

Our upbringings had a lot to do with our views about life, work, and money. While my parents were political conservatives, they were of a "job mentality," which translated into "get a good education, a job, and save your money." On the other hand, my wife Ruth's parents are political liberals, but she was told growing up, "You can be anything you want to be." Visiting her parents I suggested we wanted to build a business to become millionaires, her parents said, "Go for it. You can do it!" Saying the same thing to my parents, on the other hand, they gave us "that look" that said, "You shouldn't do that. What if…" and the conversation would get around to all sorts of things that could go wrong owning a business. What a difference between families concerning the same subject.

Circling back to the discussions Jimmy and I had, the subjects around earning money and wealth seem to have had a familiar ring: what does God say about earning money and having wealth? Is He opposed to wealth? What does He want us to do with our wealth, no matter the amount?

God, the Bible, and Bible thoughts

Tough questions for tough times.

As Albert Einstein said, "If I had an hour to solve a problem and my life depended on it, I would use the first 55 minutes determining the proper question to ask, for once I know the proper question, I could solve the problem in less than five minutes." So the quest begins. For the believer in God who wants to please Him in their work, one must ask the proper questions because *higher quality questions result in higher quality answers.* The process: formulate tough questions, then go to the Bible for answers.

There's a familiar comment in Jewish circles: "Ask two Jews, you get three opinions." It is not just the Jewish liturgical emphasis on asking questions. It is the value in and of Jewish traditional learning placed upon engaging different opinions; the emphasis on debate and discussion is pointed out in the Bible.

> Prov 27:17 Iron sharpens iron, So one man sharpens another.

The Complete Jewish Bible[32] says of this verse, "Just as iron sharpens iron, a person sharpens the character of his friend." The principle of this verse is about growing and improving ourselves to our fullest extent, not just for ourselves, but for others, too. The evidence is in the Israeli and U.S. military. "As an Israeli entrepreneur Jon Medved—who has sold several startups to large American companies—told us, 'When it come to U.S. military résumés, Silicon Valley is illiterate. It's a shame. What a waste of the kick-ass leadership talent coming out of Iraq and Afghanistan. The American business world doesn't quite know what to do with them."[33] This "sharpening one's character" attitude has blended into Jewish society and by all accounts, into American startups and military veterans. But it is far less so in current American business systems of "conformity" and "standardization."

---

32 biblestudytools.com See *Complete Jewish Bible* translation of a verse.

33 *Startup Nation*, by Senor and Singer, pg 79

New research[34] suggests that stress may be bad for you, but *only if you believe* that stress is bad for you. When you change your mindset about how you view stress and your response to it, you change your body's response to stress. This change in stress perception encourages stress resilience. Bottom line: caring about something, such as a cause or something bigger than yourself, creates stress resilience. In other words: resilience = growing!

The Bible and Truth. The Bible *tells* the truth 100 percent of the time, but it does not *contain* 100 percent Truth. When reading the Bible you need to determine if the context is telling *the truth* (telling the truth *for* us), or is it telling *a Truth* (telling the truth *to* us directly), i.e. what God wants us to follow or do. Both instances are good for learning: the first to learn from other people's mistakes and avoid, and the second is something to seek after and work to do.

The example of these concepts above is where God tells Adam about the fruit from the tree of knowledge of good and evil, God tells *a Truth* to Adam.

> Gen 2:17, but from the tree of the knowledge of good and evil *you shall not eat*, for in the day you eat from it you shall surely die. [emphasis added]

God's Word tells *the truth* and records the difference in what Eve says.

> Gen 3:3, but from the fruit of the tree which is in the middle of the garden, God has said, "You *shall not eat from it or touch it*, lest you die." [emphasis added]

Eve added "or touch it" to God's "you shall not eat;" we can only surmise why. Did Adam erroneously give the command to Eve? Did the serpent appealed to Eve's biological leanings or did the serpent spread doubt about God's word?

Whatever the reason, the Fall of Man ensued with Eve first eating the fruit and then Adam. In this case, iron was not sharpening iron; it was dulling it.

For entrepreneurs,: what does God teach us about the truth of wealth and our talents? The Bible points out the good, the bad, and the ugly.

---

34 ted.com See Kelly McGonigal's TED talk *How to make stress your friend*

The letter and spirit of the law

One of the most common comments you hear from corporations, businesses, and others when discussing legal matters is, "We have done nothing illegal" or "We were within the law" with their actions. The Bible has 613 commandments or mitzvot[35] (Hebrew: תרי"ג מצוות: taryag mitzvot, "613 Mitzvot") with 248 positive (do's) and 365 negative (do not's) commandments. Some of the 613 apply only to Israel and the Temple, but about 100 are concerning commercial and business conduct.[36]

The *intent of the law* is to set high standards when dealing with the interactions of others. Some of those standards might be exact, but the *spirit of the law* goes beyond the boundary of the law itself. It does not allow one to hide behind the law to protect oneself from one's ethical/moral or unethical/immoral actions. The true test of an ethical and moral person, business, company, or organization is one who can adhere to ethical values even if everyone else fails to adhere to them. It is the basis of the *intent or spirit of the law*. It comes from one verse.

> Deut 6:18: "You *shall do what is right and good in the sight of the LORD*, that it may be well with you and that you may go in and possess the good land which the LORD swore to give your fathers," [emphasis added]

The principle of Jewish law is that it demands that one be ethical and even go beyond just the mere legal requirement, the *intent* is just as important as the *law* itself. Business people need to lead their lives according to this principle. It goes beyond the letter of the law and willing to lose money rather than take advantage of another person's misfortunes.[37]

Christians have an identical approach from Paul in the Bible, who wrote to the Romans, regarding fulfilling the law:

> Rom 13:8-10 Owe nothing to anyone except to love one another; for *he who loves his neighbor has fulfilled the law*. For this, "YOU SHALL

35 jewfaq.org/613.htm List of 613 commandments, see also at chabad.org

36 jewfaq.org/613.htm

37 jlaw.com See *The Impact of Jewish Values on Marketing and Business Practices*

> NOT COMMIT ADULTERY, YOU SHALL NOT MURDER, YOU SHALL NOT STEAL, YOU SHALL NOT COVET," [Exod 20:13-17] and if there is any other commandment, it is summed up in this saying, "YOU SHALL LOVE YOUR NEIGHBOR AS YOURSELF[Lev 19:18]." *Love does no wrong to a neighbor*, therefore *love is the fulfillment of the law.* [emphasis added]

To repeat.

Love is the fulfillment of the law

So all 613 commandments in the Jewish Torah and the Christian OT are wrapped up in this one statement. Love between customer and business.

Biblical morals and myths of wealth and poverty

Being Poor is Relative. Rabbi Lapin says that Judaism teaches that *poverty is relative.*[38] When one reads the below Scriptures, one seems like they're getting contradictory messages from God.

> Deu 15:4-5, 11 "However, there *will be no poor among you*, since the LORD will surely bless you in the land which the LORD your God is giving you as an inheritance to possess, if only you listen obediently to the voice of the LORD your God, to observe carefully all this commandment which I am commanding you today. 11 For the *poor will never cease to be in [in the midst of] the land*; therefore I command you, saying, 'You shall freely open your hand to your brother, to your needy and poor in your land.' [emphasis added]

Poor in attitude. Regarding a rich individual or and inner city individual, both had differing levels of assets, both can be *poor in attitude.* If you or someone else label or view yourself as "poor," you'll always be poor. Especially if one is or becomes ungrateful for what one has, food on the table and even a roof over their head. Yes, it may not be the food or the

38 *Thous Shall Prosper* by Rabbi Lapin, pg 149-150

roof from the Ritz-Carlton Hotel or an expensive restaurant, but compared to the third world, Americans are rich by comparison.

The first verse that says "there will be no poor among you" is about one's attitude toward oneself and your neighbor. If you're fortunate enough to have family and friends and a community that have and maintain similar values such as caring for one another, you're not poor. You're also not poor if the community keeps one's word, respects each other's property and does not "covet" your neighbor's things. Even if you do lose everything like Job did, you still have God on your side, a brain, and friends that will invest in you. It is *this combination that created your wealth in the first place.* It means you can do it again, and again, and again as long as you have this combination.

Poor in assets. If one loses their job and can't find another job and gets evicted from their home or apartment, then yes, compared with their friends and family, they're in need of help and are poor. But no matter who you come in contact with in the world, the same view of your life applies: *you will always find someone that has more and less than you.* Just as the glass is half full or half empty, same goes with whether or not you see yourself as rich or poor, it's all in your attitude and viewpoint.

In America, over 99 percent of the U.S. poor own a refrigerator, 98 percent own color television, 98 percent own a stove/oven, 84 percent own air conditioning, 79 percent own a DVD player, 76 percent own a cell phone, 60 percent have internet service, and 68 percent own a computer.[39] And when you also consider having $500,000.00 to spend on a house, what kind of house will this buy in Manhattan, NY versus what it will buy in Tupelo, MS? How many homes could be built in a third world country with this money? So now who is now rich and who is now poor?

In the American West during the 1800s, "new institutional economics" were able to "tame the wild, wild American west." These "rules that govern how people interact with one another…the property rights that determine who may use resources, how they may use those resources, and whether they may trade them" *were established by grassroots associations.* This society cooperation as American expanded West was the norm to civilizing the west. Grassroots associations "promoted law and order, efficient use of natural and human resources, and good resource stewardship," although the government created problems soon became the exception.[40] It showed how

39 heritage.org See *Air Conditioning, Cable TV, and an Xbox: What is Poverty in the United States Today?*

40 *The Not So Wild, Wild West* by Anderson and Hill, pg 4-5

those at the lowest level solved problems, grassroots from the bottom up, not dictated from the top down.

In the book *The Mystery of Capital* by de Soto, he found that what made America the world's richest is the simple fact that America codified and systematized the *visible* assets (land, horses, houses, water rights, etc.) with *invisible* assets (titles, contracts, and other records). It was documentation representing the assets and resources and then buying and selling of this documentation that made America rich. The rest of the Western world soon followed suit, but is lacking in many third world countries.[41]

Capital is born by representing in writing, a title, what is the physical or the intellectual property and now allows one to buy and sell the physical asset represented by a physical documentation title. It is when governments fail to provide and secure these necessary societal infrastructures, (private property, security of people's rights, papers, i.e. contracts, etc.) that prevents a country from achieving their highest value in the economic world market.

Wealth Myths

Human nature has not changed since Adam and Eve. The various wealth myths below do not include deceitful, fraudulent, or criminal actions in the business world that affect prosperity. Here are some of the myths:

- The most damaging is the **spiritual/church myth**, the sacred-secular divide where the church is primarily interested in church issues and less or even disinterested in how their members handle and work through workplace ethical and moral issues. Pastors are also poorly trained in both economic and business matters, inappropriately seeing their church's role as *growing a "church" business* versus *influencing businesses and the marketplace through their church.*[42]
- The **Millennial Kingdom (1,000 Year Reign of Christ) myth** is when Jesus will become the King of kings and Lord of lords at the start of His 1,000 Year Kingdom Reign. Some wealth, legal, economic and other aspects of the Gospels do not apply to today (compare Matt 5:17, "the *kingdom of heaven is at hand*" versus Matt 25:31-34, "*inherit the kingdom* prepared for you").
- The **piety myth,** or not being *spiritual enough,* is *very similar* to the Millennial myth. Well-meaning people mistakenly focus on people's

41 *The Mystery of Capital* by de Soto, pg 48-49

42 *How the Church Fails Businesspeople* by John Knapp, pg 35-38

good intentions and support bad governmental, business, and church or synagogue policies that use dollars for things the market and people do not want or need. When God hands out our *individual heavenly rewards,* who gets the reward or punishment for what we do working in the government, a business, or a church?

- A **fixed-pie myth** means some get a bigger or a smaller slice of a fixed size of a pie. In reality, the size of the pie gets bigger or smaller as a market grows or shrinks (from buggy whips to computers) based on the wants and desires of the customers and the marketplace.

- The **zero-sum game myth** is where two or more participants have a lose/lose (If I can't win, you won't either, i.e. the miser myth) or a win/win (forced shared "winnings" between others, i.e. spreading the wealth) game. This myth is spread *by force* (might, mob, organization, business or government actions and policies), not by mutual agreement.

- Capitalism and wealth usher in the **greed myth** by the poor, wealthy, politicians, social failures, and some pious Christians. Greed is based on coveting your neighbor's stuff. *Selfish*-interest is when you apply force and is the *violent means of exchange* (abusive or unjust threat or exercise of power). *Self*-interest should be the economic norm and is the *voluntary* interaction and agreement, i.e. a *peaceful and honorable means of exchange* between two individuals for a win/win transaction.

- The **money myth** says "money is the root of all evil" when in fact the actual text says, "the *love of money* is the root of all evil" (1 Tim 6:10).

- The **consumerism myth** happens when capitalism is a form of "giveupitis" or "defeatist" (becoming hopeless for one's economic future), gluttony, even idolatry, in which we make food, drink, and stuff and make it our highest loyalty and priority. Consumerism, i.e. overspending, is in contrast with capitalism, which requires a regular income portion is saved, invested, and risked for the future.

- The **change myth** is when change is bad. The Luddites[43] rejected the replacement of "artisans with less-skilled, low-wage laborers, leaving them without work." Anything new and changes the market is bad and jobs are lost, so some will inhibit change.

- The **new-and-improved myth** believes everything old is bad, and all change is believed to be good.

---

43 wikipedia.org See *Luddite*

Follow God. Then let the market and the customer decide winners and losers and let the competition of businesses meet the market demand.

Teaching and learning morals and laws

Let's start, it begins with teaching and instilling the love of learning, starting and primarily with, the parents.

> Deu 11:18-21 You *shall therefore impress these words of mine* on *your heart* and on *your soul*; and you shall bind them as a sign on your hand, and they shall be as frontals on your forehead. You *shall teach them to your sons*, talking of them when you *sit in your house* and when you *walk along the road* and when you *lie down* and when you *rise up*. You shall *write them* on the doorposts of your house and on your gates, *so that your days and the days of your sons may be multiplied on the land* which the LORD swore to your fathers to give them, as long as the heavens remain above the earth. [emphasis added]

Jewish fathers had the responsibility to teach all their family all of the necessary aspects of what God wants them to learn. Not just a one time teaching, but with ongoing repetition (Question: what did your parents teach you about money, wealth, how to earn money, pay bills, etc.?)

Just like flying an aircraft, the more time you have *logged in with God*, the more you become in tune with what He wants for you, your life, and those around you. And one's efforts to *log more time* with God's good content, the Bible, starts as a child on the right path toward wealth.

> Prov 22:6 *Train up* a child in *the way* he should go, Even when he is old he will not depart from it. [emphasis added]

Notice that the word says, "train up" a child, it does not say teach, tell, belittle, badger, cajole, or beat, but it says to train up. The word "train" means to "to imbue someone with any thing." But look at the word imbue, this word means "inspire or permeate with a feeling or quality." In other words, parents, are to *inspire and build up a child's confidence* on a regular basis on the path God has chosen them to take! Confidence in what they can learn, what they know, and what they can do, but humble enough they don't know everything nor can they do everything by themselves.

The word "way" means "way, path, direction." So the lessons of the commandments of God are to be repeatedly discussed in an inspiring and confident approach toward living with the result that they and their family's life will be long.

Because of their rougher nature, men can be harsher compared with women and are told by God on *how men are to act toward children.*

Col 3:21 Fathers, *do not exasperate your children*, so that they will not lose heart. [emphasis added]

The word "exasperate" (Greek ἐρεθίζω erethizō) means "to provoke." and is present, active, imperative, and means fathers are *commanded to actively and continually work at not provoking their children.* The english definition of "exasperate" means "irritate intensely; infuriate, or annoy to an extreme degree." Rabbi Yehuda Ben Ilal said, "Labor is important, for it brings honor to the laborer, and he who does not teach his son a trade, teaches him to rob."[44] Teaching a child to work will result in them either finding work or starting a business or having a business on the side while working a job. Teaching a child to enjoy their talented work instills in them to have a constant eye out for opportunities and creating multiple streams of income. Once they get that desire, they're on their way to be productive citizens.

Prov 1:5 A wise man will hear and increase in learning,

Failure to love learning will lead to problems in life.

Prov 13:18 *Poverty and shame* will come to him *who neglects discipline*, But he who regards reproof will be honored. [emphasis added]

Disciplined learning and practice, you improve and then can turn what you have learned into a profit.

Prov 14:23 In *all labor there is profit*, But mere talk leads only to poverty. [emphasis added]

---

44 *Rabbis of Ancient Times*, D. A. Friedman, pg 87, Judah bar Ilai

Doing smart work means you apply your brain toward the job at hand to be both effective and efficient with an eye for being profitable. There are no "get rich quick" approaches to wealth and life, no short cuts, only working at getting effective and efficient at what you do. Just like building a house, it begins with understanding the step-by-step process and a strong foundation. Working and completing each step leads to more wealth creation and wealth distribution:

Listen > Learn > Understand > Practice > Market > Wealth

So your life steps to obtain wealth are:

- the *love of listening* leads to love to learn (Prov 1:7-8)
- the *love of learning* leads to understanding (Prov 2:6)
- the *love of understanding* leads to practice what you've learned (Jas 1:5)
- the *love of practice* leads to perfect process practice (Col 3:23-24)
- the *love of perfect process practice* leads to market prices of the value you bring to the market; the higher the value, the higher the pay (Matt 13:8)
- the higher amount the market pays you, the higher your wealth (Deu 8:18)

At any step above, even starting with the first step, someone can quit, drop out, or look for shortcuts and thereby not fulfilling one's destiny to create wealth.

When it comes to practicing, while initially an amateur will practice something to *do it right once* or a few times. In reality, as a professional you practice so you *don't do it wrong* and hit your mark 99-100 percent of the time. Perfect process practice makes perfect, practicing bad habits makes you perform bad habits at a faster pace. Finding, learning, understanding, and *practicing the good, better, or best habits makes perfect practice* and increases one's value in the marketplace. It's not just the *hours you put in*, but *what you put into the hours* to improve your value in the marketplace.

It is when one aims for perfect practice at a task, job, or career that one becomes sought after by the marketplace as the market dictates. The marketplace, that *voluntary agreement* between a business and their customer (looking out for people's needs and wants), determines whether or not what one learns is worthwhile or not. In addition, the greater one finds a market solution that more and more people need or want, the greater one attracts wealth.

If you're looking for a career in the area of your talents, then you reverse the path. First, find out what you love to do. Then research what the market wants and needs and then work backwards to your talents. Then start listening.

Listen < Learn < Understand < Practice < Market

This step by step process is the same for just about anything, and you *begin with the end in mind* and work backward to the starting point of where you are. The quicker you learn and become good at what you do, the quicker you earn a better living. If you skip the above step or you search for a "shortcut" to speed it up, you'll be ill prepared for the task at hand. However, there is such a thing as ignoring the noise and poor quality content to become effective, then improve your skills to become more efficient. At some point looking for personal or business shortcuts *you become too efficient and drop below the line and become less effective.*

So what about poverty or being poor? Do the opposite of the above, because here are the results of a poverty mindset:

> Prov 13:18 *Poverty and shame will come to him who neglects discipline*, But he who regards reproof will be honored. [emphasis added]

Disciplined learning is the start of wealth, failing to learn leads to poverty. It still boils down to this one thought.

No Learn, No Earn

If you fail to learn, you'll fail to earn the money you want to earn, so one's primary objective is to learn. *If you learn wrong or bad content, you won't earn a good living.* So swap out bad content for good, better, and best content.

Bible view of theology and economics. When it comes to Bible's views about God, work, economics, law, and motivation, it starts with what the Torah or OT says first about this subject. Sauer [45] says:

- *Creativity* - "God is the creator *of* the world, and man is the creator *in* the world," Man partners with God under His direction in Creation.

---

45 acton.org See *Jewish Theology and Economic Theory*

- *Property Rights* - The eighth (shall not steal) and tenth (shall not covet) commandments both discuss property rights.
- *Wealth Accumulation* - "Wealth, accumulated honestly, is a signal of great effort, skill, and success in partnering with God in the creative process. The wealthy individual has been unusually successful in elevating the material world and in expressing the divine image."
- *Caring for the poor* - "You should not harden your heart or shut your hand from your needy brother" (Deut 15:7-8).
- *Small Government* - Concentrating and centralizing power and wealth (See also 1 Sam 8:11-18 in Chapter 7) into fewer and fewer hands means the concentration of wealth into the same number of hands yields fewer blessings for others.

The Torah/OT sets the foundation to aligned one's life to God. But the NT shows us how we're to view our work.

> Col 3:23-24 *Whatever you do, do your work heartily [from the soul]*, as *for the Lord* rather [and not] than for men, knowing that *from the Lord you will receive the reward* [consisting of] of the inheritance. It is the *Lord Christ whom you serve.* [emphasis added]

Productive members should never be a burden to the community.

> 2 Thes 3:10 For even when we were with you, we used to give you this order: if anyone is *not willing to work, then he is not to eat*, either. [emphasis added]

Here's another verse that is similar to the above one and shows how just dreaming is not enough to bring about prosperity.

> Ecc 11:4 He who *watches the wind will not sow* and he who *looks at the clouds will not reap.* [emphasis added]

Daydreamers are not visionaries. They have a "pie in the sky" vision and won't put effort into achieving their ideas. William J. H. Boetcker (1873–1962), wrote about the wealth and prosperity and human nature, often wrongly attributed to Abraham Lincoln. His comment encapsulates the purpose of both business and economics.

> *You cannot bring about prosperity by discouraging thrift.*
> *You cannot strengthen the weak by weakening the strong.*
> *You cannot help little men by tearing down big men.*
> *You cannot lift the wage earner by pulling down the wage payer.*
> *You cannot help the poor by destroying the rich.*
> *You cannot establish sound security on borrowed money.*
> *You cannot further the brotherhood of man by inciting class hatred.*
> *You cannot keep out of trouble by spending more than you earn.*
> *You cannot build character and courage by destroying men's initiative and independence.*
> *And you cannot help men permanently by doing for them what they can and should do for themselves.*

Jim Rohn was an American entrepreneur, author and motivational speaker. His rags to riches story played a large part in his work, which influenced others in the personal development industry. He said it best about reading the Bible.

> *"The Bible gives us a list of human stories on both sides of the ledger. One list of human stories is used as* examples*—do what these people did. Another list of human stories is used as* warnings*—don't do what these people did. So if your story ever gets in one of these books, make sure they use it as an example, not a warning. [emphasis added]" — Jim Rohn*

Let your life and work and business be a good example, not a warning, to others on how to live and work in this world. That is your mantra and your legacy that you're to leave this world with; something others can turn to and get inspired.

1 Thes 4:11 and to *make it your ambition* to *lead a quiet life* and *attend to your own business* and *work with your hands*, just as we commanded you, [emphasis added]

3 Jesus' humanity: His life, business, & ministry

John 2:16 and to those who were selling the doves He said, "Take these things away; stop making My Father's house a place of business."

Jimmy and I discuss business on a regular basis. In our discussions, we talked about many familiar issues: how do we market, customers, our products and services, and of course, money and wealth. Then we get around to how to balance our family and business, as husbands and fathers. Jimmy asked me a business question one day: "How much do you pay others?" I replied to him a quote that I had heard years ago, "It is better to have someone work *with* you than *for* you." Those that work with you buy into your vision and direction and will do things that those that want to work for you won't do, i.e. they only want to get paid with money.

When I think about our two-hour long discussions around business and life, I once again consider Jesus and His time here on earth. Both as His primary purpose, *divinity* dying on the cross for the sins of humanity and accepting His saving work on the cross. But just as important, His *humanity*, living His life as a human being and running His construction business. It's not ignoring His divinity, but it begs the question: how *did* Jesus pay others?

Divinity and Humanity of Jesus. Many words have been spoken and written about the *divinity* of Jesus, to the Jew first (Matt 15:24; Rom 1:16) and then to the rest of the world. But less has been discussed about His *humanity*. For Jesus Christ the balance is between His divinity and humanity, which includes His life-work balance. What was God the Father's purpose for Jesus in business? What did Jesus have to decide? Who was Jesus responsible for in business? Who did Jesus have working with or for Him? One thing you can definitely say, Jesus, even as the Son of God, did not work alone or by Himself, whether it was His ministry or construction business. It's not an *either/or* question; it's an *and* question: how did Jesus live in both His divine *and* human life. But for this book it is the connection of His divinity with His humanity and how He ran a successful business that will be explored here.

Jesus growing up as a Jewish child helped prepare Him for working in his father's craftsman or workman business which later helped Him in His ministry. Jesus was able to weave his nearly two decades of business experience and what He had learned in His Life into about 85 percent business topic parables and told others of the Good News should make us take notice.[46]

Growing up Jesus: Jewish life and work in Galilee

What was it was like economically during Jesus' time gives a very good starting point as to what Jesus was encountering, not only growing up, but working in the family business and then into His Ministry.

> *Among many, it is accepted that the Galilee in which Jesus was born and raised was plagued by grinding poverty, that his followers were primarily poor people, and that his audience was made up of the masses of the poor. Others, however, have argued that Galilee was an egalitarian and economically prosperous society. ... Galilee was economically prosperous, and the Galileans did not have it too badly because of their vigorous manufacturing and trade. They were thoroughly "Jewish," that is, Judean in ideology, and were experiencing good times economically.*[47]

At the time of the birth of Jesus, He was like any other normal child, eating, having "diapers" changed, playing with family and neighbors and interacting with others. When He reached the age of around five or six years old, he began to be taught by his father the Torah and all that it entailed. Being home schooled and attending synagogue school[48] would continue until a son reached the age of 12. Joseph, Mary, and Jesus would head to Jerusalem every year to celebrate Passover.

---

46 tifwe.org See *Examining Jesus' inclusion of work roles in His parables*

47 sbl-site.org See *The Galilean Economy in the time of Jesus*

48 historian.net/jesused.html See *Jesus' Education*

Luke 2:41-42 Now his parents went to Jerusalem *every year* at the Feast of the Passover. And when *he was twelve years old*, they went up to Jerusalem after the custom of the Feast. [emphasis added]

Jews believed a boy's basic Torah education was complete at age 12 and then Jesus would begin learning from his family of Tektons (building craftsmen) and working for his father. At this age, a boy then becomes responsible for their actions and having a good knowledge of the 613 commandments covering not only the *laws of Sacrifice* (in issues dealing with God). Equally important are the *laws of Society* (in issues dealing with themselves and their fellow man), which including the interaction with others and the ethics and laws in living one's life and conducting business.

Girls, on the other hand, with their mother's help, received their education at home that consisted in knowing how to be a good wife and mother. A girl learned the dietary laws, which had to do with the family's devotion to God, the practical side of the laws the boys studied. A girl learned how to make a home and make it ready for special holidays and the Sabbath. In such preparation, she learned the meaning of the customs and history behind the events. This heritage she would be able to pass on to her children in their very early years.[49]

Construction career of Jesus. There are only two verses in the NT that use the word "carpenter," Matt 13:55 and Mark 6:3. The word "carpenter" (Greek τέκτων tektōn) is where our word technology and technician comes from and means "the application of scientific knowledge for practical purposes, especially in industry." The Greek word is described as "builder, craftsman." But let's look further back into Biblical history.

This same Greek word τέκτων appears two dozen times in the Septuagint or Greek Old Testament. In 1 Samuel 13:19, the word τέκτων is translated here as "blacksmith," but the Hebrew word (Hebrew חָרָשׁ charash) occurs 33 times in the OT and has the root of "to work out" or "contrive" and when expanded can mean "craftsman, workman, artisan, engraver, graver, artificer, and graver."[50] Jesus more than likely worked mostly with stone and to a lesser degree with soil (laying building foundations), wood, metal in various capacities over the course of His business and life. Since wood was not as plentiful in the area, wood would have been a premium material for the middle-upper middle class to upper-

49 studylight.org See *Education in Bible Times*

50 blueletterbible.org See *Craftsman (Strongs H2796)*

class clients. As a business owner, Jesus would have connected and been involved in all aspects of being a craftsman and the various craftsman guilds and industries. Just as a today's car mechanic learns hydraulics, electronics, mechanics, and a host of other subjects, Jesus did likewise in His business, wood tables, structural beams, and metal door hinges.

Genneseret is one of the names for the Sea of Galilee and means, "garden of riches." The historian Josephus' contemporary description of Galilee:

> *Thanks to the rich soil, there is not a plant that does not flourish there, and the inhabitants grow everything...walnuts...flourish in abundance, as do palms... side by side with figs and olives...not only does it produce the most surprisingly diverse fruits; it maintains a continuous supply. Those royal fruits the grape and fig it furnishes for ten months on end. (The Jewish War, Josephus Flavius, Book 3, Ch. VI)*

While Jesus's family lived among Jews, he more than likely had rich Greeks among his clientele. Sepphoris[51] (Hebrew: Tsipori, six kilometers north-northwest of present day Nazareth, Israel) is about an hour's walk north of Nazareth, Jesus' hometown and was the provincial capital of Galilee and the city where the villagers took care of their official business. After 3 BC, Sepphoris was the center of a building boom, providing plenty of work opportunities for artisans and craftsman. The Sepphoris synagogue was discovered in 1993 (this was no "new age" synagogue). The floor mosaic pictured the chariot of Helios, Greek god of the sun, and surrounded by the twelve astrological signs of the zodiac.

Jesus became well acquainted with a whole range of cultural, economic and craftsman demographics in His work as a craftsman/builder. Joseph took primary responsibility for teaching Jesus what it means to be a Jew and a businessman. His teaching included a diverse economy and culture, and far away from the economic and religious hub of activity of Jerusalem, and it's corruption.

Jesus was a Jewish business leader

Two areas we can learn about how Jesus prospered in His Jewish business. First, is the *Jewish Torah* or *Christian OT*, the foundational basis for which He operated his business, and last, is *His experience*, the verbal

51 itsgila.com/highlightssepphoris.htm

discussions of His parables in the Gospels that were the application of the Torah to business in the Jewish and secular world.

Nearly all kids during this period would have followed in their Jewish father's and mother's footsteps, both in habits, ethics, and work. Jesus was no exception. As with any young boy, He would have apprenticed beginning around age 12 until 20, and then entered the market as a business person.[52]

Jesus observed life and the subject of His many parables reflected that observation and involvement: construction (Matt 7:24-27), farming (Mark 4:2-20), management and labour (Matt 20:1-16), return on investment (Matt 25:14-30), the futures market (Luke 12:16-21), wine making (Luke 5:37-38) and the advantage of leverage (Luke 16:1-13). They show Jesus was an astute Jewish businessman and craftsman.

Business of His craft, craft of His business

Jesus learned the *Torah*, the foundation of life itself and the start of how to live and work in the world from a Jewish perspective, including running and doing business as a Jew. Then after learning the Torah he began learning the craft of the family *business*. Learning masonry and carpentry, working in good and bad weather, how to measure, design, and work with the material and tools, etc.

Business of His craft. Jesus learned the business side of the craft, how to communicate, how to make a profit, getting paid and not getting paid, marketing, project management, sales, operations, etc. and *he did it all under Jewish law*. While Joseph and Mary were hardly wealthy, they did not shirk working for a living. Jesus followed the family trade growing up because career-hopping was rarely practiced at that time compared with a vibrant and fluid economy today; most sons, especially the firstborn, followed in their father's profession and business. The business side of his craft was: profit, project management, customer relations, taxes, giving, sales, marketing, operations, finance, money, owning property, etc.

Jesus was good in business. While there is a "record" of Jesus business during His Ministry, there is little record of Joseph and Jesus and their family business other than this statement.

> Luke 2:52 And Jesus kept *increasing* in wisdom and stature, and in *favor with God and men.* [emphasis added]

---

52 tifwe.org See *Examining Jesus' inclusion of work roles in His parables*

The word "favor" means "goodwill, lovingkindness, favor, to have favor with one," it's the word we use for grace. So Jesus was increasing "in favor with God and man." Jesus as a businessman was doing well in how he handled His business to make some profits and earn a living. He also did well in how he dealt with his customers and vendors and the surrounding areas of commercial activities and was pleasing in God the Father's eyes.

> Matt 3:17 and behold, a voice out of the heavens said, "This is My beloved Son, in *whom I am well-pleased.*" [emphasis added]

God the Father was pleased with Jesus when He began His ministry at age 30, so all of His business dealings up to that age pleased His Father.

Craft of His business. Since the construction materials near Nazareth were mostly stones, more than likely Jesus worked primarily in masonry and to a lesser degree with other building materials. Tradition suggests that Joseph died a few years prior to Jesus entering public ministry. Then Jesus, as the eldest son, would have primary responsibility for meeting the family living expenses with his brothers' work as laborers. Matthew describes Jesus' family life and His vocation.

> Matt 13:55-56 "Is not this *the carpenter's son?* Is not His mother called Mary, and His brothers, James and Joseph and Simon and Judas? And His sisters, are they not all with us? Where then did this man get all these things?" [emphasis added]

The phrase "carpenter's son" means Jesus was his father's apprentice, but would eventually take over the family business.

Mark 6:3 says differently, Jesus is referred to as "the carpenter."

> Mar 6:3 "Is not this *the carpenter,* the son of Mary, and brother of James and Joses and Judas and Simon? Are not His sisters here with us?" And they took offense at Him. [emphasis added]

Jesus would have had about 24+ years of Torah teaching and 18+ years of a combination of a commercial and business education and application of Torah teachings with dealing with all sorts of people on a daily basis. But it all started with Torah teaching.

> Luke 2:49 And He said to them, "Why is it that you were looking for Me? Did you not know that *I had to be in My Father's house?"* [emphasis added]

Jesus was raised by an average working couple devoting His days to getting his hands dirty with building materials as a "blue collar" construction worker. His family lived and worked far away from the temple precincts and never grew up or learned in a priestly household.

Jesus was not physically sissified. Doing manual labor for almost two decades, Jesus knew how to run the family business and knew His customers. More than likely He had a "lean and mean" physical body as well. His hands would have been rough, calloused, and strong in order to handle stone, wood, and possibly metal. Physical labor made Him strong, lugging rocks and wood in baskets or wagons around to build furniture, stone walls, fences, and houses. If you were to shake His hands today, his grip would have been very firm. Jesus would have got blisters and calluses on his hands, occasionally splinters in His body working with wood. Maybe dropped a few rocks or planks of wood on His toes or feet, and because of the area He worked in, He got dirty working six days a week in His dad's business. His manual labor was not much different than today's manual labor.

In other words, Jesus was able to have and run a profitable business with and later without his father and *never sinned against the Jewish law.* It meant that Jesus' approach to business as the best model of any businessman. Satisfying his various customers and clients, both good and bad and all the while making a profit to grow his business and make a living.

Jesus extols business in His parable of the talents

Jesus was pro free market. Of primary issue at this point in Jesus's Ministry is He extols the virtues of business in the parable of the talents in Matt 25:14-30. You'll find some statements here in Matthew by Jesus about business that stand out and shows His positive view of the true, and not skewed nor swindling, nature of business.

When reading and interpreting any text you want to "read out" from what's there and be careful that you don't "read into" something that is not there. One can read "between the lines" or "parallel to the lines" a bit and surmise, versus speculate, what most likely happened during this period.

But of most concern is what can we learn and how do we apply this parable to our businesses and lives? It is from here we examine this parable.

Lessons Learned, read Matt 25:14-30:

- the master *entrusted* his slaves with his capital. Entrusted means "to give over into (one's) power or use; to deliver to one something to keep, use, take care of, manage," in this case, the master's resources were given to the slaves. He delegated responsibility, authority, and accountability to his slaves.
- the master *entrusted his slaves with his property;* it was not theirs. Private property is important (see the eighth and tenth commandments, and neither is our body our private concern, 1 Cor 6:19 "Or do you not know that *your body is a temple of the Holy Spirit who is in you*, whom you have from God, and that *you are not your own*? [emphasis added]"). Our talents and resources are God's; we're stewards of the Lord's property, our bodies and what property we own under our names are His.
- the master's view and treatment of his slaves was each had an *equal opportunity* to be as productive individuals given capital to work with, not *equal pay* for work, despite their title or station in life.
- the *attitude* of the two slaves was they were "in business for themselves" trading with their master's capital, not *whining about, complaining, envious, or covetous* of what the other slaves received from their master in capital.
- a *talent* was the *largest unit of currency*[53] in Jesus's time, up to 200 lbs[54] of gold/silver. At 75 lbs, one gold talent today is worth $1.32 million ($1,100.00 an ounce). The five talents would have a total worth of $6.6 million today (Note: 1 denarius = a day's wage, 5,298 denarius = 1 talent[55], working 6 days/week would take 16.98 years to reach the value of 1 talent. See also the talent reference in Matt 18:24; 10,000 talents = $13.2 Billion at today's gold price).
- Jesus discussed here the *largest currency* of the day, not the average or smallest, because God wants His children to *think and see larger amounts and numbers*. Not for what we can earn and get, but how many more opportunities we can serve for His Kingdom and glory.

---

53 christianity.about.com See *What Is a Talent?*

54 See blueletterbible.com reference for the Greek word τάλαντον

55 See the conversion rate at translatorscafe.com

- the trust engendered by the master with *this amount of money* required the slave's integrity and honesty and *skill and fidelity in the use of earthly goods.*[56] It is also applies equally toward one's skills and talents, being empowered to use them to the benefit of the master's business.

- each slave had *different numbers and levels* of talents, aptitudes, and skills (thus different potential for pay/income/rewards), meaning there are *inequalities between individuals* (See also Rom 12:3, 6; 1 Pet 4:10).

- the two talent slave didn't bemoan and whine about the fact they didn't get five talents, *they took what they were given and worked it.*

- the five and two talent industrious slaves were prepared (Pastors, do you prepare your flock for work and business? Eph 4:11-12) and *did not waste any time* and began *immediately trading* their talents in the marketplace (verse 16 "immediately the one" and in the Amplified Bible "went at once" and in verse 17 "in the same manner").[57]

- the slaves *traded* what they were given, "to trade, to make gains by trading, 'do business."[58] This was all that could be expected of them.

- the master *did not set any sales quota* for them, but set expectations (verse 26, "you knew," shows a leader's responsibility is to develop others). The two slaves had an *internal drive* (confidence, positive self-esteem) and the *business discipline to be profitable, productive and successful for material gain* (See Luke 16:19-31, specifically verse 29, "They have Moses and the Prophets; let them hear them," the Bible has answers to guide us in life and business).

- the master gave each slave *differing amounts*. But each slave may have chosen *different industries or markets based on their talents and decision-making abilities* for their masters's investment to *earn a return* (we're not given this in the text, but not beyond the realm of possibilities).

- the master *did not "fire" the one talent slave to hire another five talent slave*, he worked with what each slave was able to bring to the table. It was after the one talent slave "failed to produce" that he was "fired."

- the work of a slave in the ancient world *was regularly a thankless and praiseless* job (Luke 17:9, "He *does not thank the slave* because he did the

---

56 *The Expositors Greek New Testament*, Vol 1, pg 301

57 *The Expositors Greek New Testament*, Vol 1, pg 302

58 *The Expositors Greek New Testament*, Vol 1, pg 302

things which were commanded, does he?," this slave did *what* he was told, but *not more* than he was told). The master goes against this norm.

- the master was a *capitalist*, not directly doing the work, but *invested enormous amounts of capital* in his slaves and looked forward to their individual results.

- the master "settled accounts" is a "commercial phrase for settling the books, both in terms of the extent to which each one has fulfilled his duty and the remuneration due each one."[59]

- the slave says to the master, "behold, see" as he presents his results to his master "as if inviting him to satisfy himself by counting."[60]

- the two slaves achieved a 100 percent ROI (Return On Investment), unheard of in most of today's businesses environment. Both slaves *maximized their efforts to do their best* with what they were given to work with, just as each of us with our God-given talents should be today.

- the master's *expectations* were for the slaves to be productive *no matter what the circumstances* the slaves encountered in the marketplace or laws that were on the books.

- the master's *encouragement and praise* to both productive slaves were *exactly the same comment regardless of each of their results.*

- the master said, because of their success, he was going to put them *in charge of many things* (think Millenium Kingdom), it's also about more responsibilities, and he was "going to make extensive use of the talents and energy of the talents of one who had shown himself so enthusiastically and trustworthy in a limited sphere."[61]

- the master was *joyful for their productivity*, notice he did not keep them *in their place* with a lack of a promotion or future opportunities.

- the master *was not selfish, fraudulent, or stingy and dangle more potential rewards* so they could be even more productive (i.e. getting the five to produced ten, or the two to produce five. See also about Jacob's wages from Laban in Gen 31:41).

- the master *commanded* the slaves to *enter into (and share in) his joyfulness.* The word "enter" (Greek εἰσέρχομαι eiserchomai) is in the imperative mood, a command he gave to the slaves. The Amplified Bible says, "His

---

59 *Exegetical Commentary of the New Testament* by Grant Osborne, Matthew, pg 925

60 *The Expositors Greek New Testament*, Vol 1, pg 302

61 *The Expositors Greek New Testament*, Vol 1, pg 302

master said to him, Well done, you upright (honorable, admirable) and faithful servant! You have been faithful and trustworthy over a little; I will put you in charge of much. Enter into *and* share the joy (the delight, the blessedness) which your master enjoys." The master promoted them! He *shared, not hoarded,* his joyfulness and rewards with the results of those that worked for him. Joy shared is joy multiplied.

- the master empowered them with opportunities to *improve and develop* to their *natural limits,* versus their self-imposed or other imposed limits of performance and production (five talents vs. two vs. one).

- the master *authentically recognized and praised them* for their *hard and productive work.*

- the master *provided knowledge and training* (we have the Bible to learn from) to the slaves and his expectations. The *lazy slave was provided for and he had no excuses* of not knowing what was expected from him.

- the lazy slave was not "dishonest—the master had not misjudged as to that—but "*indolent, unenterprising, timid.* What he did was often done for safety. The master might have done it himself, but he wanted increase as well as safety."[62]

- the master was angry at the lazy slave because he *did not apply himself,* he was good enough because the master did invest, $1.32 MILLION, in him. The slave *failed to work, failed to be productive.* But, what *did* the lazy slave do all this time while the master was gone on his "long journey"?

- a trustworthy bank is a *legitimate institution of business.*

- the lazy slave recognized the property rights of the master by saying it was "*your talent,*" the slave's attitude was "see, you have what belongs to you."[63] The slave failed to take ownership of working what the master gave him and multiply and increase the results of the capital he was provided.

- the "wicked" slave is "too general of a meaning: mean-spirited or grudging would suit the connection better."[64] In other words, this *slave saw himself as a victim.* Satan works to spread this bad attitude on those that are on God's team so we're "taken out of God's marketplace" and either less or non-productive for Him.

---

62 *The Expositors Greek New Testament,* Vol 1, pg 302

63 *The Expositors Greek New Testament*, Vol 1, pg 303

64 *The Expositors Greek New Testament,* Vol 1, pg 302

- the master in essence said to the lazy slave, "you call me hard, I call you churl; with *no heart for your work*, unlike your fellow-servant who put his whole heart into his work."[65] The master practiced good leadership and servant-ship.
- the master *comes from a place of abundance, not of scarcity, for everyone.* An abundance or scarcity attitude, whether a slave/worker or a master/ business owner, becomes an individual choice. "Everyone who has shall more be given, and he shall have an abundance" in verse 29.
- the word "unprofitable" means "useless, good for nothing," and used only twice in the NT, here and Luke 17:10. The Amplified Bible of Luke 17:10 gives a more complete view of the attitude of laziness, "Even so on your part, when you have done everything that was assigned and commanded you, say, We are unworthy servants [possessing no merit, for we have not gone beyond our obligation]; we have [merely] done what our duty to do." Three views of one's duty: *not doing* what you're told, *only doing* what you're told, and *doing more* than you're told. The master *expected a profit, not a loss or to breakeven,* from his investment in his slave's creativity and productivity.
- and finally in verse 29, it is a "general principle on which the direction rests point to a law of life, hard, but not inexorable."[66] This law applies equally to both the spiritual and physical realm.

What is the message from Jesus? Step out! Risk! *Live courageously for Him!* Take constant chances with your life, talents, and goods for His name's sake. Your eternal rewards await when Jesus "settles accounts" with each of us.

Jesus left business at the priestly age. Often we wonder why Jesus waited until age 30 to start His ministry. Why did Jesus work about 18 years in His construction business and then start His ministry when He turned 30? Because the Torah/OT said that is what was supposed to happen.

> Num 4:2-3 Take a census of the descendants of Kohath from among the sons of Levi, by their families, by their fathers' households, from *thirty years and upward, even to fifty years old*, all who *enter the service to do the work* in the tent of meeting. [emphasis added]

---

65 *The Expositors Greek New Testament*, Vol 1, pg 302

66 *The Expositors Greek New Testament*, Vol 1, pg 304

4 God designed you

Gen 1:27 God created man in His own image, in the image of God He created him; male and female He created them.

Met Jimmy at his shop one day to help him with his business and was preparing for our work. He called me out of one of his rooms to meet a friend of his. We both got around to asking his friend what he loved to do, which he replied he loved to plan various events. Since Jimmy's friend was considering starting his own business, we both reflected on how we each started our businesses and what we would have done differently. Mainly we shared and discussed our talents and how we used them in business. Since Jimmy and I were both "older and wiser," we shared our stories so that this "young buck" could learn from our life experiences.

How does an individual find their talents, skills, and spiritual gift and then use them for God? Start with how God designed you, He added to your talents giving you a spiritual gift at the point of your salvation. When you know what your talents and gifts are, now it is up to each whether or not you follow God and His leading. Just as Jimmy became a Navy SEAL and I an Air Force Aircraft Maintenance officer, each of us is not only different as individuals go, but we each have differing paths we take.

Joke. One day a group of scientists got together and decided that man had come a long way and no longer needed God. So they picked one scientist to go and tell Him that they were done with Him.

The scientist walked up to God and said, "God, we've decided that we no longer need you. We're at the point in our progress where we can clone people and do a number of miraculous things, so thanks for everything, but we can take over from here."

God listened very patiently. After the scientist was done talking, God said, "Very well, how about this? Let's say we have a man-making contest." To which the scientist replied, "Okay, great!"

But God added, "Now, we're going to do this just like I did back in the old days with Adam."

The scientist said, "Sure, no problem" and bent down and grabbed himself a handful of dirt.

God looked at the scientist, "No, no, no. You go find your own dirt!"

"In the beginning…"

God started it. He created the universe, our world, the plants, the animals, and finally Adam and Eve.

> Gen 1:27-28 God created man in His own image, in the image of God He created him; male and female He created them. God blessed them; and God said to them, "*Be fruitful and multiply*, and *fill* the earth, and *subdue it*; and *rule over* the fish of the sea and over the birds of the sky and over every living thing that moves on the earth." [emphasis added]

Work and Rest. Specifically, the Jewish view of work notes the symmetry between Genesis 2:1-3 and Exodus 31:1-11—the same term melakha ("work") is used in both places, and that in Genesis 2:1-3 what God was "ceasing from" was "creation" or "creating."[67]

The Jews note further that the first part of Exodus 31:1-11 provides detailed instructions for the construction of the Tabernacle, and that it is immediately followed by a reminder to Moses about the importance of the Shabbat, quoted above. The Jews note that in the provisions relating to the Tabernacle, the word "work" (Hebrew מְלָאכָה mĕla'kah) is also used. The word is usually translated as "workmanship," which has a strong element of "creation" or "creativity," therefore the idea is to cease from creating. The takeaway here is to *stop being creative for one day and listen to God* on the day of rest. Listen to God for more opportunities to grow, both as an individual, and if one is an entrepreneur, in one's business. If you're constantly working, you don't have time to listen. Hence, the reason to listen just one

---

67 wikipedia.org See *Activities prohibited on Shabbat*

day out of the week means you're getting guidance from God for the coming week.

You also see something else when God creates man and woman.

> Gen 2:5 Now no shrub of the field was yet in the earth, and no plant of the field had yet sprouted, for the LORD God had not sent rain upon the earth, and *there was no man to cultivate* [work] the ground. [emphasis added]

Adam and Eve were "entrepreneurs." God's very first words were, "Be fruitful," but God has a purpose for Adam and Eve: to work. If you notice a trend, God is saying that while He was the first to create, Man should follow His path and be creators, too. *Entrepreneurs are creators, so Adam and Eve's first "job titles" were "entrepreneurs."* An entrepreneur or a creator, takes something of low value, raw materials and resources, and creates something of higher value. Something that is in it's natural or steady state and with thoughts and actions, creates something new.

Do you think if we had cameras recording a "reality TV" conversation between Eve and Adam sometime early in their married life that a conversation might have gone something like this? "Hey, Adam, instead of eating the apple (haha), lettuce, tomatoes, and onions separately we simply cut them all up and put them all together and throw in some sunflower seeds and some herbs and spices and call it a salad? Doesn't that just sound scrumptious?" as she giggled and looks to him with a sparkle in her eye. Adam would have looked straight at the camera and given us "that look" and said, "Hmm…, last time I listened to her about eating something, we got kicked out of the Garden and I had to go to work."

After the Fall of Man, there was work to be done.

> Gen 3:17-19 Then to Adam He said, "Because you have listened to the voice of your wife, and have eaten from the tree about which I commanded you, saying, 'You shall not eat from it'; Cursed is the ground because of you; *In toil* you will eat of it *all the days of your life.* Both *thorns and thistles it shall grow* for you; And you will eat the plants of the field; *By the sweat of your face* you will eat bread, till you return to the ground, because from it you were taken; for you are dust, and to dust you shall return." [emphasis added]

The phrases "be fruitful" and "in toil," you see they indicate that we are to be productive in life. It will take creativity and work/effort, and this will never end until the day we die. In fact, the word toil means "work extremely hard or incessantly." Notice there are no retirement expectations from God in the Bible. In Hebrew there is no word for "fair," or "vacation," or "retirement," or "coincidence,"[68] so if you love what you do, it's not work. It's not a coincidence that you need to find work you love, pay will not be equal, and if you love your work, why take a vacation or retire?

The word "toil" means "pain, labor, hardship, sorrow, toil." It is a pain similar to Eve's pain in childbirth, but Eve only experiences pain in childbirth, Adam will always have pain in the effort with his work. Hence why God says, "All the days of your life." Adam, and by extension us, will always have to work, so there will and should be no retirement.

Joke. But, both Adam and Eve are to be the team to work on and in the new "world" and "be fruitful and multiply." But as with all members on a team, conflicts do arise and need resolution.

A reality TV camera is following Adam and Eve in the Garden of Eden. In the Garden, Adam often wandered the fields until late in the evening. One evening, Eve became suspicious. "Why are you always out so late? Are you seeing another woman?" she asked.

"Nonsense," Adam responded irritatingly. "You're the only woman for me. In fact, you're the only woman on earth." The quarrel continued until finally Adam rolled over and fell asleep. He awoke to someone poking him in the chest. It was Eve.

"What do you think you're doing?" Adam demanded.

"Counting your ribs," said Eve.

First, for Him

God formed you and prepared you before you were born.

> Isa 44:2 Thus says *the LORD who made you*, And *formed you from the womb*, who will help you, 'Do not fear, O Jacob My servant; And you Jeshurun whom I have chosen. [emphasis added]

To love God is a freewill choice. But you're able to love God because He loved you first. In essence, it is when one fully understands love from

68 *Business Secrets from the Bible* by Rabbi Lapin, chapter "Secret #37"

God's perspective can one truly love God, oneself, and then love their neighbor.

> 1 John 4:8 The *one who does not love does not know God*, for *God is love.* [emphasis added]

Learning what love is from the world's perspective is skewed, and in some cases, abnormal. God created you for His pleasure, even though one's life and the decisions made may make life rather difficult. It does not matter. God is the same in the Torah, the Old Testament.

> Deut 6:5 You *shall love the LORD your God* with all your heart and with all your soul and with all your might. [emphasis added]

As He is in the NT.

> Luke 10:27 Thou shalt *love the Lord thy God* with all thy heart, and with all thy soul, and with all thy strength, and with all thy mind; [emphasis added]

God comes first; He is the source of all, of you, and of blessings. He is looking for someone that He can share with, to have a relationship with.

> 2 Chron 16:9 "For the *eyes of the LORD move to and fro throughout the earth* that *He may strongly support those whose heart is completely His.* You have acted foolishly in this. Indeed, from now on you will surely have wars." [emphasis added]

Did you catch it? Did it jump out at you? God wants to "strongly support those whose heart is completely His!" The God of the Universe wants to *strongly support you!*

Not only as an individual, but also in your business. What a concept!

Sad, but also so very true, there is a competitor to God: Satan.

Satan has a number of names: Accuser (Rev 2:10), Adversary (1 Pet 5:8), Angel of Light (2 Cor 11:14), AntiChrist (1 John 4:3), Deceiver (Rev 12:9), Devil (1 John 3:8), King of Tyre (Ezek 28:12), Lucifer (Isa 14:12-14),

Wicked One (Eph 6:16), and a number of other names that aptly describe who and what the Devil and his demons want to do to us and get us to do.

Satan and his demon army are fighting God's purposes, i.e. a spiritual warfare. Just like any organization, there is an angel/demon hierarchal structure (see Daniel chapter 10, verse 13 and the term "21 days"). Satan disguises himself as an Angel of Light (2 Cor 11:14). He does not have as strong or as large an "army" of fallen angels (demons) as God has angels on His side. But Satan is more cunning, sly and willing to lie, woo, and ensnare those who give in and appeal to their weaknesses and thwart God's plans. Same goes for business and the marketplace.

> Job 1:7 The LORD said to Satan, "From where do you come?" Then Satan answered the LORD and said, "From *roaming about on the earth and walking around on it.*" [emphasis added]

When you align yourself with God, Satan is going to attack you, not only in your life, but also your business. But there is a way to fight him.

> Jam 4:7 Submit therefore to God. Resist the devil and he will flee from you.

Prepare for this now so you can prepare your life and your business going forward.

Talent is God-given, be humble. Fame is man-given, be grateful. Conceit is self-given, be careful.

There is an American Indian story that helps explain the above idea. **Cherokee Indian Story.** One evening an old Cherokee Indian told his grandson about a battle that goes on inside people. He said, "My son, the battle is between two 'wolves' inside us all. One is Evil. It is anger, envy, jealousy, sorrow, regret, greed, arrogance, self-pity, guilt, resentment, inferiority, lies, false pride, superiority, and ego. The other is good. It is joy, peace, love, hope, serenity, humility, kindness, benevolence, empathy, generosity, truth, compassion and faith."

The grandson thought about it for a minute and then asked his grandfather, "Which wolf wins?"

The old Cherokee simply replied, "The one you feed."

Feed your faith and your doubts will starve

Grooming yourself for failure or success takes the same amount of effort. Which side will you decide to feed? What side of your motivations will you support with your talents and time? You reap what you sow, sow beans, get beans, not potatoes. Sow good, you'll get good.

> "*Your* smile *is your* **logo**, *your* personality *is your* **business card**, *how you leave others feeling after an* experience with you *becomes your* **trademark"** – Jay Danzie

Then, from Him

Some individuals think they're alone in their talents and skills that they're without any accountability toward someone else in their life, especially God. Nothing could be further from the truth when it comes to one's life, talents, and skills, because God tells us what is happening in one's life and talents and time.

> Deut 8:17-18 Otherwise, you may say in your heart, "*My power and the strength of my hand made me this wealth.*" But you shall remember the LORD your God, for *it is He who is giving you power to make wealth,* that He may confirm His covenant which He swore to your fathers, as it is this day. [emphasis added]

Both your explored and unexplored talent capital and wealth is not of your doing, but it has come from God. He designed and created you and put in you what you have to make wealth and to be prosperous. He put into each of us the design of what we're to be doing. Then we're to thank Him with testimonials and with the fruits of our labor, the first fruits, the best, of what we've produced.

> Exod 23:16 Also you shall observe the *Feast of the Harvest* of the *first fruits of your labors* from what you sow in the field; also the Feast of the Ingathering at the end of the year when you gather in the fruit of your labors from the field. [emphasis added]

Not the seconds, thirds, lasts or the worst of what we earn, but the *first fruits of our labor.* What you give God is to be *first and the best*, no scrimping on the offerings you give God, because He did not scrimp on creating you, so why gyp, swindle, or cheat God? He knows when you give less and not the best that He asks for. Read Psalms 139, God knows.

Second, for yourself

The outside of you is a reflection of what is inside you.

In the event of cabin decompression in an aircraft, you're told to put the oxygen mask on yourself first, then put the mask on others if they're having trouble. Why do they tell you this sequence? Because you're no good to your kids or others *if you are not alive*, so take care of yourself first before you help someone else. C.S. Lewis says it correctly, "True humility is not thinking less of yourself; it is thinking of yourself less."

> 1 Cor 7:17 Only, as *the Lord has assigned to each one*, as *God has called each, in this manner let him walk.* And so I direct in all the churches. [emphasis added]

When you read the above verse, you see that God assigns to each of us our grace talents and gifts, no one else. When you think about an individual, how many think of a business title rather than how valuable each individual is that God created?

Your life purpose: you are God's smart specialist

In Proverbs, you read God highly values wisdom, and it shows in your career, because smart work is more valuable than hard work.

> Prov 12:8 A *man will be praised according to his insight*, But one of perverse mind [Literally: heart] will be despised. [emphasis added]

It's what you're good at and the discipline to work it that others will praise your efforts. "It is my duty and mission to put to work what I am good at, rather than to do what I love to do."[69]

---

69 *Half Time* by Bob Buford, pg 28

You are special. How special are you? The odds of you being you, with your sets of parents, are 1:400 TRILLION![70] That's right; you're that special! You ARE UNIQUE! You are God's specialist!

Your life purpose in five minutes.[71] Amazon lists over 150,000 book and other items that refer to how you can learn your life purpose. The Gallup Organization surveyed over 198,000 people and found *only 20 percent* said "that their strengths are in play everyday."[72] So current businesses are failing to maximize their people's talents and skills. Here in five questions is how to help you define your life purpose.

1. *Who you are?* - This is the start of your quest.
2. *What do you do?* - What are the few things you love to do and are supremely qualified to teach and help others? It is what others would find it difficult to do themselves, but is effortless with you.
3. *Who do you do it for?* - Who specifically needs your talents, skills, or information?
4. *What do they want or need?* - What is it that people are looking for and would gladly pay you to do it for them?
5. *What do they get out of what you provide?* - How are they changed or transformed as a result of what you give them?

Now put all of the above answers to the questions into one sentence and you have your elevator speech to talk with other about what you do. However, what is the difference between the five questions? The first two questions are about who you are and are *inward facing;* the last three questions are about your neighbor and are *outward facing.* The reason? Making other people happy, i.e. serving them, results in your happiest life.

When someone asks you, what do you do, you now know. Question five is your ultimate purpose or result. By focusing on telling others of your results, they are more than likely will ask more questions about what you do. In the end, it is all about results, and how you improve their results.

Jacob's 12 Tribes. So, how unique are you? Let's see God's view of your uniqueness. Jacob, through his two wives and his two concubines had twelve biological sons: Reuben (Gen 29:32), Simeon (Gen 29:33), Levi (Gen 29:34), Judah (Gen 29:35), Dan (Gen 30:5), Naphtali (Gen 30:7), Gad (Gen

---

70 blogs.law.harvard.edu See *What are the chances of your coming into being?*

71 youtube.com See *How to Know Your Life Purpose in 5 Minutes: Adam Leipzig*

72 *Now Discover Your Strengths* by Buckingham and Clifton, pg 6

30:10), Asher (Gen 30:12), Issachar (Gen 30:17), Zebulun (Gen 30:19), Joseph (Gen 30:23) and Benjamin (Gen 35:18). But notice that when Jacob gave *his blessing to each son, each blessing was different*, no two blessings were the same (Gen 49:3-27).

> Gen 49:28 All these are the twelve tribes of Israel, and this is what their father said to them when [and] he blessed them. He blessed them, *every one with [Literally: according to his blessing] the blessing appropriate to him.* [emphasis added]

While each individual and tribe is unique, that uniqueness is a strength when you compare it with the other individuals and their strengths. But let's not stop here in the OT, let's look at the NT.

Body of Christ: 1 Cor 12-13. When it comes to the Body of Christ, you find in Paul's letter to the Corinthians that he discusses the uniqueness of an individual. In verse 11, "But one and the same Spirit works all things, *distributing to each one individually* just as He wills [emphasis added]." He goes on to say that the Body of Christ has many members, but we're one Body. An individual's uniqueness is their strength, but by themselves they are not effective. It is *only when we all cooperate with each other* that the synergy of "when two or three are gathered together in My name" begins to happen.

Apostles uneducated and untrained? Since you're God's specialist, it is not a requirement that you have an education to make a living, but you need to ensure that you learn from the best, here's the evidence.

> Act 4:13 Now as they *observed the confidence* of Peter and John and understood that *they were uneducated and untrained men*, they were amazed, and began to recognize them as [Literally: that they had been] having been with Jesus. [emphasis added]

You need education to become a doctor, lawyer, or an engineer, but it should never stop you from learning and doing what God has gifted you to do. God gave you His permission when He created you, now go do it.

"If your actions inspire others to dream more, learn more, do more and become more, you are a leader." – John Q. Adams

Nature or nurture?

There is a common question about an individual. Is a person's personality based on nature, being born that way, or is it nurture, through various life experiences become what they've grown up to become? In most cases, it's considerd an either/or proposition, but in reality, which is it, nature or nurture?

In fact, it is both. You're born with your personality as God has designed you, man or woman, extrovert of introvert, but you are also influenced by life experiences. Some of those experiences are positive and enhance your personality, negative events or circumstances can also adjust your personality. Becoming a stutterer means some negative emotion events(s) triggered you to create that habit.

Your Personality, Your Desire. When it comes to God designing who you are, there are distinct personalities as well as talents that make up that unique person of you. In order to find out how you are, there are a number of tests that you can take to reveal just what type of person you are. But they can also help you with understanding your family, friends, and others.

Here is a list of some of the various tests that you can take:

- **The Big Five** - Is more scientific regarding one's personality than the others, you can find a test either here outofservice.com or here sapa-project.org. The purpose is the help identify your personality strengths.
    - Closed/Open to new experiences
    - Disorganized/Conscientious
    - Introverted/Extroverted
    - Disagreeable/Agreeable
    - Calm/Nervous
- **Myers-Briggs** - you can visit this location to take the test at 16personalities.com or find a local consultant and get the results of your personality. It focuses on four areas:
    - Extrovert or Introvert (E/I)
    - Intuitive or Sensing (I/S)
    - Thinking or Feeling (T/F)
    - Perceiving or Judging (P/J).

- **DISC** - the DISC[73] test is based on four different personality traits and simply focuses on whether you're an introvert/extrovert, and you're task/people. All individuals have some of each, most have dominant primary and secondary letter.
    - Dominance/Drive (extroverted and task orientated)
    - Inspiring/Inventive (extroverted and people orientated)
    - Submission/Supportive (introverted and people orientated)
    - Compliance/Controlling (introverted and task orientated)
- **Strengths Finder** - In the book *Now, Discover Your Strengths* by Marcus Buckingham and Donald O. Clifton, the authors give a test for finding what strengths you're to operate in.

Are these tests insightful? Yes. Are they definitive? Good enough. But what about life experiences? How does one's life experiences help an individual progress through their life? The point of these tests is to give one a general idea as to who they are and that life can affect our personalities in some shape or fashion. The better one knows themselves and others, the better one can work together in a team environment.

---

73 wikipedia.org See *DISC assessment*

5 God designed you for others

Phil 2:4 do not merely look out for your own personal interests, but also for the interests of others.

While Jimmy and I discussed our various experiences in the service, there is always some service rivalry and bantering, and this will never go away because competition is good. What has improved is how well the services are working together at accomplishing missions. Serving in the U.S. Air Force like myself, or serving as a US Navy SEAL like Jimmy, all service members are taught and trained to serve others in their jobs. For those in the military, it's about serving the people of the United States of America.

That commitment to service runs deep in each service member and carries over into the civilian world when you get out. It is always a matter of having a "higher purpose or calling." No matter what your calling, you will always serve someone in some capacity. Whether you're in the military, the CEO of a Fortune 500 company or you're the CEO of Solopreneur Inc., you will always serve someone, somewhere, providing something to them.

Joke. Adam and Miriam Epstein were arguing who gets to make the coffee in their house. Both of them were very particular about how they liked their cup of Joe – the fact that they got a fancy new coffee machine also may have complicated matters. Adam wouldn't relent to brew coffee the way he liked it, and neither would Miriam, so they decided that the only way to resolve their dispute was to go and visit their Rabbi.

In their meeting with Rabbi Rosenberg, Adam made a passionate plea, "Rabbi, the obligation of a man to brew the coffee is commanded by the Torah itself!"

"Really," said Rabbi Rosenberg, surprised. "Where exactly does it say that?"

"It's in our very name, Rabbi," said Adam. "HEBREWS!"

There is a familiar term in the startup community of being called a solopreneur, one who works alone, going "solo," or running their business single-handedly. An entrepreneur might even have contractors for hire, yet they still require full responsibility for the running of their business. But in reality, no one goes it alone because in business there has to be at least two people involved: the business person and either a vendor or a customer. In most cases, three: business, customer, and vendor.

In Luke 10:27, it says to love "your neighbor as yourself." If you don't love your neighbor, look to see if you love yourself first.

> Mat 7:5 "You *hypocrite*, first take the log out of *your own eye*, and *then* you will see clearly to take the speck out of *your brother's eye*. [emphasis added]

Love yourself. What's one of the most important words in that phrase? Most say the word "love" is the most important word. That is true. If someone does not know how to love themselves first, they can't love others. You can't give to others what you don't have or own yourself. So to learn how to love and to love oneself is the first and most important word. But the word love is a verb that requires action, the Bible gives us the answer here:

> 1 Cor 13:4-7 Love is patient, love is kind and is not jealous; love does not brag and is not arrogant, does not act unbecomingly; it does not seek its own, is not provoked, does not take into account a wrong suffered, does not rejoice in unrighteousness, but rejoices with the truth; bears all things, believes all things, hopes all things, endures all things."

So loving oneself is the first part, so replace the word love with your name to see if you do those actions with yourself. Is ______ patient with themselves? Is ______ kind to themselves? Is _____ not jealous with themselves? Does _____ not brag about themselves? Is _____ not arrogant? Does _____ not act unbecomingly? ____ does not seek his/her own? Is _____ not provoked? Does _____ not take into account a wrong suffered? Does _____ not rejoice in unrighteousness? Does _____ rejoice with the truth? Does _____ bear all things, believes all things, hopes all things, and endures all things? Applying the love action words to your life is your first responsibility.

Love your neighbor as yourself. The second most important word is *as* and is a conjunction word used to connect clauses or sentences together, in this case, connecting two people. Since the word *as* joins two people together, it is important how the two people come together; love your neighbor as yourself.

Look inside to see your talents, but look outside yourself to observe opportunities to use your talents to serve, with love, your neighbor. When you serve others in the marketplace, you'll earn a living. Notice the sequence below: learn, work, earn, then build your house.

> Prov 24:27 *Prepare your work outside*, And make it ready for yourself in the field; Afterwards, then, build your house. [emphasis added]

Here is an additional verse that expands the "as yourself" phrase.

> Lev 19:15 You *shall do no injustice* in judgment; you *shall not be partial* to the poor nor *defer to the great*, but you are to *judge your neighbor fairly*. You *shall not go about as a slanderer* among your people, and you are *not to act against the life of your neighbor*; I am the LORD. You *shall not hate your fellow countryman* in your heart; *you may surely reprove your neighbor*, but *shall not incur sin* because of him. [emphasis added]

Jesus gives an example of who your neighbor might be in Luke 10:29-37, the parable of the Good Samaritan. To *be the best* at something is one thing, to *have the best* is another. But it's how you take the *be* and *have* and *take actions* at being the best toward your neighbor. Or how you connect with them at any point in your life that makes the difference in God's eyes.

> 1 Pet 2:18-20 *Servants*, be submissive to your masters *with all respect, not only to those who are good and gentle, but also to those who are unreasonable* [Or, perverse]. For *this finds favor* [Or, grace], if for the sake of conscience toward God a person bears up under sorrows when suffering unjustly. For what credit is there if, when you sin

> and are harshly treated, you endure it with patience? But if *when you do what is right and suffer for it you patiently endure it, this finds favor with God.* [emphasis added]

In the first-century church there were slaves, sad that there are still slaves in the world today. Being a "slave" it is still well within the focus of serving your fellow human being and is more of an attitude today, not of title.

> Phil 2:4 *do not merely look out* for your *own personal interests*, but also for the *interests of others.* [emphasis added]

In the verse above, the word "look" (Greek σκοπέω skopeō) means "to look at, i.e. care for, have regard to, a thing." It is present, active, imperative, meaning you're commanded to continually look out for your neighbor's interests just as you do your interests. A good business principle here.

When it comes to your neighbor's interests, put your heart into it.

> Col 3:23-24 Whatever you do, *do your work heartily* [Literally: from the soul], *as for the Lord* rather [Literally: and not] than for men, knowing that *from the Lord you will receive the reward* of the inheritance. It is the *Lord Christ whom you serve* [emphasis added].

Cooperation, not condemnation or opposition

Jesus gives the reason or motivation for being in business.

> Mat 20:25-26 But Jesus called them to Himself and said, "You know that the *rulers of the Gentiles lord it over them, and their great men exercise authority over them.* It is not this way among you, but *whoever wishes to become great among you shall be your servant,*" [emphasis added]

Being in business means you are to serve your customers.

There is a reason that you and every other individual is specifically different, and it is for one reason and one reason only we each have unique talents: to cooperate! Viewing both 1 Corinthians 12 (the "spiritual gift" chapter) and 13 (the "love" chapter) together, love is the cooperation and unity that is needed for the Christian Body to perform it's job here on earth. The body, i.e. we as individuals, are *required, in love, to cooperate with each other* in order for God's work to get done, His common goal. Whether that goal is between a business and the customer, neighbors in the neighborhood or a church or larger community. The emphasis is about working together, even if it's between two people, benefiting each other; this is the core issue in any business or endeavor.

When you can do a better job at raising and milking cows and I can do a better job of raising vegetables, we both benefit and raise our standards of living when we allow each other to do what they do best. These individual talents and strengths raises the level of society and an economy when everyone is allowed to pursue a living based on their developed strengths.

Spiritual faith or physical position is never about favoritism. Your position in life is your talents, skills, and spiritual gift. Sin creeps in when individuals who are better at one talent or skill prevents or attempts to shut down or control all others from working at their fullest capacity for God.

> Jas 2:1 My brethren, *do not hold your faith* in our glorious Lord Jesus Christ with an *attitude of personal favoritism.* [emphasis added]

The phrase "personal favoritism" (Greek προσωπολημψία prosōpolēmpsia) is used four times, here and once each in Rom 2:11, Eph 6:9 and Col 3:25. An expanded translation of favoritism is, "respect of person, partiality, the fault of one who when called on to requite or to give judgment has respect to the outward circumstances of men and not their intrinsic merits, and so prefers, as the more worthy, one who is rich, high-born, or powerful, to another who is destitute of such gifts."[74]

The Amplified Bible expanded translation of this verse, "My brethren, pay no servile regard to people [show no prejudice, no partiality]. Do not [attempt to] hold and practice the faith of our Lord Jesus Christ [the Lord] of glory [together with snobbery]!" While the above verse is a picture of one's faith in the church, it applies equally toward one's talents in the marketplace. In fact, to be bold, church teaching should positively influence

---

74 See blueletterbible.org for this Greek word.

and impact the marketplace with the same ideas. And James goes on to say in these verses.

> Jas 2:4-6 have you not *made distinctions among yourselves*, and become *judges with evil motives [reasonings]?* Listen, my beloved brethren: *did not God choose the poor* of [to this] this world to be rich in faith and heirs of the kingdom which He promised to those who love Him? But *you have dishonored the poor man.* Is it not the rich who oppress you and personally [they themselves] drag you into court [courts]? [emphasis added]

Some of the rich happen to think their social and economic position does not come without it's responsibilities. Notice David in 2 Samuel 12:1-14 when Nathan catches David in sin. Nathan relates a story about a rich man who takes a poor man's ewe lamb by might and force because the rich man "was unwilling to take from his flock or his herd (verse four)." David creates his own sentence for his adulterous sin saying what was just.

> 2 Sam 12:6 "He must make restitution for the lamb fourfold, because *he did this thing and had no compassion.*" [emphasis added]

David's sin is of someone who uses their economic title, position, power and might for gain, not as it should be a voluntary and mutual exchange that is supposed to happen in business.

There is a familiar saying about Las Vegas that can be changed here for believers in the church.

What happens in church, stays in church!

May it never be!

We're not to hide or seek refuge in the local church, but we are to take our Christian positive and polite influence beyond the church walls and into the marketplace not an "in your face" bold. We're to change lives that lead to changed behaviors, change from the inside out, not outside in.

Jesus spoke via parables, earthly examples with heavenly connections, but their foundation starts with a physical and earthly example.

Jas 2:8-9 If, however, *you are fulfilling the royal [law of our King] law* according to the Scripture, "YOU SHALL LOVE YOUR NEIGHBOR AS YOURSELF," you are doing well. But *if you show partiality, you are committing sin* and are convicted by the law [Law] as transgressors. [emphasis added]

When one shows either *favoritism, prejudice or unpleasantness toward another individual*, one is committing a grave error, and God points it out.

Jas 2:13 For *judgment will be merciless* to one who has shown no mercy; *mercy triumphs [boasts against] over judgment.* [emphasis added]

There is inequality in the marketplace as we have shown in the parable of the talents above and will never change, but when it comes to how one treats another person, it becomes a different matter.

Take care of yourself first, because you need to be your best in order to help others. Increase the strength of your inside, self-esteem and self-worth, so that you can become self-sufficient to help others.

Phil 4:11 Not that I speak from [according to] *want*, for I have *learned to be content [self-sufficient]* in whatever circumstances I am.

The word "want" means "want, poverty." The word "learned" means "to be in the habit of, accustomed to." The word "content" (Greek αὐτάρκης autarkēs) is the only time this Greek word is used. It means "contented with one's lot, with one's means, though the slenderest." The Amplified Bible puts it like this, "Not that I am implying that I was in any personal want, for I have learned how to be content (satisfied to the point where I am not disturbed or disquieted) in whatever state I am."

Happiness. A Finish proverb that says, "Happiness is a place between too little and too much." Happiness and joy depend on what you decide.

Ecc 9:7 Go then, *eat your bread in happiness* and *drink your wine with a cheerful heart*; for *God has already approved your works.* [emphasis added]

Do all in the name of the Lord.

When you work for others in a job, doing work, or running your own business, you're working for the Lord, so when you serve them, you serve the Lord.

God's will for your life? Add productive value

Search out and prepare that you establish your career before you build a house (and get married), that is what this next verse is saying.

> Prov 24:27 *Prepare your work* outside. And make it ready for yourself in the field; Afterwards, then, build your house. [emphasis added]

God's will for your life: be constructive and productive with *all* of your God-given talents and skills you're born with and your spiritual gift given at salvation by cooperating with others and adding value to everyone's lives following God's lead.

Take the word talent used as a form of currency and look at the parallel of the term as your "talent" to describe you and your life. It means you're to take advantage of all of the opportunities of using your talents and skills that God has given you. Work them to the fullest in a team with others that are strong in your area of weakness.

First: the master, Jesus, has given you your talents. Just like the talents in the parable, you've been given *talent capital* that God has created in you for His purpose. Since God uniquely created you, it means you are of *high-value-talent* to God. And suffice it to say, everyone has more than one God-given talent. Most people probably have a good idea or inkling of what their many talents are, and just like in the parable of the talents, you need to put your talent capital toward God's use and glory. If you don't know, the next step is…

Second: explore, "dig up," and uncover all of your many talents. In most cases, everyone needs to "dig up" undiscovered talents and discover all that they love to do through trial and error to determine their God given talents. Try something, anything, to see if you love it, like it or haven't a clue why others find it so easy to do it while you struggle with it. If you've tried it over a period and can't do it well enough after a lot of practice, you probably don't have the talent. Even if you're not in the top 10 percent, an average talent is still very useful to God, *do not neglect any of your abilities* and always put them all to good use.

In some cases, people have to "take off" or "shed" the "emotional clothes" or "mental fat" of dirt to rediscover their buried treasures of talents. Even those with "ascetic religiousness" (they "give their talent up" for God) of sabotaging behaviors. When you "take the negative off," it means you need to "put on" something different, the positives. Take off the cynical thinking and attitudes and put on better attitudes and habits.

> Prov 18:21 *Death and life are in the power [Literally: hand] of the tongue,* And those who love it will eat its fruit. [emphasis added]

Some individuals have learned to *bury their talent capital,* sometimes buried very deep. It requires lots of digging to bring their talents out in the open; some have never seen the light of day, or, others need to bring them back out into the open again. People are taught to speak erroneously and act to nullify their talents through guilt, false or erroneous pretenses, life goals or various expectations put onto them by others (See the Kieves story above). You can see these results with what God tells the Jews regarding their sins and iniquities and how sin and negativity is passed into future generations, until you break the cycle through Christ.

> Exod 20:5 "You shall not worship them or serve them; for I, the LORD your God, am a jealous God, *visiting the iniquity of the fathers on the children, on the third and the fourth generations* of those who hate Me, [emphasis added]

People's awareness of the problem is the beginning to a changed life. Next, "mine" the dirt of the sin and "baggage" that you are carrying around and toss it off (1 John 1:9). And as you mine, you will "unearth" your "vein of talent gold," then you will work it following God's path and create beautiful jewelry of added value for others.

Third: prepare for and nullify stumbling blocks. Talent nullification is brought on by well-meaning or malicious individuals, which frustrates the will and purpose of God. You can see that in the parable and how the master dealt with the lazy slave. The master's frustration is mostly against those that are on the wrong path of their life rather than following what God has for them to shine for Him. Other people can give you false advice or misdirections and mentorship so that your efforts and path goes contrary to what God wants for you. Have you noticed how Jesus responded to Peter regarding His Father's purpose for His life.

> Matt 16:23 But He turned and said to Peter, "Get behind Me, Satan! You are a *stumbling block to Me*; for you are not *setting your mind on God's interests, but man's.*" [emphasis added]

But more importantly, Jesus give a dire warning to others that put stumbling blocks into another person's path:

> Luke 17:1-4 He said to His disciples, "It is *inevitable that stumbling blocks [temptations to sin] come*, but *woe to him through whom they come!* It would [is] be better for him if a millstone were hung around his neck and he were thrown into the sea, than that he would cause one of these *little ones* to stumble. Be [take heed to yourself] on your guard! If your brother sins, rebuke him; and if he repents, forgive him. And if he sins against you seven times a day, and returns to you seven times, saying, 'I repent,' forgive [you shall forgive] him." [emphasis added]

The word "inevitable" (Greek ἀνένδεκτος anendektos) is the only use of this word in the NT, it means "that cannot be admitted, inadmissible, unallowable, improper, it cannot be but that they will come." The Amplified Bible says of verse one, "And [Jesus] said to His disciples, Temptations (snares, traps set to entice to sin) are sure to come, but woe to him by *or* through whom they come!"

The phrase "little ones" *becomes very important here;* it means "small, little, of influence or rank." While most would view this word for children, it also means others of low economic or social status. The Amplified Bible says, "It would be more profitable for him if a millstone were hung around his neck and he were hurled into the sea than that he should cause to sin or be a snare to one of these little ones [lowly in rank or influence]." If you use your "superiority" to take advantage of someone who is weaker, you've put yourself in danger. Using your superiority as a weapon against someone who is weaker is of cause for alarm. Those of higher status that makes someone of lower status fall (insult, demean, put down, etc.), woe unto you and the punishment that will come.

And here's further proof on how we are to act toward other individuals and believers and their God-given talents.

> Rom 14:13 Therefore let us not judge one another anymore, but rather *determine* this—*not to put an obstacle or a stumbling block in a brother's way.* [emphasis added]

The word "judge" means "deciding between the righteousness and unrighteousness of men; those who judge severely (unfairly), finding fault with this or that in others." The word "determine" means "to determine, resolve, decree." The Amplified Bible says it this way, "Then let us no more criticize *and* blame *and* pass judgment on one another, but rather decide *and* endeavor never to put a stumbling block *or* an obstacle or a hindrance in the way of a brother."

The parable of the talent is more about those that have discovered what their talents are and those associating with them are to encourage others to improve their talents over time. But don't stop there, "dig up" those long ago buried talents and dreams that God had put in you. They are still there; it's just a matter of when you choose to dig them up and work them.

You will feel *much better* about yourself when you find your God-given talents that come easy to you, work to improve them, improve your productivity with them, and then become productive and prosperous serving others. Every person should be on a quest to determine what talents God has given them, and since we all have more than one, we're to *pour gas on those small flames* of talent motivation doing God's will with them. Sometimes it can take a while to figure out what your primary talents are, but dig we must if we're to be the most productive for God and to add value to His Kingdom.

Fourth: an experience can be a solution for others. In Romans, we find how both good and bad work together.

> Rom 8:28 And we know that *God causes all things to work together for good* to those who love God, to those *who are called according to His purpose.* [emphasis added]

Notice that is does not say that *all things are good*, but during various events of life *in the end that all things work together for good.* And any pain associated with an experience is not necessarily a judgment, but view pain like the pain of growth. When one is physically working out, the pain experienced is one of tearing down old muscles to build up new muscles, it's the same with growing our various talents. Growing involves pain.

Any experience that you have gone through and had a breakthrough and share with others will be a shining light to another person's path who might be going through the same thing. You could write a book or give speeches about your experience to sell and reach others about how you went through your situation. This experience talent results in *having a breakthrough* and to the other side of the event or experience. When you share your story with others, it adds value, hope, and motivation to someone else's life.

Fifth: Be as productive as you're able. Just as you read in the parable the talents the inequality of the disbursement of the talents, so it is with being productive with your talents.

> Mat 13:8 And others fell on the good soil and yielded a crop, *some a hundredfold, some sixty, and some thirty.* [emphasis added]

One thing is clear, if Jesus Christ talks about business in a moral and good light through the parable of the talents, then those religious people that bemoan what good businesses do are in the wrong. Are there bad businesses? Yes. Are there people in business that do bad things? Yes. Is profit bad? No. Are their businesses that have the love of money? Yes. Jesus strongly indicates in the parable of the talents that being in business is a good endeavor to be in when you're using your talent to serve God and your fellow man. To exclude God's positive view of business from one's life is to distrust what God is saying to us and is unbelief.

God's Will + Your Good Work = God Rewards You

6 God designed you to productively serve

Psalms 37:23 The steps of a man are established by the LORD, And He delights in his way.

Arriving at Jimmy's shop for another mastermind round, we got down to business after shooting the breeze some. Having done some research about Navy SEALs, I was familiar with their tough training. After graduating from six months of BUD/S training, Jimmy was told he had two weeks off and then told to report to his next training phase, three weeks of Basic Parachute Training. He was told in no uncertain terms that during the Army's PT (physical training) he was not to run backward or to perform any other stunts to show off. They informed him of the process and timeframe of what it took to graduate and finally to get his "bird," the Trident, pinned to his chest that indicated he was now a Navy SEAL.

Jimmy's story of becoming a SEAL once again made me take a look at both of our Christian walks. What "training" do we get from parents, teachers, mentors, Pastors, and others and how do we "graduate" or get promoted from our various stages in this life? What will our physical then spiritual "graduation" look like? In fact, I would gather that most Christians rarely have heard sermons or had many discussions about the results of each our Christian decisions and actions and their respective rewards. It would be like Jimmy being told he had to do "some" training and perform "somehow," but not being told the results he was aiming for, the Trident. If you don't know what and how to achieve the goals, results, or missions, how motivated would you be to accomplish the work?

In essence, we are designed by God for the production of good works that glorify God, you are to do good in God's eyes (12 verses with the phrase "good work;" Neh 2:18, John 10:33, Phil 1:6, Col 1:10, 2 Thes 2:17, 1 Tim 5:10, 2 Tim 2:21, 2 Tim 3:17). Believers are not to be a political activist and *change the laws* to become a "Christian Nation" (although instilling legislative biblical principles is essential to our nation). We're to *change individuals* from the inside out, not from the outside in.

Be the lamp stand, change lives

God has outlined a specific step-by-step process on how to live out our lives, starting from scratch and moving up from there.

> Ezra 7:10 For Ezra had *set his heart to study* [Literally: seek] the law of the LORD and *to practice it*, and *to teach* His statutes and ordinances in Israel. [emphasis added]

Observe Ezra's sequence: study, practice, then teach it to others. He made a willful decision to *study*, which requires many hours of smart and hard work to ensure success in gaining a proper understanding of God's will for godly living. Once Ezra understood, he then *practiced* and fumbled like any person does when starting something new until he grew in strength in all areas of his life. Because of his increasing successful living, God built a foundation that supported Ezra's ministry to *teach* others what he had learned. His words had the ring of authenticity and authority because he was following God's words with actions. This is the start of the process for doing good works and entering business for God.

If you had the cure for cancer, would you keep it hidden from someone that has cancer? No! You'd do everything in your power to get that solution to someone with that problem because it will help their lives. We're never to hide a talent lamp and it's results.

> Luke 8:16-18 Now no one *after lighting a lamp covers it* over with a container, or puts it under a bed; but he *puts it on a lamp stand*, so that those *who come in may see the light.* For nothing is hidden that will not become evident, nor anything secret that will not be known and come to light. So *take care how you listen*; for *whoever has, to him more shall be given; and whoever does not have, even what he thinks he has shall be taken away* from him. [emphasis added]

While most believers know this verse to be about how to obtain salvation and to get to heaven, 100 percent true. But it is equally applicable to one's talents here on earth and providing a solution for someone that needs it. If you have a God given talent whereby you can solve someone's problems or build someone up, then it is your obligation to work at it and make it happen. That is how you serve your neighbor.

Take advantage of your given talents and skills. Otherwise, your efforts will be at the very least pruned (less productive and bad habits cut off so better habits flourish) or if you don't bear fruit, you're cut off.

> John 15:1-5 "I am the true vine, and My Father is the vinedresser. Every branch in Me that *does not bear fruit*, He *takes away*; and every branch that *bears fruit*, He *prunes it* so that it may *bear more fruit*. You are already clean because of the word which I have spoken to you. Abide in Me, and I in you. As *the branch cannot bear fruit of itself unless it abides in the vine*, so neither can you unless you abide in Me. I am the vine, you are the branches; *he who abides in Me and I in him*, he *bears much fruit*, for *apart from Me you can do nothing*. [emphasis added]

Reviewing the above verse you see that, again, one is to be productive, to produce good fruit, and good fruit means to do good works. If you notice that there are two different views of a branch above:

- If the whole branch *does not bear fruit*, i.e. not productive, then the branch is removed from the trunk (support is removed).
- If the whole branch *produces fruit*, i.e. it is productive, it is pruned (bad habits removed, good habits instilled) to produce more.

Each individual chooses how productive or not in life they are with the talents God has given them. God wants you to be more productive, being effective and efficient, not pack more and more into your life so you as an individual become overtaxed with things to do. You hire out or delegate the work to those that need the work, to give them dignity to their life.

Bearing fruit: 100X, 60X, 30X, Matt 7:17-19

At the most basic level, Jesus talks about the "fruit" (over 50+ "fruit" references in the NT alone) of your productive life with the actions you take. It means that all of your good efforts are and will be recognized and rewarded.

If you have ever noticed when you grow fruit that not all of the fruit is the same. Each piece of fruit is a different size, shape, color, or matures or ripens at different times. When Jesus talks about bearing fruit, not all of our good works will be the same, some small, some big, but from a position of love, it will all be good.

> Mat 13:23 And the one on whom *seed was sown on the good soil*, this is the man who *hears the word and understands it; who indeed bears fruit and brings forth, some a hundredfold, some sixty, and some thirty.* [emphasis added]

As you can see, when you take action on hearing the Word and do good, you are fruitful. But as you can see from the comment from Jesus, there is inequality with being fruitful, not everyone will be as productive doing good as another person. Some will be 100X (100 times), others 60X or 30X. Productivity will be the differentiator between all believers and their works judged with what God has given them.

Fruitful performance rewards. So being fruitful with our time on earth will be based on how we love our neighbors as ourselves, so how do we partner with our neighbors in the work we do? What about eternity? How does what we do on earth affect how we're judged in the afterlife? What will be our rewards be after we die?

> Tit 3:13-14 *Diligently help* Zenas the lawyer and Apollos on their way so that *nothing is lacking for them.* Our people must also *learn to engage in good deeds [occupations] to meet pressing needs*, so that they *will not be unfruitful.* [emphasis added]

The word "learn" (Greek μανθάνω manthanō) is in the present tense, imperative mood. It means we're commanded to continually be "to be in the habit of, accustomed to" learn and grow. The word "pressing" means "what one can not do without, indispensable." The word "engage" means "to care for, give attention to." The word "unfruitful" (Greek ἄκαρπος akarpos) occurs eight times in the NT and means "destitute of good deeds." The word destitute in english means "without the basic necessities of life."

The Amplified Bible quotes verse 14 as, "And let our own [people really] learn to apply themselves to good deeds (to honest labor and honorable employment), so that they may be able to meet necessary demands whenever the occasion may require and not be living idle *and* uncultivated *and* unfruitful lives." Honorable labor refers to both businesses and working at a job, and we're to work "to meet necessary demands."

> Col 1:9-10 For this reason also, since the day we heard of it, we have not ceased to pray for you and to ask that *you may be filled with the knowledge [Or, real knowledge] of His will* in all spiritual wisdom and understanding, so that *you will walk in a manner worthy* of the Lord, to [Literally: unto all pleasing] please Him in all respects, *bearing fruit in every good work* and increasing [Or, growing by the knowledge] in the knowledge [Or, real knowledge] of God; [emphasis added]

The phrase "bearing fruit" means "to bear, bring forth, deeds: thus of men who show their knowledge of religion by their conduct." The Amplified Bible says, "That you may walk (live and conduct yourselves) in manner worthy of the Lord, fully pleasing to Him *and* desiring to please Him in all things, bearing fruit in every good work and steadily growing *and* increasing in *and* by the knowledge of God [with fuller, deeper, and clearer insight, acquaintance, and recognition]."

But of primary concern is verse nine, "you may be *filled with the knowledge of His will* in all spiritual wisdom and understanding [emphasis added]." It is accurate spiritual knowledge of what is good (knowing good content and training) that produces (practice quality training) good fruit (perfect practice). Quality content + quality practice = Quality results, being fruitful in God's eyes.

Other verses regarding the production of fruit, i.e. good works: Mar 4:20; Luke 3:9; Luke 6:44; Luke 8:14-15; Luke 13:1-9; John 4:34-38; John 12:24; John 15:1-11; John 15:16; Rom 7:4-5; Gal 5:22; Eph 5:9; Phil 1:11; Col 1:6; Heb 12:11; Heb 13:15; Jam 3:18; and Jude 1:12.

Temporary: earthly work/rewards, earning income

God cares for His own at all times and is the source of all blessings.

> 1 Sam 2:7 The *LORD makes poor and rich;* He brings low, He also exalts. [emphasis added]

Have you noticed that you never find the word retirement in the Bible? The word "work" is translated as "occupation, work, business." The first recorded incidence of it occurs here.

> Gen 2:2-3 By the seventh day God completed His *work* which He had done, and *He rested on the seventh day from all His work* which He had done. And *God blessed the seventh day*, and sanctified it: because that in it he had *rested from all his work* which God created and made. [emphasis added]

While there is no retirement in the Bible, there is rest. So God created, but then rested from His work, business, or occupation. So in essence God started the pattern we're to follow, and God *blessed* the seventh day.

While God started the pattern, we follow, i.e. work six days and rest on the seventh, it is also important how we're to view work, too.

> Psalm 128:2-3 When you shall eat of the *fruit of your hands*, You will be *happy* and it *will be well with you.* Your *wife shall be like a fruitful vine*, Within [Literally: In the innermost parts of] your house, Your *children like olive plants*, Around your table. [emphasis added]

The word "fruit" literally means "labor, toil" that one does. Please God in your work, He will reward your efforts.

> 1 Cor 10:31 Whether, then, you eat or drink or *whatever you do, do all to the glory of God.* [emphasis added]

Whether one is a plumber, lawyer or a fast food worker, be the best at it because God watches you. You're God's ambassador and a light to others in whatever position you're in, so do what is right and pray for the opportunity to share the light with others. You're not to be a burden to others.

> 2 Thes 3:10 For even when we were with you, we used to give you this order: *if anyone is not willing to work, then he is not to eat, either.* [emphasis added]

So when you do the work God wants you to do, you may not become a millionaire, but God will supply everything, nothing more, nothing less, you need to accomplish His goals.

Phil 4:19 And my *God will supply all [every need of yours] your needs* according to His riches in glory in Christ Jesus. [emphasis added]

God is the ultimate angel investor, venture capitalist, and business investor, because if you're doing His will, He'll provide to get the job done.

Eph 2:10 For *we are His workmanship*, created in Christ Jesus *for good works*, which *God prepared beforehand* that *we should walk in them.* [emphasis added]

Good works is about serving others with your talents and profit is the result of serving them and the measure of how well you've done it. It is when you're not serving others well that problems earning money occur.

Prov 10:4 *Poor* is he who *works with a negligent hand*, But the *hand of the diligent makes rich.* [emphasis added]

The contrast between both the lazy and hard worker is readily apparent: if you work smart and hard, you'll do good, if you're lazy you'll be poor.

Prov 24:16 For a *righteous man falls seven times, and rises again*, But the wicked stumble in time of calamity. [emphasis added]

Eternal: finish your race, receive eternal rewards

Experiential Truth: We earn eternal crowns, good works, recognition, and rewards. Once you become a believer, your eternal security is secured. Now your *experiential truth* is to *work for your rewards*, including running your own business which God has called you. If you do the right work, you'll get the right rewards, so *God is your angel investor.* There are five crowns for those believers that qualify for them: Rejoicing, 1 Thes

2:19; Incorruptible Crown, 1 Cor 9:25; Righteousness, 2 Time 4:8; Glory, 1 Pet 5:2-4; and Life, Jas 1:12. God cause all growth to happen.

> 1 Cor 3:6-8 I planted, Apollos watered, but *God was causing the growth.* So then neither the one who plants nor the one who waters is anything, but God who causes the growth. Now he who plants and he who waters are one; but *each will receive his own reward [Or, wages] according to his own labor.* [emphasis added]

Here are the steps from the above verse:

1. Follow God's will.
2. We do the work on a team.
3. God causes the growth.
4. God gives us the rewards we deserve.

When you look at the four steps above, God handles three out of the four, we just do the work and God does the rest. How great is that?

The word "reward" (Greek μισθός misthos) means "of the rewards that God bestows or will bestow, upon good deeds and endeavors." The english word occurs 51 times in 50 verses in the NASB while the Greek word μισθός occurs 29 times in 28 verses in the Greek concordance of the NASB, showing the difference in translation. A reward is similar to a military service member's award medals and ribbons and will be given out based on each's efforts.

Whatever your Godly actions, whether you plant or water, God causes the growth, and you will receive your reward. In the believer's case, the rewards or "military ribbons" that each person will get some are listed here.

> 1 Cor 3:10-15 According to the grace of God which was given to me, like a wise master builder *I laid a foundation*, and *another is building on it.* But each man must be *careful how he builds on it.* For no man can lay a foundation other than the one which is laid, which is Jesus Christ. Now *if any man builds on the foundation* with *gold, silver, precious stones, wood, hay, straw, each man's work will become evident*; for the day will show it because it is to be revealed with fire, and *the fire itself will test the quality of each man's work.* If any *man's work* which he *has built on it remains*, he *will receive a reward.* If any *man's work is burned up,*

> he will suffer loss; but he *himself will be saved*, yet so as through fire. [emphasis added]

Jesus Christ laid the salvation foundation of grace of which our good works build upon. We will be evaluated on how we used our freedom here on earth. Because having freedom, we must take the responsibility for our thoughts, motivations, actions, and every decision we make. Being free in Christ is the greatest responsibility the world has ever known.

The word "careful" (Greek βλέπω blepō) means "to discern mentally, observe, perceive, discover, understand" and is in the present tense, imperative mood, so one is commanded to continually be careful. Ensure you have a *strong foundation* (having an accurate view of salvation) otherwise the foundation won't support your works (errors in motivation, etc.) and both will crumble. First, understanding a good, strong foundation based on an accurate view of God. Second, understanding the salvation message (obtaining eternal life, how to get to heaven). Lastly, with these two key elements, we create eternal rewards based on good and honest work and business practices.

The word "if" in "if any man builds" is in the first class condition and can be translated as "if and it is true." It means "it's true that all Christians will build upon the foundation" and will receive recognition and heavenly rewards of the heavenly good works God determines they do. The word "build" means "to finish the structure of which the foundation has already been laid, i.e. in plain language, to give constant increase in Christian knowledge and in a life conformed thereto." Everyone's individual rewards will be different in *quality* (gold, silver, precious stones) and *quantity* (of the number of works we accomplish), but *all Christians* will get heavenly recognition and rewards for their righteous work and these rewards will be eternally permanent. Jesus even states we will do *greater quantity, not greater quality*, of works, because we can never exceed the quality of His works.

> John 14:12 "Truly, truly, I say to you, he who believes in Me, *the works that I do, he will do also;* and *greater works than these he will do;* because I go to the Father [emphasis added]

Works that glorify God and Christ are the gold, silver, and precious stones, those that glorify us as individuals are the wood, hay, and straw and will be burned up when God applies His perfect judgment to our works.

The word "test" means "to test, examine, prove, scrutinize (to see whether a thing is genuine or not), as metals." God will test our works, not using *pressure* to test the strength, but test for *purity*, the genuineness of the purity of one's works. The word "quality" (Greek ὁποῖος hopoios) means "of what sort or quality, what manner of" and occurs seven times in the NT (Gal 2:6; 1 Thes 1:9; Jas 1:24). The Amplified Bible says of verse 13, "The work of each [one] will become [plainly, openly] known (shown for what it is); for the day [of Christ] will disclose and declare it, because it will be revealed with fire, and the fire will test and critically appraise the character and worth of the work each person has done." Smelting metal is extractive metallurgy, producing metal from its ore. Jewelers test the quality of a gold ring by rubbing it on a touchstone pad or "test stone." Then use various acid concentrations (10k, 14k, 18k, and 22k solutions) to determine the level of the gold's purity. God will use fire to test for the purity of our motivations doing His Works.

Judgment Seat of Christ: Providence, People, Profit. The purpose of the Judgment Seat of Christ is to reveal the quality and quantity of one's works for God, even when it comes to how you handle your business.

> 2 Cor 5:10 For we must all appear before the *Judgment Seat of Christ*, that each one of us [royal family of God] *may receive what is due him* [rewards] for the things accomplished while in the body, whether *good [of intrinsic value] or worthless [evil]*. [emphasis added]

This is the evaluation of the believer's performance in the plan of God during their time on earth. One decision decides eternal life, but many decisions to receive the various recognitions, decorations, honors, and rewards (gold, silver, precious stones, crowns, etc.) that are coming to us.

In 1 Cor 3:13, our works will be judged for purity by fire, whether our motivation is for God or only ourselves. Those works performed to please God will remain, those works to *please only ourselves* will be forever lost. While nearly all Christians will receive rewards, some will receive more in quality and quantity than others because of their decisions. For example, the graph "# of Rewards" shows an idea of how it might look to us when God "settles our accounts." It shows that we perform 60 "gold" works for God and 40

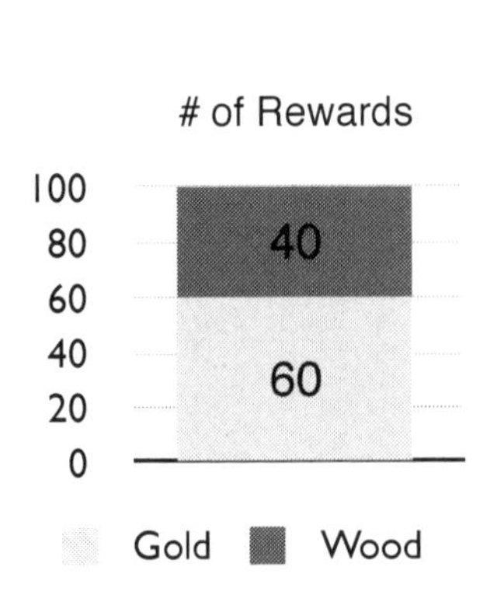

works of "wood" for ourselves, i.e. 60/40. Our *regret* will come when we see that we *could have done a total of 100 works for God.* We'll still receive 60 rewards on eternal display, but we'll lose the 40 because we decided to please ourselves and not God. No one will receive 100 percent "gold" because we're all sinners, each will have a different "split" between "gold" and "wood." Instead of 60 gold/40 wood they might have 70/30, or 40/60, 20/80 or lower. Paul says, "I count all things lost," which are the "wood, hay, and straw" because they are burned up at the Judgement Seat.

> Phil 3:8 More than that, *I count all things to be loss* in [Literally: because of] view of the surpassing value of knowing [Literally: the knowledge of] Christ Jesus my Lord, for [Literally: because of] whom I have suffered the loss of all things, and *count them but rubbish so that I may gain Christ* [emphasis added]

We're to "be careful to engage in good deeds" so as to please God, which includes making money at a job or profit in a business. Our good works are about a moral business that ensures that it pleases God first, people who are our customers second, and profits third.

> Tit 3:8-9 This is a trustworthy statement; and concerning these things I want you to speak confidently, so that *those who have believed God will be careful to engage in good deeds.* These things are *good and profitable for men.* But *avoid* foolish controversies and genealogies and strife and disputes about the Law, for *they are unprofitable and worthless.* [emphasis added]

The word "careful" (Greek φροντίζω phrontizō) is the only time this Greek word is used and means "to think, to be careful." The word "profitable" (Greek ὠφέλιμος ōphelimos) means "profitable" and is only used three times in the NT (1 Tim 4:8, 2 Tim 3:16, Tit 3:8) and the negative of this word is used twice (Tit 3:9, Heb 7:8). The Amplified Bible expands these verses to say, "This message is most trustworthy, and concerning these things I want you to insist steadfastly, so that those who have believed in (trusted in, relied on) God may be careful to apply themselves to honorable occupations and to doing good, for such things are [not only] excellent *and* right [in themselves], but [they are] good *and* profitable for the people." We're to have "honorable occupations," meaning work or a business because it is profitable to you, both here on earth and in heaven.

Finish your race to receive your full reward. Paul talks about running a race in 1 Corinthians 9.

> 1 Cor 9:23-25 I *do all things for the sake of the gospel,* so that *I may become a fellow partaker of it.* Do you not know that *those who run in a race all run,* but only one receives the prize? *Run in such a way that you may win.* Everyone who competes in the games exercises self-control in all things. They then do it to receive a perishable wreath, *but we an imperishable.* [emphasis added]

The Amplified Bible says in verse 24b, "So run [your race] that you may lay hold [of the prize] *and* make it yours." We run our race based on what God has designed us to do. We *do not run someone else's race* and we *do not dictate to others how they're to run God's race for them* to run, we run only our race in our individuals lane.

> Heb 12:1-2 Therefore, since we have so great a cloud of witnesses surrounding us, let us also *lay aside every encumbrance and the sin* which so easily entangles us, and *let us run with endurance the race* that is set before us, *fixing [Literally: looking to] our eyes on Jesus,* the *author [Or, leader] and perfecter of faith,* who for the joy set before Him endured the cross, despising the shame, and has sat down at the right hand of the throne of God. [emphasis added]

The word "encumbrance" is the only time this word is used and means "what is prominent, protuberance, bulk, mass, hence a burden, weight, encumbrance." Discern and then drop all things that burden your Godly motivated work. Jesus will continue to support us in our race and will help us finish it until the day *we cross our finish line.* We cross or own finish line in one of two ways:

- Called Home - when the Lord calls us home at our appointed time.
- Called Up - when we're called up with other believers to meet Him at the Rapture.

We're not to lose heart, focus, or quit before our race ends. Each of us has our own race, our own lane, to run in. This verse below outlines how we should view the race we're running.

> 2 John 8 *Watch yourselves*, that *you do not lose what we have accomplished*, but that *you may receive a full reward.* [emphasis added]

When reading the verse you see John saying to watch what each of us is doing so that any ground that has been gained for Christ is not lost. But what stands out is the word "full." It means "full, i.e. complete; lacking nothing, perfect" and is the only reference of this word regarding the subject of rewards. The below commentary outlines the focus and attitude of John and his view toward both the followers of Christ and their current efforts ("what we have accomplished") and their potential eternal rewards ("full reward"). This word is also significant in that it addresses our motivational efforts.

> *"St. John here addresses not only Kyria but her family and 'the Church in her house.' He views them as his fellow-laborer in the Lord's vineyard: 'We have worked together: see that you do not forfeit the reward of your labor. Get a full wage. Be not like workman who toward the close of the day fall off, doing their work badly or losing time, and get less than a full day's pay. 'We have been fellow workers thus far, and I mean to be faithful to the last; see that you also be so.' "*[75]

The Bible is saying that we'll get rewards, so God through John says that we're not to slow down or let up toward the end of our race. When we follow God's will for our life, He will continue to support us to do good work until that faithful day when we're called home or called up.

> Phil 1:6 For I am confident of this very thing, that *He who began a good work in you will perfect it until the day of Christ Jesus.* [emphasis added]

Serving others at work or in business you elevate their *and* your situation and it is honorable, right and good from God's perspective.

---

75 *The Expositor's Greek New Testament* by W. Robertson Nicoll, Vol V, pg 202

Pleasing God, doing good, you'll get rewards that will last throughout eternity, and we're to encourage those on the Team of Christ to stay in their race and to complete it to the end.

> Heb 10:35-36 Therefore, *do not throw away your confidence*, which *has a great reward.* For *you have need of endurance*, so that *when you have done the will of God,* you *may receive what [Literally: the promise] was promised.* [emphasis added]

The word "reward" means "payment of wages due, recompense" of rewards. Do good at work and in business that glorifies God. Jesus is waiting to reward each of us for our *all of our good and righteous efforts.* Don't quit, encourage each other so everyone finishes their Godly race in their own lane. It is when we change from flesh lanes to God lanes or back to flesh lanes that we will lose our full rewards for our efforts and time here on earth. Keep in the Godly lanes so as to receive your full rewards.

> Rev 22:12 Behold, I am coming quickly, and *My reward is with Me, to render to every man according [Literally: as his work is] to what he has done.* [emphasis added]

7 God designed you & teams to serve others

Col 3:23 Whatever you do, do your work heartily, as for the Lord rather than for men,

There is an unspeakable brotherhood bond when you meet another veteran, even when they are from a different branch of service, whether the Air Force, Marines, Army, Coast Guard or Navy. But once one determines the branch, the familiar sister service harassments begin. Soon after, we get to the heart of our new found brother: where and when did you serve and what did you do while serving?

When Jimmy and I would talk, invariably there would be a comparison between how the Navy and Air Force worked and how we each accomplished our various missions. Rarely stopping there, we'd bounce back and forth between what we did in the service and the current state of our businesses. Where we were and where God was leading us, but it also narrowed down to how each of us was handling what God was up to in our lives.

Jimmy and I have similarities and differences. One of our very first business meetings was at his shop. When I arrived, he told me to be quiet until he finished (those "directive" commands military people do, either with or without yelling or a smile). He outlined his "ideafest" on his small white board with icons, images, lines, and arrows connecting them all together. It took about 10 minutes or so to show what he was thinking, and it was comprehensive. Wow. And that is just one part of who Jimmy is.

Now me, on the other hand, I see how ideas connect with current market forces and the marketplace, and as he was talking, I saw how to implement it in the real world. I saw how his ideas would and could work, but also how each of our individual strengths worked together to make things happen. Just like Paul talks about how the Church has many members, but one body, so, too, did the interactions between Jimmy and I showcase this perfectly. I could not be Jimmy, and Jimmy could not be me, but together working toward a common mission we are a team. He makes me better and I make him better.

Joke. Maurice has a business appointment, and he arrives a little early. The receptionist points to a comfortable, easy chair and asks him to be seated for a while. Maurice settles down, picks up a magazine and tries to read. However, he finds that he cannot concentrate because he is distracted due to a ruckus coming from behind one of the doors leading off the reception area. Maurice goes over to the receptionist and asks, "What's going on in there?"

She replies, "It's the partners' meeting."

"But why are they shouting at each other?" Maurice asks.

"It's a high stakes battle of wits," she replies.

Maurice asks: "Between who?", and she answers, "Horowits, Lebowits, Rabbinowits and Abramowits."

The Church: many members, mentors; never alone

The purpose of the church. When it comes to the church, the role of a pastor/teacher (P/T) is to shepherd and teach Christ's flock how to live lives according to Christ's model of behaviors and life. The P/T is to be a shepherd, not a commander, CEO, or a coach P/T. The role of a P/T is to equip the saints for the work of service, i.e. preparing the Body with how to perform their work that God has designed each of us to perform in the marketplace.

> Eph 4:11-13 And He gave some as apostles, and some as prophets, and some as evangelists, and some as *pastors and teachers*, for the *equipping of the saints [Or, holy ones] for the work of service, to the building up of the body of Christ*; until *we all attain to the unity of the faith, and of the knowledge* [Or, true knowledge] of the Son of God, to a mature man, to the measure of the stature which [Literally: of the fullness] belongs to the fullness of Christ. [emphasis added]

The P/T correctly fulfills their role in the church when they provide everyone with the necessary information and tools to perform their various God-given purposes. The church becomes a fully functioning team when individuals know their role, but each other's role, too. Much like having a team of football players follow the team playbook or Navy SEALs successfully complete a team mission. For Christians, the P/T is to expound the playbook, the Bible, and what Christ envisions things to be so that we can each fulfill our destinies.

Many mentors and due diligence. God tells us multiple times to seek out those that provide good advice and mentorship.

> Prov 15:22 Without consultation, plans are frustrated, But *with many counselors they succeed* [Or, are established]. [emphasis added]

Being in business for yourself means you are battling competitors, including some that are not in God's family and are secular. So you need good Godly advice in order to combat them. Nothing is taken for granted – all arguments are to be considered and debated. Learn to ask why and to make sure you understand the issues.

> Prov 24:6 For by wise guidance you will wage [Literally: make battle for yourself] war, And *in abundance of counselors there is victory.* [emphasis added]

Paul, who was a Pharisee, tells us how the Church should see itself.

> 1 Cor 12:13-14 For by [in] one Spirit *we were all baptized into one body,* whether Jews or Greeks, whether slaves or free, and we were *all made to drink of one Spirit.* For *the body is not one member, but many.* [emphasis added]

Paul goes on to say in chapter 12 that there are many members in the body of the church, but not all have the talents to do the same thing. Every individual needs to find out what they love, like, can, have, and dislike with their mind, body and soul of what and who they are. In most cases, kids may not have a clue and parents need to guide them to not only learn reading, writing, and math, but also about what talents and skills God has instilled in them. Sometimes even adults may not have a clue to what inspires them, or were so pushed into something they don't like that their talents need to be resurrected and released to make them shine. But how does one find out?

Follow God, follow your talents, and use your head

Find God's direction. Take action. Do something. Get moving.

Psal 127:1 Unless *the LORD builds the house,* They labor in vain who build it; Unless *the LORD guards the city,* The watchman keeps awake in vain. [emphasis added]

A familiar refrain by some is to "step out in faith." Faith is the starting point. That is what you need to get moving with first. A simple illustration is this: God can't steer a parked car. Here is the story of the parting of the Red Sea and how God gave direction to Mose and the Jews.

- God tells Moses that He fights for them (Exod 14:14), "The Lord will fight for you while you keep silent."
- God tells Moses to tell the Jews to quit crying and take action (Exod 14:15), to "move forward."
- God tells Moses himself to take action (Exod 14:16), "stretch out your hand over the sea and divide it."
- God is glorified in the results (Exod 14:25), the Egyptians said, "Let us flee from Israel, for the LORD is fighting for them…"

God gives us our talents and spiritual gift, His direction, we move and take action, and someone else will partner with us in this endeavor.

Benjamin Franklin rather poetically and succinctly said, "Hide not your talents, they for use were made, what's a sundial in the shade?" He also said, "If passion drives you, let reason hold the reins." If you've never tried to do something, how would you know if you have the talent? It means trying something many times, even at different times in your life. It's not saying "No" to any individual at any age and what are their interests. It's saying "Yes" to just about anything and everything. The emphasis is to find out *how many talents each person might have* and then ignite their fuse, their inspirations, and their talent insights and apply them in the marketplace. It's determining *what you can do and cannot do.* What you can't do, find someone who is talented in what you're weak at and work as a team.

What you don't want to do is have someone tell you that you have a talent when you don't. You see this constantly on the TV talent shows like

American Idol where most contestants can't carry a tune in a wet paper bag. Whatever one's reasons to go on these shows, you need God-given talents, your spiritual gift, and skills first, then you need to work on improving them for the marketplace.

If you have singing voice, you can't deny it. If someone has that talent, it is that person's responsibility and the obligation of those around them to encourage, push, and develop their talent to their fullest. And once one knows and fully develop and apply their talents, at some point you will be recognized by others for your performance.

> Prov 18:16 A *man's gift makes room for him*, And brings him before great men. [emphasis added]

Your improved talents will put you in front of those that need your talents, because they need your help. To do what you love, get paid for it, then you need to share your wealth with those that need your help. It is a shame to have your talents and then to misuse them for our personal glory rather than for God's.

> Psm 119:97-98, 102 O how I love Your law! It is my meditation all the day. *Your commandments make me wiser than my enemies*, For they are ever mine. I have not turned aside from Your ordinances, For *You Yourself have taught me.* [emphasis added]

Work primarily in your strengths, talents, and gift. A few years back I took the test in the book *Strengths Finder* by Tom Rath (More about your strengths at Gallup's website, gallupstrengthscenter.com). The test nailed what I love to do. When my wife took it. Her number one strength was she was a deliberator; she mulls over information before she makes a serious decision. I was eager to compare notes since we both have taken the test. Wanting to know more about how she felt about the test, I eagerly asked her, "Well, well, what did you think of the test results?"

She paused for a moment as if in deep thought (yep, deliberating), and then said, "I'll have to think about it."

I laughed out loud.

A hearty laugh, but not quite a snort laugh.

When I finally stopped laughing, I looked back at her, and she looked bewildered and said, "What's so funny?"

Still snickering some, I said to her, "Do you realize that your comment about your results just validated the test?"

I watched for her reaction.

She paused, deliberating what I said, then gave me her silly smile and playfully hit me and said, "Stop teasing me."

She got it. Now we move on knowing more about ourselves and learning how to apply it in our marriage and the marketplace.

Needless to say, because of how accurate the tests were at helping us understand ourselves and each other we were able to find out where each other's strengths and weaknesses were and work them into our lives. We were now working *with* each other as a married team with common goals and working less *against* each other, fighting for our selfish selves, trying to control one another versus working toward our agreed upon goals. The test results show I'm a high-level idea thinker, and my wife is a detail oriented individual, I'm an extrovert she's an introvert. Do you see how we both can use how God designed us to help each other? That's how it's supposed to work in marriage, in life, in a job, at a business, in a church or synagogue.

Motivated talents. When you read about Cain and Abel, you read a rather interesting comment coming from God.

> Gen 4:7 If *you do well*, will not *your countenance be lifted up*? And *if you do not do well*, sin is crouching at the door; and it's desire is for you, but you must master it. [emphasis added]

When you read the Complete Jewish Bible[76] of this verse, it gives a bit different view: "If you are *doing what is good*, shouldn't you *hold your head high?* And if you don't do what is good, sin is crouching at the door—it wants you, but you can rule over it [emphasis added]."

Talents, like tools such as a pen, can be used by a person to do good or to do bad and leads to one issue: freewill. What do you intend to do with what you have, both in talents and tools? Follow your talents and use your head and do good.

Discover your talents, gift; skills then support them

What do you love to do? Does working with numbers excite you? Do you love to drive for hours? Do you love to write? Do you love babies and

76 biblestudytools.com

everything about them? Do children steal away your heart and soul? Can you teach those around you absolutely anything? How about crafts? Can you sing like a songbird? Play the guitar? Do you love to build? A house? A boat? A commercial building? Do you like the outdoors? Hunting and tracking? Do you like martial arts? Boxing? How about sports? Are you into rock climbing? Snowboarding? Do you love food? Do you cook like a chef? Are you good with colors? Clothing material? Do you love fashion and styles? Do you love to work with colored oil or watercolors?

Your talents and gifts are those that you find easy to do and others find difficult. You have to listen to what your talents are telling you. Write down all those things that you have a strong interest in and begin finding an affinity of your talents and skills and then find an affinity of what the market needs and wants. When you're "zoned" in with your talents and working for God's Team, you'll never be afraid or timid. It builds confidence.

> 2 Tim 1:7 For *God has not given us a spirit of timidity [Or, cowardice], but of power and love and discipline* [Or, sound judgment]. [emphasis added]

Paul writes and tells us that our physical life is just as important as our spiritual life and not to discount our physical work (brain and brawn) here on earth as worthless.

> 1 Tim 4:8 for bodily discipline is only of little profit, but *godliness is profitable for all things, since it holds promise for the present life and also for the life to come.* [emphasis added]

Our physical efforts come in second after our Godly, reverence, spiritual and heavenly motivations and focus.

> Phil 4:13 I can do all things through Him who strengthens me.

Strengths and Talents. God designed you with both strengths and weaknesses. Why both? Because based on "love your neighbor as yourself" it means you *need others to fulfill each of our missions in life,* you never do it alone. You could be a genius, but even if you could to it all, you only have one brain, two hands, and two legs and 24 hours in a day. To be productive in this world, *you will require help from others.*

Creating and making a pencil requires four basic components: lead, wood, metal, and an eraser. But it requires many people from across the world to create just one pencil. Read the article *I, Pencil* by Leonard E. Read[77] to get a good basic economic idea as to what it takes to produce a simple pencil. Creating staples, paper clips, or paper all require many steps and resources to produce what we find in our local store.

In 1 Samuel, David with his God given talents and skills as a shepherd was able to kill a lion and a bear and to take care of his father's sheep. Taking supplies to his fighting brothers, he was given the opportunity by Saul to help out on the battle front.

> 1 Sam 17:38-39 Then *Saul clothed David with his garments and put a bronze helmet on his head*, and he *clothed him with armor*. David girded his sword over his armor and tried to walk, for he had not tested them. So David said to Saul, "*I cannot go with these, for I have not tested them.*" And David took them off. [emphasis added]

Saul gave David his armor and clothing to fight Goliath.

Lessons Learned:

- *Saul's view of David.* King Saul had been fighting all along with the necessary equipment and training needed to conquer the enemy with their current view of military doctrine and strategy of military force.
- *David's view of himself.* David already had training as a shepherd taking care of sheep and protecting them from lions and bears and other enemies of the sheep. He listened to what King Saul had to say, and based on his young experience, decided against following the King's word. David rejected the King's way of doing things and followed what was best for him to accomplish the task before him.
- David's goal or target did not change, just the process of how it was going to be done.
- David's goal did not change, but having no experience with what tools Saul had given him he would have not been as productive. David was only productive with what God had trained him in using.

77 econlib.org See *I, Pencil* by Leonard E. Read

Operating outside your talents and gift is soul-sucking

When you read the Kieves' story above and the unhappy life she had, while she was able to push through and be productive and accomplished, law was not her cup of tea. So you can see when we operate outside of what God has called us to do, we will be frustrated, depressed and in some cases we can become destructive. While we all might not like to clean house or wash dishes for a living, it still needs to be done. When you get attacked, and you love what you're called to do, most of the time you can handle it. But when you don't love what you're doing, the work becomes soul-sucking.

I once had a conversation with a "gear-head lady," she loved working with motorcycles, but because of a back injury, she found another job in another field, which she completely disliked. I gave her some tough questions to answer. While she might not be able to do 100 percent of what she loved, she could do 75 or even 50 percent of what she loved or liked versus 100 percent of what she disliked. Another friend was on the path to becoming the "next big singing star" in her state. But after becoming a Christian, because of her new "religiousness," she decided to "give it up for God." We need to realize that *our natural talents don't change once we become a Christian,* the only change that should occur is when we just switch from working for Team Self to working for Team God.

> *Working hard for something we don't care about it is called stress. Working hard for something we love is called passion. – Simon Sinek*

When you operate outside your calling, spiritual gift, and talents your energy is *sapped*, sucked away, and depleted. Fighting off all of the various negatives, both outside in your environment and inside you, it becomes the most disheartening thing to any person. Living and working around your skills, talents, and spiritual gift is like being *zapped* and struck by a lightening bolt. You come alive with energy and could do it all day long and never tire of it, the naysayers and cynics eat your dust. This is the true meaning of operating in your calling.

> Prov 12:25 *Anxiety in a man's heart weighs it down*, But a good word makes it glad. [emphasis added]

The idea regarding talents is that once you understand what you were born with, you can now search the market for how you can serve someone and connect with others that do what you don't like to do to serve them.

Positive vs. negative views of failure and success

Positive. While we were designed to do good and when we do good and follow God's plan for our lives, He delights in us.

> Gen 6:8 But Noah *found favor* in the eyes of the LORD. [emphasis added]

He does not like us to habitually and continually do bad and then expect Him just to take us back without consequences.

> Hos 6:6 For *I delight in loyalty* rather than sacrifice, And in *the knowledge of God* rather than burnt offerings.[emphasis added]

He wants us to want to do good. The Amplified Bible expands, "I desire *and* delight in dutiful steadfast love *and* goodness, not sacrifice, and the knowledge of *and* acquaintance with God more than burnt offerings."

> Psa 100:2 *Serve the LORD with gladness*; Come before Him with *joyful singing*. [emphasis added]

God loves and delights in His relationship with you.

> Jas 2:23 and the Scripture was fulfilled which says, "AND *ABRAHAM BELIEVED GOD*, AND IT WAS *RECKONED TO HIM AS RIGHTEOUSNESS*," and he was called *the friend of God*. [emphasis added]

Abraham *believed* God it was *accounted* to him as righteousness, and he was *called the friend of God*. Abraham's faith first was what placed him as a friend of God, works were the results of this friendship. When two individuals get to know each other well, don't they become friends? And the more time you spend together, the better that friendship becomes? It's the same with God.

> Psa 37:23-24 The *steps of a man are established by the LORD*, And *He delights in his way*. When he falls, he will not be hurled headlong, Because the *LORD is the One who* [Or, who sustains him with His hand] *holds his hand.* [emphasis added]

He, God, *delights in your way!* The Amplified Bible gives a stronger view, "The steps of a [good] man are directed *and* established by the Lord when He delights in his way [and He busies Himself with his every step]."

What?

Did you see that?

He, God, delights in your way and busies Himself with your every step!!!

WOW! The first keyword that God tells us in the Amplified version: *WHEN!* When you choose the path God wants you on, God delights in what you're doing. The second keyword is BUSY! God busies Himself and enjoys watching every detail of your life. When you align with God, you will not be alone in your work. Even if you fall, God has you so you won't hurt yourself because even if you fall, He'll keep you from hurting yourself.

> Isa 64:8 But now, O LORD, You are our Father, We are the clay, and You our potter; And *all of us are the work of Your hand.* [emphasis added]

Once God designed us, when we were born, our next step is we're to grow in what he has designed us to do, both in our talents and skills. We are not animals, but as humans we must learn, create, and connect with Him first, with ourselves second, and others third.

> Psal 14:2 The LORD has looked down from heaven upon the sons of men, To see *if there are any who understand [act wisely], Who seek after God.* [emphasis added]

He politely waits for us to turn to Him; it reads *if there are any.* God is a gentleman, so should we be ladies and gentlemen toward God, ourselves, and others. What should be our ambition, even in business?

> 2 Cor 5:9 Therefore *we also have as our ambition*, whether at home or absent, *to be pleasing to Him.* [emphasis added]

If God has created you with your abilities and talents, the above verse says He understands how He created you, and there is one thing that stands out the most about His creation, you.

> *As a believer, God gave you His permission to perform your best with your talents, which He gave you at your birth, and your spiritual gift, which He gave you at the moment of salvation, to do good that pleases Him.*

So go forward and do good.

Negative. Guilt drives some people, so does sin, resentment, anger ("clam up" or "blowup"), fear, materialism, a need for approval and a host of other negative motivations.

There are three views of failures:

- *Dwelling on it* ("Pity Party") - Don't get "stuck" (emotionally or otherwise) in sins or failures and forever hold onto the negative past. When it comes to sin and failure, expect it to happen, but never, never, never allow it to become a self-fulfilling prophesy for your future.
- *Dealing with it* ("Man/Woman Up") - Take ownership and learn what went wrong; make changes, so you can redefine what failure is. Getting a vaccination inoculates you from certain diseases; learning from failure helps inoculate you from future failures when you learn. Focus on the part of the experience to make you stronger and grow from it. The more time you spend in God's word and connecting with Him, the fewer opportunities that you'll have to create problems.
- *Denying it* ("Macho Man/Woman") - By not facing your problem, you will potentially and repeatedly fail, in the same way, in the future.

Often when reading other writings, a thought or an idea enters one's mind and any good person asks: what does God say about this? When you find something that strikes you, compare it with what the Bible says about the idea. The reason: you don't throw the baby out with the bathwater, because the Bible does not cover all subjects in depth. While Satan talks in half-truths, it is only through discernment with learning 100 percent truth can one understand where the errors are in the half truths.

Too much fearful focus on either the *future* "what ifs," or of the *past* "coulda, shoulda, woulda" creates guilt, regret, resentment, bitterness and all forms of non-forgiveness and leads to obsessive mental loops that will drain your energy and build anxiety. Too much future and past focus are deleterious to your performance.

How often does God say, "do not fear" to His people? Does God not give us hope for our future? Paul says in Philippians.

> Phil 3:13 Brethren, I do not regard myself as *having laid hold of it yet*; but one thing I do: *forgetting what lies behind* and *reaching forward to what lies ahead*, [emphasis added]

In one verse, God outlines that too much fearful looking into the future and too much fearful living in the past stifles our present efforts. When looking at failure, how should one view it?

Failing to learn and grow from failure is the real definition of failure.

Observe. Assess. Learn. Let go. Move on.

Conclusion: decide to grow despite what you face. Those individuals with a *growth mindset* see talent is improved from work and grow much faster and better. Those with a *fixed mindset* says talent is innate, that says there are limits.[78]

Sin and failure will always be in a person's life. We each determine how it will affect our future efforts. The *negative* of one's life without God goes from "How much *pleasure am I* getting out of life?" to a *positive* one with God of "How much *pleasure is God* getting out of my life?"

In a recent LinkedIn post[79] James Cutrin interviewed Admiral Eric T. Olson, U.S. Navy (Retired). He had reached the pinnacle of leadership in the United States military, the first Navy SEAL as Commander, U.S. Special Operations Command (USSOCOM). Admiral Olson shared, "If you want to make it through Navy SEAL training, don't quit." But it does not stop there, what determines whether one succeeds or one quits? The

---

78 YouTube.com See *Why You Need to Fail* by Derek Sivers

79 linkedin.com See *The No. 1 Lesson from Navy SEALs: 'Don't Quit in Anticipation of Future Failure'*

characteristics of being successful SEALs, they are driven, focused, always want to be better, and are problem solvers who look at things from different angles. But what about the quitters, what about them?

> *Most quit over breakfast or lunch. They quit in anticipation of the difficult conditions to come. ... They self-eliminated, not because they didn't have the abilities to perform the tasks ... [the Navy SEAL organization] learned that the competitive athletes [competitive water polo players or wrestlers (in that order)] who also excelled as chess players were three times as likely to graduate as those who didn't play chess. Chess players are always thinking two or three moves ahead ... they are less emotional, less knee-jerky, and are always thinking about longer-term problem-solving. Put another way, chess players don't quit over breakfast or lunch. [So] don't quit in anticipation of future failure. Decide now to not quit, decide to keep going with the confidence that you can do more than you think you can do [despite what you are facing].*

While nearly all of us may not aspire to become Navy SEALs, these successful characteristics can boil down the above commentary to this for each Christian.

> Phil 1:21 For to me, *to live is Christ* and *to die is gain.* [emphasis added]

As believers, we live lives fully for Christ, but securely knowing death is a gain, both living and dying, we're covered, and that gives us confidence.

Clear the rooms of your mind of the enemy. To summarize:

Every saint has a skeleton past, and every sinner has a new potential future.

Let God use His Word to get into your life and let His Word work its magic on your thoughts, motivations, and actions. God gave it to us for a reason, to guide us in our quest to do His will.

> Heb 4:12 For the *word of God* is living and active and sharper than any two-edged sword, and piercing as far as the *division of soul and spirit*, of both joints and marrow, and *able to judge the thoughts and intentions of the heart.* [emphasis added]

God's Word helps you with the thoughts and intentions of one's heart. It can help illuminate where you're having issues and where are the root problems you're having. It's like seeing a mental health professional for free. It will only cost you time and effort to get rid of your "mental fat" and "bad habits" with the Great Counselor, God, helping you out.

> Phil 3:13-14 Brethren, I do not regard myself as having laid hold of it yet; but one thing I do: *forgetting what lies behind* and *reaching forward* to what lies ahead, I *press on toward the goal* for the prize of the upward call of God in Christ Jesus. [emphasis added]

Letting go is difficult, but the "Love chapter" tell us the *why of letting go.*

> 1 Cor 13:5 does not act unbecomingly; it does not seek its own, is not provoked, *does not take into account a wrong suffered,* [emphasis added]

The Navy SEALs, Delta Force, Army Rangers, and other U.S. Special Operations give us a strong indication of *how quickly we need to let go to move on.* These men train to enter buildings, room by room, to secure it, and capture it from the enemy. If they fight in one room, they have to take care of what's in the current room before advancing to the next room. Four steps need to happen when entering a room. *First,* neutralize the threat in the room by whatever means dictated by the Rules of Engagement (ROE). *Second,* if a team member gets injured, they need to attend to them so that they can survive and thrive. *Third,* they need to learn from and forgive their errors of the room they're in (keep a short account). *Lastly,* determine what is new or different, quickly learn the differences, then prepare to engage this new situation in the next rooms. It's all done in mere seconds, especially the third step, learn and forgive quickly from the negatives and move on.

Christians should be just as quick with sins and errors (1 John 1:9). We need to let God the Holy Spirit and His Word secure and clear the rooms and recesses of our minds from negative thoughts, habits, and sins and replace them with His good thoughts and move on. We're to let go, forgive ourselves and others for our past, learn better thoughts and habits, and look to the future, i.e. *we're to keep a short accounts of wrongs, Special Operations short.*

Then begin and keep renewing your mind.

> Rom 12:2 And do not be conformed to this world [age], but be *transformed by the renewing of your mind*, so that you *may prove [approve]* what the *will of God is*, that which is good and acceptable [well-pleasing] and perfect.

While your talent should be the first thing that drives you, often is the case that we're imprinted from outside motivations that affect our internal motivations, in both positive and negative ways.

Skills and improvement. Skills are what you pick up as your life progresses, such as learning to write, make a peanut butter and jelly sandwich, digging a hole in the ground, or even driving a car. Whatever the case, you've learned to do something that will help you with your life. And everything you learn can help you or your neighbor at some point, so don't discount what you learn, even things you may not quite like. Why? Because you'll at least understand how it gets done and anyone who loves doing it more than yourself, you want to connect with them.

Your talents provide you with a baseline of what to do, your responsibilities with your talents is to make improvements in them over time. It would be like being given the talent to sing and not put it to good use nor to learn how to be better with your talents serving customers.

> John 15:2 Every branch in Me that *does not bear fruit*, He takes away; and every branch that bears fruit, He prunes it so that it *may bear more fruit.* [emphasis added]

God prunes us so we can be more productive with the talents He has given us, so don't take all pressure as judgment. He also stretches us to produce more and getting rid of stuff that negatively affects your Godly production, such as skills that others can do better than you.

Christian spiritual gifts and love: 1 Cor 12-13

A spiritual gift, which is different from the physical talents and skills that you were born with, is *received at the point of salvation* and is a gift from the Holy Spirit.

> 1 Cor 12:11, But *one and the same Spirit* works all these things, *distributing to each individually just as He wills.* [emphasis added]

A spiritual gift is never earned, deserved, or initially developed through any form of experience. The Holy Spirit has decided what to give you. You can never seek or ask for it. In some parts of the Christian community, a spiritual gift is something to *strive for, over promote, or seek out.* Every individual's spiritual gift relies 100 percent upon the Holy Spirit, including your growth in your spiritual gift. It is only after you have received your spiritual gift and work with it do you grow with His reliance and guidance.

1 Cor 12:13 For by one Spirit *we were all baptized* into one body, whether Jews or Greeks, whether slaves or free, and we were all made to drink of one Spirit. [emphasis added]

The word "baptism" (Greek βαπτίζω, baptizō) is aorist, passive, indicative. The aorist tense means at a point in time (at the moment of your belief in salvation, never after or "second chance"), passive voice means *God did it to you* (you could not help it along, ask for it, pray for it, or seek it, because it is a grace gift pre-planned from eternity past for God to give to you), and the indicative mood means it's a fact, that it was permanently done, you don't have to question it. This Greek word is not the same as the Greek βάπτω baptō. From the notes about this Greek word:

> *This word should not be confused with baptô (G911). The clearest example that shows the meaning of baptizo is a text from the Greek poet and physician Nicander, who lived about 200 B.C. It is a recipe for making pickles and is helpful because it uses both words. Nicander says that in order to make a pickle, the vegetable should first be 'dipped' (baptô) into boiling water and then 'baptised' (baptizô) in the vinegar solution. Both verbs concern the immersing of vegetables in a solution. But the first is temporary. The second, the act of baptising the vegetable, produces a permanent change.*[80]

The idea here is the baptism of the Holy Spirit, which occurs for every Church Age believer *at the moment of salvation* means this baptism, the Spirit's impartation of salvation and our spiritual gift, is permanent. It can never be sought post salvation, after you have believed, and *can never be undone.*

Scriptures for spiritual gifts: listed and explained (Rom 12:6-8, 1 Cor 12:4-30); came from God (James 1:17); assigned sovereignty (1 Cor 12:28); cannot be bought (Act 8:18-20), always for edification (Rom 1:11);

80 blueletterbible.org See notes at Strong's G911

counterfeited by Satan (2 Cor 11:13-15); spiritually discerned (1 Cor 12:2-3); and love is supreme (1 Cor 13:1-13). Your spiritual gift is grace given, is permanent, and is in addition to your physical talents and skills you get at your physical birth and developed over the years.

Grieve and quench the Spirit. Notice something significant here. Every Christian has a spiritual gift to be used for God's glory. In the Christian world there are two words regarding the Holy Spirit, that we *grieve* and we *quench* Him. Let's take a look at these two words.

> 1 Thess 5:19 *Do not quench* the Spirit; [emphasis added]

The word "quench" means "to metaphorically to quench, i.e. suppress, stifle divine influence."

> Eph 4:30 And *grieve not* the holy Spirit of God, whereby ye are sealed unto the day of redemption. [emphasis added]

The word "grieve" means "to grieve, offend."

When it comes to grieving and quenching the spirit, we most often think of it from God to ourselves and how we stifle His influence over our lives. Do we hinder what God wants to do with our lives on a regular basis? How much do we listen to God so that we can do His will in our lives?

See Chapter 12 below about grieving and quenching the Holy Spirit for more details regarding this issue. Because it's not all about you.

8 Serve God, serve yourself, serve others

Lev 19:18 'You shall not take vengeance, nor bear any grudge against the sons of your people, but you shall love your neighbor as yourself; I am the LORD.

Jimmy showed up "on time, on target" for our meeting at a local restaurant for coffee. He sat down with a grin on his face when he saw for the first time, and my first time ever growing, my "battle beard" (I have never grown a beard, so not shaving for 8 weeks I wanted to know what it and I looked like). He joked that it "looked good," but per my wife, I had too much gray and looked much older than I should. Oh well, it was fun while it lasted, and I checked that off my bucket list.

As service members and military Veterans, you first learn to be a part of a team, Jimmy for a Navy SEAL platoon and me for a USAF Aircraft Maintenance Squadron. You learn to depreciate yourself and become a team member and then learn how your specific training fits the team environment and mission. However, becoming an entrepreneur in most cases means you become "the team" and wear many hats. In many ways, you're alone in your endeavor to start your business and the business talks Jimmy and I had shows this happens to all solopreneurs. But our talks gave us a chance to become a "team" with similar emphasis, serving our customers, but also to share our knowledge and experience on how to grow each of our businesses.

When God created Adam, He said, "It is not good for the man to be alone, I will make him a helper suitable for him" (Gen 2:18). God shows us that we're not to "go solo," whether in life, work, or in business. We need each other. God designed each of us with different talents and innate skills based on our physical attributes, personality, and mental capabilities. He indicates that we are to be on a team with Christ as the team leader. One of the greatest aspects about serving in the military is that you become well acquainted with the idea that you take on a cause that is greater than yourself. As a Christian it's by serving God and someone else, just like when Jesus spoke about the two great commandments.

Joke. It was mealtime during a flight on El-Al , Israel's national airline.

"Would you like dinner?" the flight attendant asked Moishe, seated in the front row.

"What are my choices?" he asked.

"Yes or no," she replied.

We're given more talent choices at birth than the joke indicates. But we are all charged with discovering all of one's talents and encourage and pour gas on each person's talent spark to fulfill their God-given purpose.

This verse shows the basic premise of what you're to do with your talents and life.

> Deut 6:18 You *shall do what is right and good* in the sight of the LORD [emphasis added]

Love and serve are action verbs

Notice that both the words "love" and "serve" are both verbs in Hebrew, words that require action. Action requires that two or more are involved, whether it is between God and me and me and my neighbor, always two will be involved.

The verb *love* (Hebrew אָהַב 'ahab) is a root word. Its basis comes from Leviticus 19.

> Lev 19:18 You shall not take vengeance, nor bear any grudge against the sons of your people, but *you shall love your neighbor as yourself;* I am the LORD. [emphasis added]

Inherent in this word the Great Commandment emboldens individuals to treat each other as equals which first requires valuing oneself in order to be able to mirror the love of yourself onto others. You cannot share or give what you do not own yourself.

Love between individuals is not give and take, but give and receive, which the word take has the idea to apply force.

While Job's servants served him, he views them as an equal to him as God created them both.

Job 31:13-15 If I have despised the claim of *my male or female slaves*, When they filed a complaint against me, What then could I do when God arises? And when He calls me to account, what will I answer Him? *Did not He who made me in the womb make him*, And the *same one fashion us in the womb*? [emphasis added]

The verb *serve* (Hebrew עָבַד 'abad) is a root word and is defined as "to serve or work for another." Entrepreneurs perform duties or services for (another person or an organization); provide (an area or group of people) with a product or service; attend to (a customer in a store); supply (goods) to a customer; or be of use in achieving or satisfying another individual. The results are receiving payment in most cases in the form of money. The more people you serve and serve well, the more money you make.

If you get into business solely to make money, you won't. If you try to make a real difference, you'll find true success. —*Richard Branson*

So going into business means you serve someone else with your talent and skills. In 2 Corinthians, we get the basis for how one is to live their lives, but also the basis to be in business.

2 Cor 1:3 Blessed be the God and Father of our Lord Jesus Christ, the Father of mercies and *God of all comfort*, who comforts us in all our affliction so that *we will be able to comfort those* who are in any affliction with the comfort with *which we ourselves are comforted by God.* [emphasis added]

Do you find comfort in a specific solution, whether it is a medical condition or a tool that makes your life easier to function in life? Do you not think someone else might get the same comfort using the same solution? Isn't it neighborly to share something with someone else who needs what you have found?

Here is the basis for all entrepreneurship.

> Phil 2:3-4 Do nothing from [Literally: according to] selfishness [Or, contentiousness] or empty conceit, but with humility of mind regard one another as more important than yourselves; *do not merely look out for your own personal interests, but also for the interests of others.* [emphasis added]

Serve God: Deut 8:3, 18

What did God tell the Jews regarding His Word?

> Deut 8:3, 18 *He humbled you and let you be hungry,* and fed you with manna which you did not know, nor did your fathers know, that He might make you understand that *man does not live by bread alone, but man lives by everything that proceeds out of the mouth of the LORD.* 18 But you shall remember the LORD your God, for it is *He who is giving you power to make wealth,* that He may confirm His covenant which He swore to your fathers, as it is this day. [emphasis added]

The Jews weren't the only ones God told this to; Jesus used the same verse when He was tempted by the devil in Matt 4:4 and Luke 4:4.

What it is important: the first is to learn, the second is to act on what you've learned. To know what to do, learn or be educated on what it is that you're to be doing. In most cases, the education comes from your family.

> Isa 48:17-18 Thus says the LORD, your Redeemer, the Holy One of Israel, "*I am the LORD your God, who teaches you to profit, Who leads you in the way you should go.* If only you had paid attention to My commandments! Then your well-being [peace] would have been like a river, And your righteousness like the waves of the sea." [emphasis added]

The word "profit" means "to be benefited, to receive help from any thing." It is a universal truth in that God will lead you in the direction He needs and wants you to go, it is up to each one of us to follow His lead.

Follow His path and you'll be prosperous, follow any other and you won't be.

12 steps to better serve your neighbor as yourself

Being an entrepreneur, the totality of God and who you are that determines a good foundation grounds oneself in the hectic pace and path of entrepreneurship. Of the various parts of man, body, mind, spirit, and emotion all together make up a person. Each part of a human being is affected the other parts. What you eat or drink affects your mind, spirit, and emotion. What you put or allow into your mind and affects the other parts, what you allow in your spirit affects the others. So all in all, each part of what makes up you is affected by each of the other parts.

Your and your neighbor's life (body, soul, spirit) are a business, with "profits and losses," treat each of them with respect.

Do you want to be successful? The below text is modified from *12 Things Successful People Do Before Breakfast*[81] that provides significant good habits that others do which you can adopt to have a fulfilling life.

1. Learn better decision making: managing your emotions and stress levels. Your decisions are disrupted by an array of biases and irrationalities: overconfidence, quick decisions with incomplete or bad info, and short term emotions starts us agonizing over our decisions.[82] However, the military and NASA train people to face uncertainty and the unknown, and it boils down to one critical aspect: arousal control, i.e. training others in the art of not panicking. Succumbing to short term emotions, one begins to make mistakes, and astronauts flying 150 miles above the earth facing a crisis situation or Special Forces facing the Taliban is not the time or place to lose one's head. Putting people "through the paces" of what they'd experience produces a level of familiarity, a powerful feeling of confidence, and helps inoculate a person towards higher stress levels.

Experience is better than training, training is better than knowledge, knowledge is better than ignorance.

81 entrepreneur.com See *12 Things Successful People Do Before Breakfast*

82 *Decision* by Chip and Dan Heath

In the military there's a saying, "The more you sweat in training, the less you bleed in combat." A few factors which significantly help your decision-making. *First*, train in USAF Colonel John Boyd's OODA Loop (Observe, Orient, Decide, Act)[83], the ability to get "inside" the thought process and make quick decisions (it's not for the military any more). *Second*, understanding what "Stress vs. Performance" levels do to a person's body[84] and the color codes that help define what they are: 1. Green/White=bored or unprepared, 2. Yellow=prepared or relaxed alert, 3. Orange=you alerted to something, 4. Red=strong anxiety, taking action, 5. Black=a complete meltdown or you are overwhelmed and freeze up. *Third*, control your stress through Tactical breathing,[85] a breathing process that throttles the body's response to pump adrenaline (erroneously referred to as "nerves," "shakes, or "emotions") into your body. It restricts the elevation of this hormone and stress into one's body during a potential flight/fight/freeze situation. This mental and emotional training prepares one to increase the correct handling of uncertainty better. *Fourth*, avoid "what if" thinking, focus on taking action on the task at hand. *Fifth*, give yourself (body, mind, emotions) a break from stress, too much stress over long periods of time reduces your effectiveness.

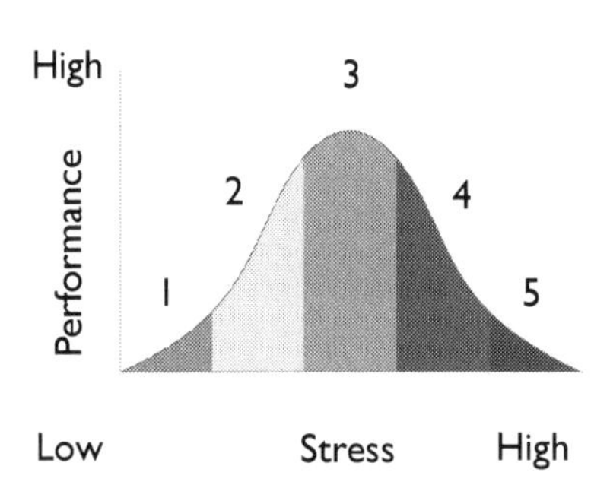

> Jam 1:19 This you know, my beloved brethren. But everyone must be quick to hear, *slow to speak and slow to anger;*

2. Manage your energy over your time. Loehr and Schwartz's book *Power of Full Engagement* gets at the heart of being productive: manage your energy over your time. Packing more things into your life today negatively affects your future life. God tells the Jews to rest on the Sabbath, to produce everything for the Sabbath to rest on that day. Loehr's states:

---

83 wikipedia.org See *OODA Loop*

84 *On Combat* by Grossman and Christensen, Chapter 4

85 *Warrior Mindset* by Asken and Grossman, pg 112

> *The performance demands that most people face in their everyday work environment dwarf those of any professional athlete we ever trained. … Professional athletes typically spend 90 percent of their time* training, *in order to be able to* perform *10 percent of the time.*[86]

As sports psychologist, his goal was to understand factors that set apart the greatest competitors in the world from the rest of the pack (in one case, it was tennis players). There were very few differences in the tennis players from the *service to the point scored.* But there were big differences between the number four and number 50 seeded tennis players when they *measured what happened in the time between the point scored and the next serve.*

In quality assurance circles this measurement is called *cycle time.* It measures from the start of a task to the start of the next task (in lean production, you improve the process and look for *cycle time reduction*). The tennis differences included how they held their heads and shoulders; the way they walked back to the baseline after a point; the pattern of their breathing; where they focused their eyes; and even the way they talked to themselves.

In the sixteen to twenty seconds *between the scored point and the next serve*, the best tennis players were able to relax, they were able to lower their heart rates by as much as twenty beats per minute. The heart rates of their competitors who didn't have the same dialed-in *rest rituals* often stayed at the same levels. In the game, if you can put in 15-30 seconds worth of rest while the other players don't, this resting time adds up during the course of hours of play. The same concept can apply in your endeavor of life, taking "short siestas" and relaxing, meditating during the day, but it also leads us into getting enough sleep and rest to be at a high performance level.

Dave Green, CEO of Hobby Lobby cites in his book *More than a Hobby* how he turned in $600.00 investment into a $1.3-billion a year enterprise. But he saw that he was not living the values God had created because stores were open seven days a week. Sunday's sales equaled $100-million in one year, to close the door to this amount of sales and potential profit was not an easy decision because it involved serious money. Not without some trepidation, he made the decision and began in a one state trial and then later expanded nationwide, closing his stores on Sunday. Sales took a dip, but very soon rebounded, then climbed higher than ever. There were additional results: no effect on sales, profits up, employees are happier, and managers are eager to work for a retailer with six days a week instead of the

86 *Power of Full Engagement* by Jim Loehr and Tony Schwartz, pg 8

usual seven. As a leader, you not only *manage your energy*, but you *manage the energy of those under your leadership*. Oh, and Green kept his TG&Y job for three years after he opened his first 300-square-foot store until he knew he could make it.[87] Find success, then scale.

3. Proper Rest and Sleep. God started it by resting on the seventh day, it's imperative we should follow His pattern and so should our neighbors. But not only are we to get a rest day, but included in that is ensuring we get enough sleep. Getting a good nights rest is, starting with one's mind, is echoed by Ben Franklin's proverb, "Early to bed and early to rise, makes a man healthy, wealthy, and wise" is the perfect and truest example of what to do to become successful. Poor sleeping habits leads to sleepiness and impairs the ability to concentrate and think clearly.

Ecc 5:12 The *sleep of the working man is pleasant*, whether he eats little or much; but the full stomach of the rich man does not allow him to sleep. [emphasis added]

Since most people sleep around eight hours, drink water before and right after sleep to keep your body hydrated. Also, setting the right temperature for sleep can help with the ability to sleep. A cooler room temperature, around 65°F (but not below 54°F nor above 75°F)[88], lets you fall asleep faster and sleep better.

Sleep studies of NASA engineers show that you cannot put in more hours to get things done without a drop in one's benefits in life.

Sleep cannot be "banked," but sleep deficits accumulate. Humans get two hours of performance for each one-hour of sleep. If there isn't enough sleep to cover performance, the brain finds a way of getting the sleep it needs. It's almost as if the brains says "if you won't give me sleep, I'll sneak it in when you're not looking,"... With fatigue, the brain's awake state becomes unstable. It lapses and micro-sleeps to interrupt performance.[89]

87 *More than a Hobby* by Dave Green, pg 10

88 alifeofproductivity.com See *The exact temperature you should sleep at to get a good night's sleep*

89 nasa.gov See *To Sleep or Not to Sleep?*

While one can actually put in a number of "late nights" to get something done or finished, the continuation of "late nighters" will soon catch up to you, your body, and your life and create a bad body clock which can affect your business or mission effectiveness.[90]

4. Eat proper food. "You are what you eat" has been more proven accurate in recent decades as mounting evidence show that what you eat does affect your body, and your body affects your mind and your outlook on life. While the poor food you eat may not severely or negatively affect you right away, such as getting food poisoning or getting sick. What is becoming clear is the fact that the poor food over long periods degrades your body's ability to repair itself. Putting poor food into your body means poor energy translates into poor productive results.

> Prov 28:19 He who *tills his land will have plenty of food,* But he who follows empty pursuits will have poverty in plenty.

Kashrut (also kashruth or kashrus, כַּשְׁרוּת) is the set of Jewish religious dietary laws. Food that may be consumed according to halakha (Jewish law) is termed kosher in English, from the Ashkenazi pronunciation of the Hebrew term kashér (כָּשֵׁר), meaning "fit" (in this context, fit for consumption).[91] In the book of Daniel we read how Daniel viewed the issue of food with what the King offered them, sticking with the Jewish dietary laws, Daniel proposes something interesting.

> Dan 1:8 But Daniel made up his mind that he would not defile himself with the king's choice food or with the wine which he drank; so *he sought permission* from the commander of the officials that he might not defile himself. [emphasis added]

Notice Daniel sought permission to test and showcase the results of their kosher lifestyle versus the King's approach. So, Daniel went on to say to the King's official regarding the test between Daniel and the King's men.

---

90 spacesafetymagazine.com See *Adjusting to Sol Takes Toll on Mars Rovers' Teams*

91 wikipedia.org See *Kashrut*

> Dan 1:12-13 "Please *test your servants* for ten days, and *let us be given some vegetables to eat and water to drink*. Then let *our appearance be observed in your presence and the appearance of the youths who are eating the king's choice food*; and deal with your servants according to what you see." [emphasis added]

And the results.

> Dan 1:15-16 At the end of ten days *their appearance seemed better* and *they were fatter* than all the youths who had been eating the king's choice food. So the overseer continued to withhold their choice food and the wine they were to drink, and kept giving them vegetables. [emphasis added]

Processed food have encroached on the supermarket shelves significantly over the last 30-40 years compared with what food was on the shelves when your grandmother or great grandmother shopped at the store. Today's processed foods have various additives, preservatives, chemicals, GMO (Genetically Modified Organism), etc. that have shown over time to contribute to many long-term health issues. While most people can eat these processed foods and not feel the affects right away, the cumulative effect on the body have long-term repercussions and could pass the effects on to future generations.

The *best principle is that the more natural (not the marketing ploys of "all natural") and organic food* one puts in their body, the better it is for the body to repair itself and to handle the onslaught of the demands of today's workforce. Imagine you have a Ferrari, you don't do regular maintenance (oil change, etc.) on it, how soon before you expect your car to start acting funny? If you don't do the required maintenance, you increase the chances of it having a catastrophic failure? Same goes with your body. If you actively read the food labels and if they have items that you have difficulty with or cannot pronounce, then the food is probably processed. If it's packaged, there's a high probability that it is processed, and you need to look elsewhere for what you eat (Note: check with your nutritionist for questions about healthy eating).

What started changing our path toward eating our way to better health occurred on a short business drive from Denver to Ft. Collins with a new business friend, Rex Wisehart, of yellowschmello.com fame. During the trip and lunch he described having to fly to the east coast to see a specialist doctor for a health issue. Rex was taking 12-15 pills a day for his pain, his doctor asked him if he wanted to feel better and be in less pain. "Of course!," Rex said. "Well, as your doctor, follow my advice for 90 days and then see how you feel. Eat only raw vegetables, fruits, and nuts for every meal. Smoothies, salads, etc., but *only raw plant-based food*."[92]

Rex told me he'd followed the doctor's advice *to the letter* and did not deviate once from what the doctor ordered him to do. Rex wanted to prove the doctor wrong, and Rex, being a bit tenacious, thought his doctor just might be pulling his leg and wasn't telling him the whole truth.

Rex didn't need a total 90 days to find out what he needed to know; he knew *within 30 days* that this was the path to take to improve his health! The results: Rex cut *nearly all* of his pain meds out and was able to exercise more, and his physicals showed he is in much better health than he was years ago and for those his age. All because he moved more toward a plant-based lifestyle change. Other than adding some animal protein, he has stayed away completely from processed food and has never felt better.

In fact, if you watch the videos that Paul Gautschi has posted at his web site backtoedenfilm.com you'll see what he learned from God regarding organic gardening and organic food using sustainable methods of food production: God's way of food production. Rex also recommends watching the videos forksoverknives.com and fatsickandnearlydead.com to get some additional views about eating more natural/organic, plant-based foods versus processed foods or foods that have food additives in them.

NOTE: Please consult with your doctor before embarking on any changes in your health decisions in your diet or health regimen. In addition, research the above information to confirm that it is both accurate and true. Don't throw the baby out with the bath water, there is a difference between a philosophy and a fact. Facts should be indisputable, philosophies should be based on facts, not start with a philosophy and then interpret the facts.

5. Proper Exercise. Getting exercise gives your body the extra "umph" and is by far the best "anti-depressent" there is.

> 1 Tim 4:8 for *bodily discipline* is only of little profit, but godliness is profitable for all things, since it holds promise for the present life and also for the life to come. [emphasis added]

92 See your local farmers market or grow your own.

The Amplified Bible gives a better comment, "For physical training (useful for a little), but godliness (spiritual training) is useful and of value in everything and in every way, for it holds promise for the present life and also for the life which is to come." Physical exercise is great for while we're here on earth, the better we are at being in physical shape, the more productive we are. Just a 30 minute walk three to four times a week can do wonders for one's mental and physical health. Check with your doctor before starting an exercise regime.

6. Time Block Top Priority Tasks. Work in batches or "time block" your tasks and never try to multi-task.[93] Switching from one task to another your brain has to switch task context. The switch causes your brain to "download" and then "upload" the context of the task, this takes time.

> *"Multitasking, specifically for knowledge workers, causes at least a 15% penalty in productivity. It is much higher for tasks (such as troubleshooting or design for instance) that require complete immersion before the resource can actually make progress."*

In addition, at the end of the day before going to bed, if there is a need, prepare what you're going to work on in the morning. Then, when you rise early, the first thing you do is work uninterrupted for an hour or two on a business project that requires focused efforts. This uninterrupted time allows for concentrated work and to be at your most productive.

> Ecc 3:1 There is *an appointed time for everything*. And there is a time for every event under heaven [emphasis added]

7. Personal Passion or Hobby Project. This project connects outside of your current areas of life. It could be a community project, write a book, coach little league or girl scouts, or do an art project. Whatever the case, it's a project that is outside what you normally do that inspires or provides you with another outlet of your talents. Research has shown that hobbies get your creative juices flowing. From an inc.com article.

> *The analysis showed that those who engaged in a creative hobby performed between 15-30 percent better at work. The team offered several possible*

---

93 *Slack: Getting Past Burnout, Busywork and the Myth of Total Efficiency* by Tom DeMarco

> *explanations for why this might be so. Taking time to indulge in your favorite creative pursuit might help you recharge before heading back to work, or could also be a means to learn more about your strengths and weaknesses, knowledge that will benefit you professionally as well. Those who engaged in a hobby also reported greater feelings of control and mastery.*[94]

It is these creative activities like knitting, cooking, painting, or gardening that can positively affect work performance.

8. Quality Spouse Time. Have a regular date night with your spouse. Relationships are like bank accounts, if you don't make deposits by doing nice things for and with your spouse, at some point you won't be able to make a withdrawal. Spend time now with your spouse *before* your kids leave home for the real world means staying connected and you'll still have a marriage when the empty nest happens.

9. Quality Family Time. Spending time with your family requires effort to give them the necessary time they need to connect with you. As you have heard, no one every said on their deathbed, "I wish I spent more time at the office." It could be eating dinner together one to three nights a week for the whole family, you need to devote time with your family.

10. Network. Networking to connect with others in your industry, outside your industry, and other areas. Connect so that if there is ever a need by someone you can help them and they can return the favor.

11. Be grateful, have personal quiet time, and read. It's a matter of being appreciative of what you have in life and being open to more opportunities that avail themselves to you. Spending quiet time by yourself allows one to recharge yourself and to ground yourself in who and what you are and your purpose in life. Airlines tell you to put on your oxygen mask first before helping your children and others. can't do that if you're not healthy or alive.

> 1 Cor 7:5 Stop depriving one another, *except by agreement for a time, so that you may devote yourselves to prayer*, and come together again so that Satan will not tempt you *because of your lack of self-control.* [emphasis added]

This is especially true on a day of rest, being able to listen to what God is saying to you about what He wants you to do. Doing little or nothing for

94 inc.com See *How Your Hobbies Impact Your Work Performance*

a whole day, you're able to listen. Reading, versus skimming, 30-45 minutes per day reduces stress significantly, keeps your brain functioning into old age, but most important, increases comprehension.[95]

12. CEO day and Master Mind meeting: plan ahead, strategize. Once a month you need a CEO day and a Master Mind meeting. A CEO day gets you away from your typical day and life in general. Gather up some coffee or tea, a notebook, Post-Its (from 3x3 inch to easel size), and your business goals and ideas and do a mental dump from your head onto paper. Stand back and get a 10,000 foot look and begin to see what you've done and what you need to do going forward. It is well documented in numerous articles that Bill Gates takes two, one week "think weeks" every year, and family, friends, and Microsoft employees were banned from his retreat. He has said that he may read 100 papers during this time and would answer employee suggestions, too. But the basic idea – to read and think during time alone – to review ideas from the creative thinking of yourself and employees – should remain constant. A Master Mind meeting is committing and connecting with 6-12 other like-minded business people on a regular basis to help each other with their businesses. Do a "round robin" as you go around the table to discuss business issues and search for solutions.

Serving Others. The same steps of opportunities outlined above that you get with your life should have equal status with others. Your neighbor is an equal, allow them the same equal opportunities and responsibilities that you do for yourselves, to deprive them is not to treat them like an equal.

> 1 Pet 4:10 As *each one has received* a special gift, *employ it in serving one another*, as *good stewards* of the manifold grace of God. [emphasis added]

There is no greater satisfaction than when we serve another human being, and they are satisfied.

> Eph 2:10 For *we are His workmanship*, created in Christ Jesus *for good works*, which *God prepared beforehand so that we would walk in them.* [emphasis added]

---

95 mic.com See *Science Has Great News for People Who Read Actual Books*

The word "workmanship" means "that which has been made," and the Amplified Bible says of this verse, "For we are God's [own] handiwork (His workmanship), recreated in Christ Jesus, [born anew] that we may do those good works which God predestined (planned beforehand) for us [taking paths which He prepared ahead of time], that we should walk in them [living the good life which He prearranged and made ready for us to live]." Before you were born, God designed you and your career, listen for what He has in store.

Examples of entrepreneurial service. *Liter of Light* [96] solves the lack of lighting by placing a one liter, sealed water filled plastic bottle into a sealed hole in a tin roof (top 1/3 of the bottle outside the roof and the bottom 2/3 of the bottle inside the home). It provides the solar equivalent of a 50 watt light bulb allowing families to live and work inside and moving up the economic ladder because their lives have been improved.

Dry Bath [97] was created by 17 year old Ludwick Marishane who lived in Limpopo, South Africa, northeast of Johannesburg. Globally 2.5 million (450 million in Africa, 5 million in South Africa) do not have access to good, clean water. The disease trachoma affects 350 million people worldwide and makes 8 million people blind each year. One thing solves this problem: wash your face! Using an old cell phone, an allowance of 50 South African Rand a week ($5.00 US dollars), and four years of work, Marishane invented Dry Bath. His solution saves about 80 million liters of water and two hours per day fetching water each time someone uses Dry Bath. Getting back two hours a day means that time can be devoted to other more important things for both adults and children. Marishane was named the Global Student Entrepreneur of the Year in 2011.

Pancreatic cancer tests. Teenager Jack Andrak's[98] close friend of his family died of pancreatic cancer, it has a five-year survival rate of 6 percent. Andrak invented a small dipstick probe using nanotubes, 1/50,000 the diameter of a human hair, using just a sixth of a drop of blood, takes five minutes to complete, is 400 times more sensitive, is 100 percent accurate in early stages, and reduces the test cost from $800 to $0.03.

Barefoot College.[99] In Rajasthan, India, a school founded by Bunker Roy teaches rural women and men (some illiterate) to become solar engineers,

---

96 youtube.com See *A Liter of Light*

97 ted.com See *Ludwick Marishane's "A bath without water."*

96 smithsonianmag.com See *Jack Andraka, the Teen Prodigy of Pancreatic Cancer*

99 ted.com See *Learning from a barefoot movement*

artisans, dentists and doctors in their own villages via grassroots learning. None of the teachers have diplomas or certificate from schools.

With all your might and trust in Him

God gives the basis for one's living.

Deu 6:5 "You shall love the LORD your God with all your heart and with all your soul and with all your might."

Notice that there is an action verb, to love God. God goes into what those actions looks like, but Grant Perry gives an insightful view and writes in his web article *Loving God and Doing Business*[100] of what it means,

> *According to Rabbi W. Gunther Plaut, author of* The Torah: A Modern Commentary, *the reference to "your heart" refers to one's intellect; "your soul" refers to one's life; and "your might" refers to one's physical strength -- and by tradition to one's "material possessions." Thus, loving God requires harmonizing one's mind, spirit, and conduct.*

When you think of the Hebrew view of language of one's heart, soul, and your "might" (versus the Greek view), think of an illustration of a target with three concentric circles, one within another, of one's interests:

- the inner circle is your *heart* (one's intellect, will, and emotions).
- the middle circle is your *soul* (the total you, your mind and body, the full embodiment of a person, the whole self, "me"), which is everything that makes up who you are.
- the outer circle is your *might* (all that you influence, all that you have stewardship over in the world, all of your available resources), it is your connection with the outside of you, your world, your sphere of influence.[101]

To love God with your "might" means almost literally putting your resources, your time, talent, and treasure (money) where your mouth is. Your "might" is your strength, your strength is your labor, and your labor

---

100 myjewishlearning.com See *Loving God and Doing Business* by Grant Perry

101 skipmoen.com See *Circular Reasoning*

produces resources for others to purchase and ultimately you earn your livelihood. It's about your actions speak louder than your words so that your heart, mind, soul, and actions are congruent and authentic.

The basis of one's business and ultimately livelihood is this: if a person believes in God with more than lip service, then the person believes that God will provide him with a livelihood. Anyone who rigidly clings to his money betrays a lack of confidence that his wealth can grow. Thus, he clutches it tightly as if it is not replaceable. *If a person believes that God provides their livelihood, then what reason is there for someone to cheat or be stingy, either as a customer, vendor or as a business? NONE!*

In James 5:4, when we read the word "withheld" in the sentence, "the pay of the laborers who mowed your fields, and which has been withheld by you," it means "to withdraw or keep back a thing by fraud." While the context refers to the rich who have an economic might against the poor, defrauding anyone on either side of a business transaction is wrong. *A person who cheats, whether it's selling or buying, shows that they do not believe that God will take care of them.*

Manna from heaven, one's needs are met. A very good and decades long example for us to learn from when it comes to God taking care of each one of us. While we might not get the quality of the Ritz-Carlton hotel, He still does take care of us in the right way.

> Deut 29:5 "I have led you forty years in the wilderness; *your clothes have not worn out* on you, and *your sandal has not worn out* on your foot. [emphasis added]

Do you think God can take care of you? The Master of the Universe? Of course He can, He took care of all of the Jews in the desert, didn't He? He provided them with clothing, now look where He started to take care of the Jews in the desert providing manna to them.

> Exo 16:4, 31 Then the LORD said to Moses, "Behold, *I will rain bread from heaven for you;* and the people shall go out and gather a day's portion every day, that *I may test them, whether or not they will walk in My instruction [law]*. 31 And the house of *Israel named it manna,* [emphasis added]

And when God started taking care of the Jews, He also ended it when other opportunities arose, and they began transitioning into their new land.

> Jos 5:12 The *manna ceased on the day after they had eaten some of the produce of the land,* so that the sons of Israel no longer had manna, but they ate some of the yield of the land of Canaan during that year. [emphasis added]

And in the NT, Paul writes in Philippians how God will provide.

> Phil 4:19 And *my God will supply all [every need of] your needs* according to His riches in glory in Christ Jesus. [emphasis added]

Notice he said *needs* and not *wants,* there is a difference in the perspective of both need and a want.

One of those factors was John the Baptist was preparing and telling the Jews of the day was what it was like with their attitude and what was going to happen to them.

> Luke 3:7-8 So he began saying to the crowds who were going out to be baptized by him, "You *brood of vipers,* who *warned you to flee from the wrath to come?* "Therefore *bear fruits in keeping with repentance,* and do not begin to say to yourselves, 'We have Abraham for our father,' for I say to you that from these stones God is able to raise up children to Abraham. [emphasis added]

John the Baptist was telling the Jews that who they were and their "status" as God's chosen people was not an "entitlement" or to be reveled in (include Christians that say "I'm a Christian!" versus being Christ-like today). But who they were was to be used for the production of doing good as a *child of God* and not for *selfishly gaining a better life over others,* i.e. to be a *brat of God.* When you read "who warned you to flee the wrath to come," he tells them to "bear fruits in keeping with repentance." John was getting at the heart of their attitude.

When you read "in keeping" means "befitting, congruous, corresponding to a thing." The Amplified Bible version, "Bear fruits that are deserving and consistent with [your] repentance [that is, conduct worthy of a heart changed, a heart abhorring sin]. And do not begin to say to yourselves, We have Abraham as our father; for I tell you that God is able from these stones to raise up descendants for Abraham."

The Jewish denominational attitude (and today's Christian's with theirs) is one of "heritage," and "lineage" with Abraham (or being a child of God). "Going through the motions" of faith in God was/is not what God wants, He wants a *change of heart* resulting in a *change of actions* from individuals. God does not want *displays of* or an image (Matt 23:2-5, Jas 2:2-3) of a person's faith, He wants *deeds from* or actions coming from a person's faith.

> Jas 2:20 But are you willing to recognize, you foolish fellow, that *faith without works is useless?* [emphasis added]

Faith without works, i.e. faith without taking action, is useless. The business world rephrases the Bible verse.

Ideas are a dime a dozen; it's all about execution!

Seems like the business acumen that is spoken of today is really thousands of years old, so the "new" is really the old and is considered a "tried and true" method of getting things done. Faith without works is dead, ideas without execution is worthless. Both the spiritual and physical have the same problem: getting someone to do the work.

> Eccl 1:9 That which has been is that which will be, And that which has been done is that which will be done. *So there is nothing new under the sun.* [emphasis added]

So it seems that marketing, sales, operations and making a profit based on what the customer wants has been around for years, so the basic principles have not changed much because you're still dealing with Man.

Abraham pays fair market value for a burial plot. Of prime examples is of Abraham when Sarah, his wife, dies in Genesis 23. But let's take a look at what Abraham does here. First, he approaches those he is neighbors with because he is a foreigner and did not start out living there.

In verse six, it is recorded, "Hear us, my lord, you are a mighty prince among us." They recognize the blessings of Abraham, but he does not take advantage of his position as a one of great wealth. While he was offered less than market value for a burial plot, he does not bite at the offering.

> Gen 23:9 that he may give me the cave of Machpelah which he owns, which is at the end of his field; for the *full price let him give it to me* in your presence for a burial site."[emphasis added]

Abraham still negotiates for a burial plot, despite his profound grief and his wealth. After some discussion, he *pays fair market value* for what he receives despite the wealthy natives wanting to give him the plot for free ("My lord, listen to me. A plot of land worth 400 silver shekels—what is that between me and you? Just bury your dead.").[102] Abraham counters to what most "celebrities" that look for "free" stuff for themselves. Abraham pays full retail, thus showing his neighbors he does not play favorites and is transparent when it comes to business. He could also be wary of "you get what you pay for" free and it may not have had been the best plot of land for Sarah, so he could have been suspicious. In other words, all are alike to Abraham and he does not take advantage of anyone because of his wealth or status or with God. Business is business.

102 biblestudytools.com See *Complete Jewish Bible* of Genesis 23:1-20

9 God's blessings economy is about serving

1 Pet 3:9 not returning evil for evil or insult for insult, but giving a blessing instead; for you were called for the very purpose that you might inherit a blessing.

After working with Jimmy for a few months, he offered me the chance to attend one of his training sessions, an all day Saturday event. Of course, I said yes, who wouldn't want to learn from the world's best. On the appointed day, I arrived along with about 10-15 other folks. Watching him teach and in action was amazing. He showed us what we were going to learn, trained us, then tested us. *Oh man!* Did he ever test us! It was like nothing I had ever been through before, or since, and was well worth it. But the most important part was that his training was a blessing to me and those that attended. Blessings are actions that mutually improves and benefits both sides, and Jimmy's training did just that. Not only mine, but I was able to show my wife what Jimmy had trained us in, his content was both superb and timely.

Jimmy's training benefited me and my wife because he was able to elevate our situation and life because of what he knows and what he was able to impart to us. But it was not only him providing my family a benefit, but as he told me, so did my time with him benefit him and his life. It is this mutual blessings benefit that not only as Christians we're to espouse, but also how we're to see each of our businesses. If one does not improve or provide a benefit to someone else, then why would you want to promote or sell it to you neighbor? Work, business, and the economy are made to improve lives.

Joke. Mr. and Mrs. Rubenstein were teaching their 4-year-old son Eli the importance of making brachot – blessings before you eat.

"For example," said Mr. Rubenstein, "before I eat this piece of cake, I need to make a bracha to thank God for this wonderful cake."

Mrs. Rubinstein motioned to the food on young Eli's plate. "Go ahead," said Mrs. Rubinstein, "Why don't you make a bracha, blessings on those vegetables on your plate."

Eli looked down and waited–and waited. After a long silence, little Eli looked up at his parents and asked, "If I thank God for the broccoli, won't He know that I'm lying?"

God is your Angel Investor: 2 Cor 9,16; John 15

God has plans for you; but He wants you to do the work.

> Prov 16:3 Commit your works to the LORD, And your plans will be established.

And here are the results.

> 1 Cor 3:6 I planted, Apollos watered, but *God was causing the growth.* [emphasis added]

Pitching God for an investment. In the Angel Investment and Venture Capital world you're always pitching your idea to someone with the resources and money for your idea. If they think your idea has merit, they'll invest, if not, you won't get the money.

In the case of pitching to God for His resources, He already knows what you want and need, He's just waiting for you to come around to His view of your business, His Business. The more you know His business, the better off you'll be at getting the resources and money you need to accomplish His Goals.

God points it out perfectly when it comes to giving. It starts in the OT and giving to the poor,[103] or having a business transaction where you pay a roofer, doctor, dentist, or a dog sitter.

---

103 *The Expositor's Greek New Testament* by W. Robertson Nicoll, pg 92-94

> Deut 15:10 You *shall generously give* to him, and *your heart shall not be grieved when you give to him*, because for *this thing the LORD your God will bless you in all your work and in all your [Literally: the putting forth of your hand] undertakings.* [emphasis added]

God through Paul reemphasizes it in his letter to the Corinthians.

> 2 Cor 9:6-8 Now this I say, he who *sows sparingly* will also *reap sparingly*, and he who *sows bountifully* will also *reap bountifully*. Each one must *do just as he has purposed in his heart*, not grudgingly or under compulsion, for *God loves a cheerful giver*. And God is able to make all grace abound to you, so that always *having all sufficiency in everything*, you may have an *abundance for every good deed*; [emphasis added]

But do you know that *God wants to be your Angel Investor?* Your business Partner? In 2 Cor 9:8, the Amplified Bible says, "And God is able to make all grace (every favor and earthly blessing) come to you in abundance, so that you may always *and* under all circumstances *and* whatever the need be self-sufficient [possessing enough to require no aid or support and furnished in abundance for every good work and charitable donation]." Giving is the lifeblood of abundance, but there's more.

> *"God designed grain to be sown and to yield its return; God arranged Christian life in good works and in giving in the same way. It is he who wants us to have the blessing of the harvest. This is his beautiful way of bestowing his blessing. … All that he thus gives us is intended for great increase. … It is not because of the lack of generosity that so many of us remain poor. … How can God pour 1,000 bushels into a receptacle that holds no more than one? … The other way which the world has ever found is to enrich oneself by robbing others, by grinding the face of the poor, by withholding the workman's wages, etc. … God lets you yourself say in advance in what way, what kind of harvest, and how much you want to reap. One sows with one idea alone: on the idea of blessings—-blessings, praises to God; blessings, benefactions to men; return blessings to ourselves."*[104]

---

104 *Interpretation of I and II Corinthians* by R. C. H. Lenski, pg 1168-1170

If one is stingy with their wealth, no matter whether one earns $4,000, $40,000 or $400,000 income a year, those who "sow sparingly" will also "reap sparingly." If you're a farmer, and you have enough seeds to plant 10 acres of land and you only plant two acres, how much would you reap planting the two acres versus compared with planting all 10?

The hole you give through is the hole you receive through.

Do you see that if you stop planting, or investing in yourself and others, you stop the flow of blessings?

Hoarding wealth and stuff. Properly stored planting seeds last between two and five years, depending on the seed. If you hoard the seed and do not plant it, and exceed the "shelf life," the seed will be ruined, and all of that effort and resources getting the seed will have been wasted. Hoarding seeds (capital) versus planting (i.e. reinvesting your capital) decreases your reaping (business profits and financial wealth). Hoarding takes many forms, by far the most prominent habit of hoarding is buying more "stuff" that you and your family do not need and then putting it in storage costing you even more money.

Another significant Bible verse regarding God and you.

> 2 Chron 16:9 "For the *eyes of the LORD move to and fro throughout the earth that He may strongly support those whose heart is completely His.* You have acted foolishly in this. Indeed, from now on you will surely have wars." [emphasis added]

Did you notice? God says that He may "*strongly support* those whose heart is completely His [emphasis added]." Is your heart completely His? Here's the point when your heart is completely sold out for God.

God is waiting to invest more in you!

Reread 2 Cor 9:8 from the Amplified Bible again in the above pages. Reread it multiple times and read it in context multiple times. Do you realize that the God of the Universe wants to invest in YOU? But wait, there's more.

God's First Investment. When it comes to earthly angel investors/ venture capitalists, they will only invest in your business venture (a shortening of the word adventure, a risky or daring journey or undertaking) if your business has a viable chance to make them more money with their investments.

God has the same mind about you.

But guess what?

God has already given you His first investment: you!

He designed you with your unique set of talents, skills, personalities, etc. which means He has already invested in you by designing you for His purposes. Now the question comes: how have you made out with His first investment, you? Have you taken His investment, you, and used it wisely to do His good works? Or have you squandered, for selfish reasons, His investment in you, much like the Prodigal Son who squandered his inheritance away?

But don't worry! If you have squandered away or decreased your value to Him, He still sees you as a good investment. You can always recover and increase His investment value by improving His investment, by improving you and following Him. Take your buried talent out of the ground and put it to good use. Jesus says it accurately as *your* angel investor.

> John 15:5 "*I am the vine, you are the branches*; he who abides in Me and I in him, *he bears much fruit*, for *apart from Me you can do nothing.* [emphasis added]

We *have to be connected* to our angel investors, God the Father, Son, and Holy Spirit to get the resources we need to be fruitful. So God is just waiting to invest more in you. But He will only invest (bless you) more if you're doing His will and good works, not continually devaluing His investment or are stingy or hoarding His investments in you. We're to be a steward and a conduit of His grace and abundant resources so there's more growth in God's Kingdom, not selfishly hoarding, guarding, or abusing what He has given us. That's the world's expectations, not God's.

As your angel investor, God hears you loud and clear.

> 1 John 5:14 This is the *confidence which we have before [Literally: toward] Him*, that, *if we ask anything according to His will, He hears us.* [emphasis added]

Maybe we will, maybe we won't ask according to His will, but He hears and answers us according to His Will. The true measure of a God-lead business owner is how they view His investments. When God invests in your business, there are two perspectives of His investment:

How many more people *can I serve versus how* much money *am I getting?*

Servants "serve people" while selfish people "get money." But we have a mentor, the Holy Spirit, which will guide us in the path we're to take.

> John 16:13 But when He, the Spirit of truth, comes, *He will guide you into all the truth*; for He will not speak on His own initiative, but whatever He hears, He will speak; and *He will disclose to you what is to come.* [emphasis added]

The Holy Spirit will make the path quicker and easier to walk; thus less time and resources are used being more effective and efficient.

God's investment in mutual funds. Recognizing your individual talents and skills and you understand the above concept that God invested in you first. Next you need to *combine God's investment in you with God's investment in others*, thus creating *God's Mutual Funds*, the equal investment "for God's own possession" for His purposes.

> 1 Pet 2:9 But you are A CHOSEN RACE, A royal PRIESTHOOD, A HOLY NATION, A PEOPLE FOR God's OWN POSSESSION, so that you may proclaim the excellencies of Him who has called you out of darkness into His marvelous light; (Isa 43:20f; Exo 19:5-6)

It is His mutual funds that we're to tap into and work together.

> Rom 12:6a Since *we have gifts that differ according to the grace given to us, each of us is to exercise them accordingly* [emphasis added]

God looks at an individual's behaviors and tells us how we should proceed with doing His business, in our industry or career.

> Luke 3:14 Some soldiers were questioning him, saying, "And what about us, what shall we do?" And he said to them, "*Do not take money from anyone by force, or accuse anyone falsely, and be content with your wages.*" [emphasis added]

If you were an angel investor/venture capitalist and you were investing in someone, you'd wait until they had proven themselves in the little things before you'd reconsider investing anymore in them, right? Same with God.

The word "content" (Greek ἀρκέω arkeō) is present, imperative. In this very instance means you as a soldier are commanded to be continually "to be satisfied, contented" with your soldier's pay, but the principle applies equally in everyone's life. The idea is not to abuse your position for false gain. But it does not limit one from working or earning more, elsewhere, just don't earn more "pay" through theft, deception, or fraud. The main idea is this: *when God promotes you, you have been promoted.*

While giving is the context of the above chapter in 2 Corinthian 9, the same principle applies in business. Those who sow (invest) sparingly, reap sparingly, because they choose to or do not want to be able to see or observe more opportunities, i.e. more opportunities to serve others. Whether or not their reasons or motivations are legitimate or not, when someone on purpose shuts down one's eyes to opportunities they're being stingy. It is unbelief. This same idea applies towards one's business, the less you invest, the less you'll receive in your Return On Investments (ROI).

"Two or three have gathered together": Matt 18

All business transactions require two individuals. For Christians, there's something significantly different when doing business.

> Matt 18:19-20 "Again I say to you, that *if two of you agree on earth about anything that they may ask*, it shall be done for them by [from] My Father who is in heaven. For where *two or three have gathered together in My name, I am there in their midst.*" [emphasis added]

While some Christians might see this verse strictly referring to a spiritual sense, and it is, this concept applies equally in the physical sense. The idea is not to see this as an "either/or" situation or principle (spiritual and not physical), life should include an "and" approach, spiritual *and* physical. While Jesus spoke in parables (a simple physical story used to illustrate a moral or spiritual lesson), *He does not "divorce" or separate the spiritual from the physical* so that our physical realm is null and void.

Seeing things *only in a spiritual sense* would be like saying, "we love God" alone and not "love your neighbor as yourself." It would be like ignoring the beauty God has created in flowers, a sunset, or amazing food for us to enjoy. While the spiritual and eternal are better in the long term with our relationship with God, we're not to ignore the physical. It is about applying both God's spiritual *and* physical bread to our lives.

> Matt 4:4 But He answered and said, "It is written, 'MAN SHALL NOT LIVE ON BREAD ALONE, BUT ON EVERY WORD THAT PROCEEDS OUT OF THE MOUTH OF GOD.'"

The Amplified Bible says it this way, "But He replied, 'It has been written, Man shall not live *and* be upheld *and* sustained by bread alone, but by every word that comes forth from the mouth of God [Deut 8:3].' " The physical *and* spiritual combined.

When Jesus says, "if two or more are gathered together in My Name," it means that for any believer that Jesus Christ, by His divine power, is *Himself in the midst of all of our efforts, including all business transactions.* So how would Jesus view your behaviors transacting business? As a customer buying from a business? As a vendor selling to a business? As a business owner toward your customer? When Jesus is watching over your business transaction, how should you be doing business that honors Him?

That means that as believers in Jesus Christ, Jesus was a Jewish businessman under the Jewish law, and it boils down to just one question for Christians:

How Would Jesus Do Business?

Would you follow His example? Will you learn how to do business His Way? In fact, the Amplified Bible say in Matt 18:19, "Again I tell you, if two of you on earth agree (harmonize together, make a symphony together) about whatever [anything and everything] they may ask, it will come to pass *and* be done for them by My Father in heaven." To harmonize between both the spiritual and the physical also means to harmonize business transactions, it means that both parties are to be in agreement about the transaction, a win/win solution, not a lose/win, or a win/lose situation.

Love is prosperity; hate is poverty. If we're to love our neighbor as ourselves, it means that we are to cooperate with each other so that both sides are prosperous. This comment is not to advocate equal income or outcome, but it does mean equal opportunities to be prosperous on both sides of the transaction. Living in spiritual and physical poverty is not love, because poverty is created when individuals or a group of people either *fail to cooperate* or are *prevented from cooperating*[105] in doing good for one another. This idea shows up in the "Love Chapter" of 1 Cor 13:5-6. The Amplified Bible says, "Love (God's love in us) *does not insist* on its own rights *or* its own way, *for* it is not self seeking, ...but rejoices when right *and* truth prevail." Right and truth prevail when both sides get the benefit from a business transaction. So, to quickly summarize these verses.

> *Love does not insist on its own rights or its own way (either as a business or customer). Which means love, i.e. doing business, is neither force or fraud.*

If both the *fail to cooperate* and *prevention from cooperating* scenarios occur, it is because of fear or arrogance and the lack of an abundance of love. The results of love are that there are faith and trust in the cooperation in the transacting of business.

Cooperation, via trust and love, has an attitude of sharing, so long as cooperative arrangements are voluntary. When we love each other, we cooperate to achieve ends that we all agree are *mutually beneficial*, though not *mutually equal* because of certain inequalities (value, price, effort, talents, skills, etc.) between two or more parties or even a whole community. The only way you and I or a group are in agreement with a new arrangement is if each of us is mutually better off with the agreed upon results.

Specialization and Cooperation. Cooperation is specialization of one's skills and shows up when your certain skills are better than mine. While I could do the job or task myself, you do it better or cheaper because you achieve a higher level of performance because of your skills and talents. When you perform better at the task than I do, then I should pay you for what you do. It also means I am free to specialize in what I do best and you in turn will pay me for what you need. Specialization is about cooperation with others around individuals and their unique talents and skills.

---

105 fee.org See *The Case for Voluntary Private Cooperation* by Michael Munger

Capitalism is moral, crime is immoral

Love your neighbor as yourself, but entrepreneurship and capitalism is more then love, it encapsulates faith, hope, and love.

> 1 Cor 13:13 But now faith, hope, love, abide these three; but the greatest of these is love.

Capitalism is based on the *morality of the marketplace,*[106] and *morality depends on hope, the expectation of good, and faith, the trust or confidence in something.* Hope and faith that the product/service provided is promised and delivered as stated. To over promise and under deliver is borderline immoral, but to under promise and over deliver is the preferred moral approach. The former means a customer overpays while the latter means the business under charges or over delivers to their customer.

Being pro-free market is different than being pro-business

Pro free market means protecting both sides of a business transaction so that both sides are just and right, pro-business means there is protection of businesses over other entities.

The *hope and faith of business* happens when a business makes the right choice in investing in the right type and number of loaves of bread at the right time their customer wants to buy. Choose right with all of your business factors and "success" will be the result with the sale and profits. Choose wrong, and the business will be "punished" by the market and have to discount or dispose of the "failed" product. When a business makes the wrong choice, it means a waste of both resources and time to make a product or service. Most businesses take any stored treasure and profit and reinvest in their business to grow it. Just like growing and preparing for a rainy season or droughts, businesses have to save for any inevitable problems (taxes, fraud, crimes, etc.).

There is also *hope and faith of the customer* that the seller does not deceive them of what they are buying. They have faith that the promises of what the product will do and are concerned that what they're buying won't be a bunch of "snake oil" products from the company.

---

106 *Thou Shall Prosper*, by Rabbi Lapin, pg 162

Without the hope and faith of the market in creating something that people want, the value of a promise in an exchange, the *promise* itself, is useless. If there is doubt, suspicion, fraud, or crime anywhere on either side of the transaction, i.e. lack of trust, then there would be no transaction or a contract to do business. Doing good business brings about joy, bad business brings about grief.

> *When the morality of capitalism crosses the line into immoral territory, it is no longer capitalism, it is a crime.*

A crime is an action or activity that, although not illegal, is considered to be evil, shameful, or wrong. Immoral territory using deception, fraud, or force via the might of a crowd, a mob, a large bankroll, social media, or the government to get one's way is a crime. Just as Deut 6:18 states, "You *shall do what is right and good* in the sight of the LORD [emphasis added]," immorality crosses into criminal behavior or actions, whether it's a business, customer, or government.

Motivation of capitalism. Marcus Tullius Cicero, who lived from 106 B.C., was a Roman philosopher, politician, lawyer, orator, political theorist, consul, and constitutionalist and was assassinated in 43 B.C. He gave an answer to what a positive faith in the free market does for people.

> *Friendship improves happiness and abates misery, by the doubling of our joy and the dividing of our grief.*

Lt. Col. Grossman, the author of *On Combat*, discusses the effects on those that have experienced violence, such as Post-Traumatic Stress Disorder (PTSD). He says is a bit differently, "Pain shared is pain divided, joy shared is joy multiplied." He echoes what the Bible says.

> Prov 12:25 Anxiety in a man's heart weighs it down, But a good word makes it glad.

Grossman and Cicero's statement are apropos, when businesses legitimately and honorably help a customer, pain is reduced, and joy is enhanced for both sides of a business transaction.

Two well-respected books about economics are *Basic Economics* by Thomas Sowell and *Economics in One Lesson* by Henry Hazlitt. Sowell writes,

> *A distinguished British economist named Lionel Robbins gave the classic definition of economics:* economics is the study of the use of scarce resources which have alternative uses. … *If each resource had only one use, economics would be much simpler. But water can be used to produce ice or steam by itself or innumerable mixtures and compounds in combination with other things. … Whether the people in a given economy will be prosperous or poverty-stricken depends in large part on how well their resources are allocated.*[107]

Hazlitt says this about economic policies:

> *The art of economics consists in looking not merely at the immediate but at the longer effects of any act or policy; it consists in tracing the consequences of that policy not merely for one group* but for all groups [emphasis added].[108]

Pain is *shared* when the individual expresses it, thus pain is lessened. Because we are social beings, there is also an opportunity for the individual hearing of the pain to have *sympathy* for it and to search for and provide a solution. If a baby is hungry or thirsty, the mother and most people hearing of their cries for help and discomfort will search out for a solution to the baby's problem. It's about hearing of the problem(s) and solving them, even giving someone the pleasure of a good cup of coffee.

Adam Smith's most influential work was his book *Wealth of Nations*, which he published in 1776 and was a precursor to the modern academic discipline of economics. In his works, Smith expounded how rational self-interest and competition can lead to economic prosperity. What he is less known for is his first book, *Moral Sentiments*, which he published in 1759, the foundation for his *Wealth of Nations* book. Smith says in *Moral Sentiments*,

> *Every man is, no doubt, by nature, first and principally recommended to his own care; and as he is fitter to take care of himself than of any other person, it is fit and right that it should be so.*[109]

---

107 *Basic Economics* by Thomas Sowell, pg 1, 3

108 *Economics in One Lesson* by Henry Hazlitt, pg 17

109 *The Theory of Moral Sentiments (1759)* by Adam Smith, Section II, Chap. II

One's salvation, punishment, recognition, and rewards are an individual issue, the same can be said for one's economic self-interest. Smith goes further to say:

> *But man has almost constant occasion for the help of his brethren, and it is in vain for him to expect it from their benevolence only. He will be more likely to prevail* if he can interest their self-love in his favor, *and show them that it is for their own advantage to do for him what he requires of them. Whoever offers to another a bargain of any kind, proposes to do this.* Give me that which I want, and you shall have this which you want, is the meaning of every such offer*; and it is in this manner that we obtain from one another the far greater part of those good offices which we stand in need of.* It is not from the benevolence of the butcher, the brewer, or the baker that we expect our dinner, but from their regard to their own interest. *We address ourselves, not to their humanity, but to their self-love, and never talk to them of our own necessities, but of their advantages.* [emphasis added][110]

Capitalism creates wealth. For a man to create more wealth, he requires the most freedom to be able to produce. Here's a step-by-step process to create wealth.[111]

Freedom > Knowledge > Innovation > Growth > Wealth

- More freedom promotes the ability to learn more (new knowledge)
- More new knowledge leads to applied knowledge (innovation)
- More innovation leads to economic growth (wealth distribution)
- Economic growth leads to more wealth (wealth accumulation)

The freedom to question and think means the freedom to improve because one aggregates knowledge and information into new products and services and displace the old with the new: automobiles replaced horse-drawn carriages. Most innovative surprises (innovations are rarely planned) are far more delightful and desired than the economic uncertainty of government "oversight" of new and laborious laws and regulations. The more laws and regulations there are, the more of a burden it is on the economic engine provided by businesses, especially for startups and

---

110 *The Theory of Moral Sentiments (1759)* by Adam Smith, Chapter II, p. 19

111 pragerunversity.com See *What Creates Wealth* by George Gilder

entrepreneurs. The legal and regulatory barrier entering the market becomes too high, and innovation and economic growth slows because only larger businesses can afford the required lawyers, lobbyists, and accountants. Thus, competition is reduced and costs remain high for startup entrepreneurs and customers.

People conducting business have an important social function between all involved parties. We *approve and reward* acts that benefit or add value to us and society, and we *disapprove and punish* acts that harm or subtract value from us. Solutions that provide the greatest positive benefit to the greatest number of people create the greatest reward to those providing it, those with the least benefit or are a detriment are punished. The bigger the problem you solve, whether in quality or quantity, the bigger the reward.

Five factors that affect an entrepreneurial ecosystem[112]: Talent, density, culture, capital, and regulatory environment within a team/ community. *First*, talent is natural talents. *Second*, density is the number of people of certain necessary talents. *Third*, the culture provides the necessary support. *Fourth*, capital is the necessary funding to grow the business, and *fifth*, the right level of smart laws and regulations protecting property. Even third world micro-loan/peer-to-peer lending such as kiva.org and grameen.com provide the necessary infrastructure to improve a family and their neighbor's lives.

Social responsibility, not social justice or slavery

The definition of "responsibility" is "the state or fact of having a duty to deal with something or of having control over someone; the state or fact of being accountable or to blame for something."

When the term "social justice" is bantered around, God is mainly concerned about equality of justice, right and wrong, less so about equality of resources and incomes. In fact, if either the rich or poor earn their money justly, there is no issue with this inequality as God has made us unequal in talents and skills in life. God says about justice.

> Lev 19:15 'You shall do no injustice in judgment; you *shall not be partial to the poor nor defer to the great*, but you are to *judge your neighbor fairly*. [emphasis added]

---

112 www.up.co See *Fostering a Startup and Innovation Ecosystem* by UpGlobal

God says that we're not to feel sorry for the poor and pervert justice just to sway the decision toward the poor. The Complete Jewish Bible say of this verse, "On the other hand, don't favor a person's lawsuit simply because he is poor." We're to defend the rights of all equally.

Is Socialism in Acts? The eighth and tenth commandments support property rights, i.e. the creativity, production, selling, and even the gifting of property to others. When you read about the first Christians in Acts 2 and 4, it shows the selling of property was an act of love for community.

> Acts 2:44-45 And all those who had believed were [One early manuscripts does not contain *were* and *and*] *together and had all things in common*; and they began *selling their property and possessions and were sharing* them with all, as anyone might have need. [emphasis added]

Commentary about the view of individual property in Acts:

> *"The key to the two passages (2:42 and following and 4:32 and following), is to be found in the expression in which they both agree (2:45 and 4:35). Such expressions indicate, as we have seen, not reckless but judicious charity...they show wise management...the Christians did not act like the Greeks...cast great quantities of money in to the sea, which was no contempt of riches, but only folly and madness...But whilst men were called upon to give ungrudgingly, they were not called upon to give of necessity: what each one had was still his own (4:32)...the daily administration (6:1) seems to show that no equal division of property amongst all was intended; the act of Barnabas was apparently one of charity rather than of communism, for nothing is said of an absolute surrender of all that he had."*[113]

The act of giving away all of one's possessions in the anticipation of the Rapture of the Church coming quickly or date setting of the Rapture is in error. The doctrinal issue of *eminency* (future coming) is the correct view because history shows everything else has been wrong.

> *A tyrannical product brought on by fanaticism...But we cannot shut our eyes to the fact that there was another and fatal cause at work—love itself had grown cold—the picture drawn by James is painfully at variance with the*

113 *The Expositor's Greek Testament*, Vol 2, pg 100-102, see *Community of goods.*

> *golden days which he had himself seen, when bitter jealousy and faction were unknown, for all were of one heart and one soul.*[114]

Those left behind after the Rapture will get your property anyway, prepare those left behind and have signs, Bibles, and messages on how to prepare their souls for eternity and handle the upcoming seven years. Until then, continue to follow "love your neighbor as yourself." If any property is to be sold before the Rapture, it should make good sense.

> Act 4:32 And the congregation [multitude] of those who believed *were of one heart and soul;* and not one of them claimed [Literally: was saying] that anything belonging to him was his own, but all things *were common property to them.* [emphasis added]

Here is why there is no evidence of social justice in Acts.[115]

- *Individual property rights are assumed in the eight and tenth commandments and throughout the case law given them through Moses, socialism the government would control it. How can one steal or covet a neighbors possessions if there is not personal property? In the books of Acts, how can one sell personal property and give the money to the apostles if there were no personal property? If the apostles were somehow the heads of a communal gathering, then they would have had control over everyone else's property and not the individuals who sold their property.*

- *The context is clear, because of the common faith these converts had in Christ (see 2:41–43) they were united in their goal to spread their new faith to others. However, we know from the previous context (2:5–11) that many of the new converts were visiting Jerusalem from many other countries; therefore, in order to support the physical needs of the out-of-towners while they were being instructed in their new faith, the entire group pitched in to help pay for their needs.*

- *The couple in Acts 5, Ananias and Sapphira, had land that was their private property, as well as the money they received from the sale of their*

---

114 *The Expositor's Greek Testament*, Vol 2, pg 102, See *Community of goods.*

115 pre-trib.org See *Is Jesus a Socialist?*

> *land. It was theirs to do as they pleased. They were killed by the Holy Spirit because what Ananias and Sapphira were doing was lying about the amount they were giving to the early church. Ananias and Sapphira made it look like they had offered their entire proceeds from the sale of their land when in reality they had kept part back for themselves. Such deceit was not a fruit of the Holy Spirit and the Lord demonstrated early on that indeed the Spirit of God was in their midst because only Ananias and Sapphira would have known that they lied to the apostles.*

In a letter to the colonial's agent in London, Dennys De Berdt, dated January 12, 1768, Samuel Adams wrote regarding "wealth redistribution."

> *It is observable that…there are few men who do not agree that property is a valuable acquisition, which ought to be held sacred. … if property is necessary for the support of savage life [bows, arrows, tomahawk, hunting/fishing grounds], it is by no means less so in civil society [gold, silver, land]. The Utopian schemes of leveling, and a community of goods, are as visionary and impracticable as those which vest all property in the Crown. [These ideas] are arbitrary, despotic, and, in our government, unconstitutional.*

Who decides who gets what? In Exodus 16:15 you find Israel gathering "the bread which the Lord had given you to eat." But in verses 16-18 you find every person who gathered much *individually gave* to those who had less. Individuals were not dictated to by Moses or others, they saw it as their *individual responsibility and reward* to share with those that came up short.

According to Bible prophecy the world is moving forward to a future age in which the evil aspects of socialism/communism/totalitarianism will work toward dominating the world under the rule of Satan and the Antichrist and his fake one world government during the Seven Year Tribulation. The real utopian One World government is when Jesus Christ becomes "KING OF KINGS, AND LORD OF LORDS" (Rev 19:16) during His Millennial Reign. Free enterprise is the modus operandi of what God and Jesus supports, and so does His Word. It is about individual social responsibility, never social justice.

Six steps in God's blessings bounty

Giving is a multiple blessings event, and it starts with God first. God is always about grace giving from Him! Just like salvation is neither deserved or worked for, doing good deeds after salvation follows the same pattern:

grace first, growth second, i.e. silence to receive, sow to reap when it comes to listening to God and then growth!

> Act 20:35 "In everything *I showed you that by working hard* in this manner you must help the weak and remember the words of the Lord Jesus, that He Himself said, *'It is more blessed to give than to receive.'*" [emphasis added]

We're to work smart and hard to earn a good living, and from our earnings we're to share with others that are less fortunate, especially those that are hungry and naked. Jesus says that giving affects all sides of the exchange, but it is more than that, it affects God Himself, too.

Here is how the six blessings economy works in the proper sequence:

1. **God blessed you** at your birth with who you are (spiritual self-esteem). A pen, a rough diamond, or any object has inherent value, so were you born with inherent value. It's having an *attitude of gratitude,* for Him creating and blessing you with your talents. This is the start of this blessing economy (Psm 139:13-14, "For You formed my inward parts; You wove me in my mother's womb. I will give thanks to You, for *I am fearfully and wonderfully made*; Wonderful are Your works, And *my soul knows it very well* [emphasis added].").

2. **You increase blessings** by increasing your innate value by learning and applying yourself and increasing in knowledge, skill, experience, and wisdom (Prov 3:13 "How blessed is the man who finds wisdom, And the man who gains understanding").

3. **You earn blessings** by applying your talents and skills and add value to someone's life through your job, work, or business and getting paid for your work. While a pen has innate value, the greatest value of a pen is using it, it's the same when you apply your talents and skills serving others (Prov 12:11 "He who tills his land will have plenty of bread, But he who pursues worthless things lacks sense [heart]."). *To rob a man of his efforts and work is to rob him of his earned and full blessings.*

4. **You bless God first, then others,** *from your earned blessings* (Prov 3:9-10, "Honor the Lord with your wealth, And from the first of all of your produce; *So your barns will be filled with plenty, and your vats will overflow with new wine.*" First, give a *free will offering* to God, then hire others to help you in business. Only after hiring others do you then give of your talents, time, and treasure to those less favored. Always bless others by

hiring out work first, charity last, unless they're naked and hungry (1 Pet 3:9 "not returning evil for evil or insult for insult, but *giving a blessing instead;* for *you were called for the very purpose* that you might inherit a blessing").

5. **Exponential "domino affect" of blessings with joint associations** and joy through the power of thankfulness between the receiver, the giver, and others (2 Cor 4:15 "For all things are for your sakes, so that *the grace which is spreading* [Literally: being multiplied through the many] to more and more people *may cause the giving of thanks to abound to the glory of God.* [emphasis added]"). "It is an immoral act of ingratitude to dismiss" someone doing good to or for you, whether offering a job, work, reward, praise, thank you, time, etc.; and "any person doing good for another deserves to receive gratitude" for their efforts, especially if anyone benefits from their efforts.[116] *Failure to share and give thankfulness and gratitude fails in the exponential encouragement of future blessings.* One becomes a "blessings hoarder" when one depreciates, cheapens, withholds, belittles, or ignores the blessings one has received from others, including God Himself. If I bless you and you fail to return the blessings , you not only hoard and cut off a blessing ("Thank you for being a blessing to me") which encourages me to do more, but you have cut off *my praise to God* for being able to bless you. See the below chapter 11 in the section *God's prosperity process: Roots, shoots, fruits, and seeds* about the principles of exponential potential of blessings seeds. All praise, lastly, is sent back to God for His provision.

6. **God eternally blesses you** with *rewards and recognition in heaven for all the good works you've done* (1 Cor 3:11-15, "gold, silver, and precious stones") and will be an eternal memorial to God for doing good works for Him, "Not that I seek the gift itself, but I seek for *the profit which increases to your account* (Phil 4:17)."

Paul echoes the above steps in his letter to the Philippians what happens with their work and efforts here on earth.

> Phil 4:17-19 Not that I seek the gift itself, but *I seek for the profit which increases to your account.* But I have received everything in full and have an abundance; I am amply supplied, having received from Epaphroditus *what you have sent, a fragrant aroma, an acceptable sacrifice,*

116 *Thou Shall Prosper*, by Rabbi Lapin, pg 155

> *well-pleasing to God.* And *my God will supply all your needs* according to His riches in glory in Christ Jesus. [emphasis added]

The word "account" means "account, i.e. reckoning, score." So when Jesus says it is better to give than receive, He means it, giving multiplies the joy to others and God remembers, accounts, and scores your giving.

Warning: Blessings are diminished, become scarce, because *failure to share* stops the multiplying and exponential effect of giving, the purpose of giving, which is to turn blessings into more blessings.

10 Marketing, sales, operations in the Bible

2 Chron 16:9a For the eyes of the LORD move to and fro throughout the earth that He may strongly support those whose heart is completely His.

Jimmy gave a demonstration to a small group of men, women and kids of what and how he trains people to protect themselves and their family. After the demo, we were lined around the training room discussing what he showed us and what we would learn from him. Having read *E-Myth Revisited* by Michael Gerber, I was well aware that most entrepreneurs miss that there are three views in any business. The technician (the craft of your business, what you love to do), project management, and business ownership (the business of your craft, marketing, sales, operations, money, taxes, etc.).

During his Q&A session, I prompted Jimmy with a personal defense question, "The Tueller Drill showcases how quickly an attacker could cover 21 feet, how does your training answer this threat?" Since we had not talked much about his marketing, I thought I was giving him a leading question with him taking my lead and giving the best answer. He answered, like nearly all of us beginning entrepreneurs do: he answered with a *technical* answer of *what,* not the business ownership *marketing* answer of *why* they need his training. In the drill, the average person takes two seconds or less to travel 21 feet. Having information what to do for an attack is not good enough to protect your family, you need to train and test yourself because you never know how you'll react in any given situation. My mistake. But I was able to explain the marketing answer to Jimmy a few days later, of why someone needed his business, thus increasing the reasons customers need to hire him.

Joke. Solly Finklestein was dismayed when a brand new business much like his own opened up next door and erected a huge sign which read BEST DEALS.

He was horrified when another competitor opened up on his right, and announced its arrival with an even larger sign, reading LOWEST PRICES.

Finklestein was panicked, until he got an idea. He put the biggest sign of all over his own shop; it read MAIN ENTRANCE.

People, product, process

Every business has three main elements: people, product, process.

People. Startups are about using God-given talents and resources to serve someone in their weaknesses. If you're good with numbers, serve those that are weak with working with numbers. Good with working with your hands, serve those that have difficulty. But there are two sides to the same people coin: An *entrepreneur* on one side and their *customers and vendors* on the other side. Each individual is a person, and we're to love them as we love ourselves, never to take advantage of them in their weaknesses. Jesus doesn't take advantage of us, why should we do it to others?

Product. Once you have an understanding of your ideal customers, it's now time to create a product or service to sell to them that improves their lives in more ways than one. A product or service is an improvement that elevates your customer's lives and makes them happy and prosperous, but not in a way that hurts or tears them down.

> Rom 13:10 *Love does no wrong to a neighbor*; therefore love is the fulfillment of the law. [emphasis added]

Create a viable product from your talents is your first order of business, then sell it. If you can't sell it to 10 people, you won't sell it to 10,000.

Process. There are two parts to a process: the *process* and the *results*. Just as a formula is 1+1+1=3, so it is with a business: 1+1+1 is the process and 3 is the results. Each business process step requires a measurement to track progress. As an entrepreneur you need to *focus on both sides of the formula at the same time*. In large corporations managers focus more on results and less about the process (time, resources, etc.) while workers reverse it (how it gets done), it is when an entrepreneur loses site of the whole process picture, both process and results, that problems, sometimes big problems, ensue.

When it comes to *process*, a business is made up of a number of processes, such as marketing, sales, operations, accounts payable, accounts receivable, taxes, vendors, and all of these processes make up one *system:* Your business. Paul talks about the Church as being a body with many interconnected members that comprise the body.

1 Cor 12:20 But now there are many members, but one body.

While most talk of a business as an *organization* of various departments and processes, in reality a business is an *organism,* people whose lives are on the line with what they do. A sick person/business needs to get healthy. Most businesses get sick and die, or fail, less because of the product or service and their talents, but because of the business side of their talents.

Most businesses fail because of the business of their craft, not because of the craft of their business

Marketing

Ecc 11:6 Sow your seed in the morning and do not be idle in the evening, for *you do not know whether morning or evening sowing will succeed,* or whether both of them alike will be good. [emphasis added]

God is looking throughout the earth to find someone that is willing to accomplish His purpose; He wants to start a movement and He expects us to do the work. But it starts with God first.

2 Chron 16:9 "For the *eyes of the LORD move to and fro throughout the earth that He may strongly support those whose heart is completely His.* You have acted foolishly in this. Indeed, from now on you will surely have wars." [emphasis added]

God is looking for those workers and entrepreneurs that are willing to do His Will and Work with His Message. Marketing is about the Good News message and getting noticed among all of the other businesses with whom you compete. Warning: beware of image-only marketing.

Prov 12:9 Better is he who is *lightly esteemed and has a servant,* Than he who *honors himself and lacks bread.* [emphasis added]

It makes one wonder in an age of "selfie" portraits if God doesn't shake His head at what He sees. There's a saying in Texas cattle country, "He's just a big hat with no cattle." The book *The Millionaire Next Door* by Stanley and Danko documents this. They've researched what defines someone who is truly wealthy versus the "Big Hat, No Cattle" imagery.

> *The large majority of these millionaires are not descendants of the Rockefellers or Vanderbilts. More than 80 percent are ordinary people who have accumulated their wealth in one generation. They did it slowly, steadily, without signing a multi-million-dollar contract with the Yankees.*[117]

God moves you and your market, here is marketing in three questions:

1. *What's* my main idea? What's the core message I want to share?
2. *Why* does my customer care about this, why is it important to them?
3. *What* single action do I want my customer to take after reading this?

If God is with you and your business cause, you won't be timid, but upright with boldness. Not an "in your face," but with a straight spine standing firm with confidence.

Psa 138:3 On the day I called, You answered me; *You made me bold with strength in my soul.* [emphasis added]

If you think you don't have to market, then let's see what Jesus does with His view of His purpose.

Jesus and marketing: Matt 4:23a

What is your marketing message? Well, Jesus gives us an example of how He did it when it came to the message of the Good News.

---

117 *The Millionaire Next Door* by Stanley and Danko, pg 3

> Matt 4:23a Jesus *was going* throughout all Galilee, *teaching* in their synagogues and *proclaiming* the gospel [Or, good news] of the kingdom [emphasis added]

Jesus had to *find* His ideal clients, in His case everyone, and *went to them*, and *told* them the Gospel. He didn't stay home and say, "Where are my clients, why aren't my customers finding me? (Although people filling a synagogue becomes a captive audience)". You need to find *who* your customers are and *where* they are. Then, go interact with them (See "Business Modeling and fishing: what's common?" in the book *How to Start a Business: Mac Version*). Taking these above *action steps*, Jesus created a stir.

> Matt 4:24 The *news about Him spread* throughout all Syria; and *they brought to Him* all who were ill, those *suffering* with various diseases and pains, demoniacs, epileptics [Literally: moonstruck], paralytics; and He healed them. [emphasis added]

His results were what people needed, it "went viral" throughout the land and people were bringing more problems for Him to solve.

Marketing, God, and the Parable of the Soils: Luke 8:5-15

Now the parable is this: the seed in this parable is the word of God, the Gospel, the Good News. If your product is good for your customers and helps them with their lives, then it is good news to them, too. Good news applies equally to the spiritual and physical world. Learn from the Bible how they receive your marketing message about your product or service.

- **"Way Side" verse 5, 12** = "Those beside the road are those who have heard; then the devil comes and takes away the word from their heart." The physical world idea here is that your competitor's marketing message overshadows your marketing message. Or Satan, too, can steal your business message.
- **"Rock" verse 6, 13** = "They on the rock are they, which, when they hear, receive the word with joy; and these have no root, which for a while believe, and in time of temptation fall away." A weak product or marketing message did not grab their attention enough to hold them.
- **"Thorns" verse 7, 14** = "And that which fell among thorns are they, which, when they have heard, go forth, and are choked with cares

and riches and pleasures of this life, and bring no fruit to perfection." Your marketing was drowned out by the noise of the market or life.

- **"Good Ground" verse 8, 15** = "But that on the good ground are they, which in an honest and good heart, having heard the word, keep it, and bring forth fruit with patience." Here, *your ideal customers were ready to hear and want your solution now!* It is this customer that you need to chase after and watch for their loyalty as they are the ones that will take your business to the next level. Too often businesses chase and court after their "rock," "thorn," and "way side" customers rather than finding the "good ground" loyal customer and continually appeal and "court" them and get referrals from them for more business.

The last of the four customers hears the message and takes action on it. Major point: marketing is for the customers that are interested in your solutions, hungry for what you offer while the others are not. So find the hungry ones and let them help tell/sell others about your solutions.

Jesus and Paul didn't waste God's resources targeting some unbelievers. There is no truer saying than, "When the student is ready the teacher will appear." God wants us to spend time and resources mostly with those that are ready now and stick with them and then work with unbelievers. They may come around, but until then, focus mainly on those that are ready now, Jesus promoted this principle.

> Matt 13:58 And He did not do many miracles [Or, works of power] there *because of their unbelief.* [emphasis added]

The word "unbelief" means "want of faith, unbelief…in the divine mission of Jesus." Jesus shows that as a business owner, chase only those that are open and see and want your product and services, you'll be a good steward and save valuable energy and resources.

And Jesus tells us not to give out our good products and services to those that will ruin them.

> Mat 7:6 *Do not give what is holy to dogs*, and *do not throw your pearls before swine*, or they will trample them under their feet, and turn and tear you to pieces. [emphasis added]

The Holy Spirit guided Paul regarding directions on where to visit and "market" the Good News next. His group was forbidden to visit one area and instead guided to visit another.

> Act 16:6-7 They passed through the Phrygian and Galatian region, having been *forbidden by the Holy Spirit* to speak the word in Asia; and after they came to Mysia, *they were trying to go* into Bithynia, and the *Spirit of Jesus did not permit them*; [emphasis added]

God moves us to where we are to plant, grow, then harvest fruitful spiritual markets. One's business is no different, find ready markets, not ones that are too tough to crack.

Product pricing, brown bananas, bad restaurant table

Price versus value. Consumers think price, entrepreneurs think value and ROI. There's an old Jewish question: "Who pays retail?" That's true for pricing, but it equally applies how one looks at buying and selling. During a recent discussion, I was amongst some entrepreneurs as a lady was discussing the cost of her cell phone bill and how to reduce her costs. While reducing costs makes your business more profitable, after much discussion we found out that she was not earning enough, i.e. she was being pennywise and pound foolish. She was focusing on the *pennies of her costs and expenses* rather than on the *dollars of earning income.* She should have been focusing on earning income first and expenses second.

We know the price of everything, but the value of nothing

Some would say that paying $29.99 for a book is "too expensive" to pay. When looking at the price of book, how much would it cost you to research, write, and produce a book or have a one-on-one personal consulting time with the author? Hundreds, thousands, or even tens of thousands of dollars? What does it say of an individual who cheapens the author's work searching for a discount compared with the knowledge and time devoted to producing a product or service that costs the customer two or three ten spots?

When someone says something is "too expensive," it comes from a consumer's scarcity view, not an entrepreneur's abudance view. An entrepreneur would turn it around and say, "If I pay $29.99, would I get

$60.00-$200.00 worth of ideas out of it (or an ROI, Return On Investment, or 2-4 times or what I paid)?" If you get *more value out of it than you paid*, then it is a high value item.

Too often customers only look at the price and number of pages of a book and never the value of the content. Hence, customers know the price, but not the value of what they are buying. So next time you look at buying something, *seek value over price.*

Brown bananas. Have you noticed that there are two colors of bananas in the store: yellow ones and yellow ones with brown spots. The difference is that you'll see a marked down or reduced price of the brown spotted bananas versus the green/yellow ones because they're "defective" or "damaged" bananas. Some customers may not want these over ripened bananas, so the store reduces the price in order for them to recover some of their costs. Much like outlet malls, "seconds," consignment, second hand, or Goodwill shops dealing with used, damaged or older merchandise. The main point: there is not one thing wrong with marketing a product at a reduced price, in fact, being honest about the product and prices will probably bring in more customers.

Bad restaurant table. There is a story about a restaurant that could not get their customers to sit at a certain table. The "environment," next to their front door, was just not conducive to attracting customers to sit there. That is until their right marketing kicked in. The restaurant owner decided to "market" the table as "such and such discount off all meals at this table." Soon after the owner started marketing it, they had a line and later had to take reservations for that specific table as people wanted to get their discounted meals. While the owner's profit at that table may not have been as high as the other tables, because of his "volume" he was making a profit that was previously an under performing table.

"Inglorious Fruits and Vegetables."[118] In France, getting others to eat more fruits and vegetables was difficult and costly. They were throwing away hundreds of millions of tons of food away each year because the food "did not look normal," i.e. it was ugly, but still just as nutritious. Enter a marketing campaign of France's third largest grocery chain with "Inglorious Fruits and Vegetables," with such names as Grotesque Apple, the Ridiculous Potato, the Hideous Orange, the Disfigured Eggplant. They were as good as the perfect fruit and vegetables, but 30 percent cheaper. Results: they had 24 percent increase in store traffic had difficulty keeping the fruits and vegetables in stock.

---

118 YouTube.com See *Intermarché - 'Inglorious Fruits and Vegetables"*

16 marketing principles checklist, four tough questions

Nearly all marketers are very familiar with the AIDA copywriting formula: Attention, Interest, Desire, Action. Knowing this basic formula is the equivalent of playing the 12-Bar blues pattern on a guitar, EVERY guitarist knows it. Here is one of the simplest copywriting formulas around:

- What I've got for you
- What it's going to do for you
- Who am I?
- What you need to do next?

There are dozens more marketing formulas to use to market your product and services, so ensure you pick the one that works best for you and your product and services. Here is a top 16 checklist things to do to make your marketing 2X, 5X, even 10X (ROI) more successful:

- ☐ Headline with a hook - captures their attention.
- ☐ Lead - who is it for and why they should read more.
- ☐ Story - from failure to success.
- ☐ Sub headline - to keep them reading.
- ☐ Create urgency - set a deadline.
- ☐ Be unique - you must differentiate your product.
- ☐ Be useful - give your customers useful information in your copy.
- ☐ Benefit bullets - features tell, but benefits sell.
- ☐ Testimonials - add credibility with celebrity third-party comments.
- ☐ Use graphics and images wisely.
- ☐ Break it up - use white space.
- ☐ Make an offer - a compelling offer.
- ☐ Guarantee - reduces product returns and buyer remorse.
- ☐ Have a "Call to Action" - tell them exactly what to do.
- ☐ Include contact information - so they can contact you.
- ☐ Use a promo code to track - track what works or doesn't.

When you write your marketing, you need to ensure you get to the heart of the matter. You need to *ask four tough questions*:

1. Why should anyone read or listen to it?
2. Why should anyone believe it?

3. Why should anyone do anything about it?
4. Why should it be acted upon immediately?

If you can't answer these questions about your marketing and your copywriting, you don't want to send it out. Ask the four questions above every time you prepare an ad, letter, brochure, etc.

Sales - sell to customers

God states in the Bible surrounding making money from the sale that He expects us to run a business.

> Lev 25:14 If you *make a sale*, moreover, to your friend or *buy from your friend's hand*, you *shall not wrong one another*. [emphasis added]

Notice that God uses both words, *buy* and *sell* when it comes to business. That means that even at the most basic level, everyone is in a business. Even if it is buying or selling to your neighbor, such as farm animals, a sofa, a used bike, or even a selling a service of cutting someone's lawn. Everyone is in a business when you trade time or value for money.

Selling is about persuasion, not about manipulation

When it says "you shall not wrong" one another, the word "wrong" means used of fraud and cheating in buying and selling. When you pursue your goals either as a neighbor or as a salesperson for your business, the sale must be achieved by mutually benefiting each other on a voluntary basis. It means enriching both individuals, not at the expense of one or the other. Both must accept responsibility for their actions. And the phrase "one another" is just that, you equally win. The Complete Jewish Bible gives the translation, "If you sell anything to your neighbor or buy anything from him, neither of you is to exploit the other."

> Prov 11:26 He who withholds grain, the people will curse him, But *blessing will be on the head of him who sells it.* [emphasis added]

The idea here is not to hold out selling, especially the necessities (water, food, clothing, etc.) for a higher price. Customers needing the necessities of life, sell it to them, you may need to raise your prices some, but don't withhold your product if it belongs in the essential category.

Jesus and selling: Matt 4:23b

Once you find your market and tell them of your solution, how are you going to sell them your product? After Jesus told them through His marketing, now He had to show and giveaway His product to prove to them of the veracity of His product: Him.

> Mat 4:23b and *healing* every kind of disease and every kind of sickness *among the people*. [emphasis added]

First Jesus *told* them, then He *showed* them by demonstrating His work and results of His Good News message. But just as important, He also *gave away* His product, Himself, and the veracity of His product through healing others. An entrepreneur needs to demonstrate to their ideal customers who and what your product or service solves, unless through common sense it is readily apparent. Demonstrating your product can be done through videos, social media, but in person and face-to-face is more powerful. From God's perspective, your product and service and your marketing needs to solve a person's problem honestly and accurately, i.e. authentically.

Operations - delivery, billing, customer service

The best advice that God gives us regarding our business applies to every business is the below verse.

> Prov 27:23 Know well the condition of your flocks, And pay attention to your herds;

If you don't know the condition of your business and your business numbers, you'll eventually fail.

Jesus and testimonials and customer service: Matt 4:24

We need to look now at how Jesus performed customer service.

> Mat 4:24 The *news about Him spread* throughout all Syria; and *they brought to Him* all who were ill, those suffering with various diseases and pains, demoniacs, epileptics, paralytics; and He healed them. [emphasis added]

Testimonials. The testimonials and "buzz" that Jesus received means His work "went viral" (More testimonial comments: Matt 8:4, 12:16, 16:20, Mark 7:36, 8:30, etc.). Once He told others of His work, did the work, His good reputation spread so that more "business" was coming His way. Once others heard of His solution, Himself, others sought Him out.

God started testimonials, and giving is a testimonial to God. When God blesses you, He gives to you, He looks for a "testimonial" of what He has done for you. The *best testimonial from you to Him* is giving Him your praise, honor, glory, and the first and best 10 percent of what He gave you in earnings. Be stingy with what God has given you, and your Angel Investor may pull His funding from you. The same is true of your neighbor, if you've been blessed by someone, give a testimonial to God of them and to others. Joy shared is joy multiplied, so multiply the good that you have received. Abundance is shared; scarcity is not.

Jesus was concerned about testimonials, you find it numerous times when He healed others. Sometimes He'd tell them to keep quiet, other times to tell the priests; some did what He said, others did not. The key element was that Jesus was about telling or not telling others about what He did; He was concerned about who told what to whom and when.

> Mat 8:4 And Jesus *said to him, "See that *you tell no one*; but go, *show yourself* to the priest and present the offering [Literally: gift] that *Moses commanded, as a testimony to them.*" [emphasis added]

Testimonials for the work Jesus did are no different than for an entrepreneur who does a good job: Testimonials speak of good news to others. The person who was healed thanks God, giving Him a testimonial of the work He has done. They also shared the good news with those that worked in the Temple that saw evidence of God's good works. Giving both spiritual and physical testimonials means everyone shares in the joy that one receives.

Testimonials for entrepreneurs, when describing good products or services, spreads the good news and blessing to others that might need an entreprencur's solutions. *Blessings are always a two-way street;* they go both ways, to the one receiving and to the one giving. Testimonials are a blessing, when you as a customer give one to a business, both you and the business are blessed, this is especially true if you both are businesses. Putting one's business name on a testimonial gives recognition to others how you value your fellow business person. And with the internet, writing a book review stays online for how long? How about 24/7/365!

Testimonials spread joy and encouragement around. Even God the Father gave a testimonial and encouragement to Jesus His Son.

> Matt 3:17 and behold, a voice out of the heavens said, "This is My [Or, My Son, the Beloved] beloved Son, *in whom I am well-pleased.*" [emphasis added]

Do you give testimonials to God for His Blessings and what He has done for you? Do you give testimonials to your family? Friends? Others for their efforts and results?

Customer service. When it comes to customer service, the Bible is pretty clear on how to handle your customers and others, they're your neighbors, your family.

> 1 Tim 5:1-2 Do not sharply rebuke an *older man*, but rather appeal to him as a father, to the *younger men* as brothers, the *older women* as mothers, and the *younger women* as sisters, in all purity. [emphasis added]

Treat your customers and others like your family.

> Rom 12:18 If possible, so far as *it depends on you, be at peace with all men.* [emphasis added]

Jesus and project management: Luke 6:47-49, 14:27-30

Project management. Let's take a look at what Jesus says about the business of the construction of a building, of which he had considerable skills and knowledge about.

> Luke 14:27-30 "Whoever does not carry his own cross and come after Me cannot be My disciple. For which one of you, when he wants to *build a tower*, does not *first sit down and calculate the cost to see if he has enough to complete it?* Otherwise, when he has *laid a foundation and is not able to finish*, all who observe it begin to *ridicule him*, saying, 'This man began to build and was not able to finish.'" [emphasis added]

Jesus tells of a person who is starting a project to build a "tower" which means a "tower-shaped building as a safe and convenient dwelling." It probably was a large farm building versus an actual tower. The person building the tower needs to calculate the cost so as not to place himself in a position to be ridiculed by others if they fail to finish the project because they run out of money. God echoes the connection between the spiritual and the physical in Proverbs 24:3 "By wisdom a *house is built*, and *by understanding it is established* [emphasis added]." Jesus comment: a natural business or project best practice is to ask what the final cost is going to be before you sign up or start work on it. Jesus in the parable was utterly honest and spared no words to tell his disciples that it would cost them to follow after him. If you start a project, you need to be able to finish it.

Laying building foundations. Jesus uses the building metaphor to describe the essential aspects of laying a great foundation to build one's faith upon, and the object of one's faith is built upon Jesus Christ.

Laying building foundations. Jesus uses the building metaphor to describe the essential aspects of laying a great foundation to build one's faith upon, and the object of one's faith is built upon Jesus Christ.

> Luke 6:47-49 "Everyone who *comes to Me* and *hears My words* and *acts on them*, I will show you whom he is like: he is like a man *building a house*, who *dug deep* and *laid a foundation on the rock*; and when a flood occurred, the torrent burst against that house and could not shake it, because *it had been well built*. But the one who has heard and has

> not acted accordingly, is like a man who built a house on the ground without any foundation; and the torrent burst against it and *immediately it collapsed*, and *the ruin of that house was great* [emphasis added]." [emphasis added]

The word "dig" and "deep" both combined does not mean he *dug deep*, but *made it deep*, i.e. a wise builder "struck the rock before he laid the foundation."[119] "The foolish builder did not make a mistake choosing a foundation. His folly lay in not thinking of a foundation, but building a haphazard on the surface."[120] Securing a foundation takes work, and the hard work is worth it because in a storm the house stands strong and secure. Nothing shakes it. But since Jesus used "multiple terms [immediately, torrent, burst, ruin great] to describe the houses' collapse [it] accentuates the note of the tragedy in the image."[121] And since in most cases a house is the most expensive purchase one makes in life, this person *lost everything* because of their foolish decision.

Bottom line: Jesus was locally known, a laborer and a business owner. He understood what it meant by giving the example of building a building without ensuring that you had a good foundation to build on, otherwise all of the work, effort, and resources you put into the building will go to waste. Not to mention how one's reputation was at stake. But most importantly, this concept applies both to the spiritual and the physical. A bad physical foundation corrupts the whole building just like a bad spiritual foundation corrupts a life, and a bad spiritual foundation can cost one their eternal life.

Rest, time, and priorities

There are a number of factors that go into running a business. Scheduling your priorities and your time will become a significant issue as you begin building your business. Up first: scheduling down time, rest, holiday, vacation, or a little R&R.

An entrepreneurial joke: As an entrepreneur, you get to choose which 80 hours a week you work. You're always thinking about your business in one form or another, sometimes even on your "day off" you think about it.

---

119 *Word Pictures in the New Testament*, by Archibald T. Robertson, pg. 95

120 *The Expositor's Greek Testament*, Vol. 1, pg 509

121 *Luke* by Davell Bock, pg 130

However, that's not a good habit to start. You need time off to revive and recuperate. In fact, God rested Himself.

> Gen 2:3 Then God blessed the seventh day and sanctified it, because in it *He rested from all His work* which God had created and made. [emphasis added]

If God rested, then Man should rest, too. Not only you rest once a week, but the Bible shows that you're to rest other things as well, land.

> Lev 25:2-4 "Speak to the sons of Israel and say to them, 'When you come into the land which I shall give you, then the land shall have a sabbath to the LORD. Six years you shall sow your field, and six years you *shall prune your vineyard and gather in its crop*, but during the seventh year the land shall have a sabbath rest, a sabbath to the LORD; you *shall not sow your field nor prune* your vineyard. [emphasis added]

Even animals should get a rest, too.

> 25:7 'Even your cattle and the animals that are in your land shall have all its crops to eat.

It's universal.

So that means that an 80-hour work week means you work 14-hour days for six days, so your seventh day is for resting and recuperating.

Priorities and time. We often hear that you have to use time management wisely. There are two components to getting things done: priorities and time, with both being important, although time is often the first thing discussed. Often left behind are priorities.

As another entrepreneur has said, "Most people give more thought to protecting the stuff stored in the garage than protecting their time." Why?

Everything is replaceable but time, which is wasted or lost!

When you read the Jewish Torah you read that during the sixth day before the Sabbath begins you're to have enough food prepared on the sixth day to handle the seventh day so as to not even to start a fire to cook your meals. That means you're required to plan slightly ahead so that there would be no cooking on the day of rest.

A Jewish perspective of a rest comes from a "spark" to light the fire to cook your meal (Ex 35:3 "kindle a fire"). Their perspective of a spark also means not use a "spark" to turn on the lights, the "spark" of the battery to start a car, but more importantly, a "spark" is used for creativity and to come up with new things for your business. This is a time of rest during the one day of the week, whether it's Saturday for the Jews or Sunday for the Christians. Of primary purpose is the idea of time and priorities.

Prioritize your time to have down time.

Plan ahead for downtime so that things are done before your day of rest. When you have a spark of creativity, you create and work, and if you work, then you're not resting. Since God wants us to rest, it means:

While resting, it means you should be listening to God, getting His guidance on your day of rest for the next six days.

Resting means your mind is listening. Regardless of how far you go with a Jewish view of a spark, it's the relationship that God wants with us and you can't listen to Him if you're working. And when you listen, your Godly Angel Investor is able to give you good advice and direction.

Planning. When it comes to planning your business and your life, too often we're of the mindset that we'll live a long time. Problem is, you don't know when your life will end, no one does. From an entrepreneur's perspective, you should look to the long term and the future, but expect it to not go as you planned.

> Jam 4:13-15 Come now, you who say, "Today or tomorrow we will go to such and such a city, and spend a year there and *engage in business and make a profit.* Yet you do not know what your life will be like tomorrow. You are just a vapor that appears for a little while and then vanishes away. Instead, *you ought to say, 'If the Lord wills, we will live and also do this or that.'"* [emphasis added]

The word business means "to go a trading, to travel for business, to traffic, trade." The Amplified Bible verse says, "Come now, you who say,

Today or tomorrow we will go into such and such a city and spend a year there and carry on our business and make money. Yet you do know know [the least thing] about what may happen tomorrow. What is the nature of your life? You are [really] but a wisp of vapor (a puff of smoke, a mist) that is visible for a little while and then disappears [into thin air]. You ought instead to say. If the Lord is willing, we shall live and we shall do this or that [thing]." Our lives are in His Hands; it's His Decision to whether or not we live another day. Although we can plan, it's up to Him to allow us to live another day.

11 Stewardship of God's resources

Prov 3:9 Honor the LORD from your wealth; And from the first of all your produce.

Jimmy and I had conversations with other men, and we asked the question to each of them: what kind of training or information did you get from your parents regarding money? Nearly all said they got next to nothing or nothing at all from their parents and had to learn it all on their own. Bringing up the issue is not about finding fault with parents, but showing how bad habits are transferred through to each generation. Our discussions came to a head, and we realized that we needed to search out better content and learn better habits to improve not only the lives of our families, but the lives of those around us.

Two perspectives echoed around our money discussions: managing and earning money. First, managing money and the resources we had brought home was first. Jimmy's church, The Rock, used Dave Ramsey's Financial Peace University's as a starting place, and we figured we would add other content as we grew. Mastering the little amounts God gave us, we would grow onto handling larger amounts. Last, earning money and resources in reality has a direct relationship with how you manage money. The more you learn, the more you earn, and the more you earn, the more you need to learn how to handle bigger financial responsibilities. And there is also a direct relationship with those you hang around with and their various habits.

You become like the average of the five people you hang around the most.

And this average shows itself in not only the average of managing and earning money, but health, home, social, and other issues.

Joke. A poor man managed to get an appointment with a wealthy philanthropist by insisting that he had a foolproof way for the man to make 5 million dollars.

"So let me hear your great idea," said the philanthropist.

"It's very simple," replied the pauper. "I understand that when your daughter gets married you're planning on giving her a dowry of $10 million dollars."

"Yes," said the philanthropist.

"So, I've come to tell you that I'm willing marry her for half the amount!"

Where are your motivational thermostats set?

Motivation is a difficult thing, and we each have our own motivational and emotional thermostat settings. How do you handle your motivational thermostat settings when it comes to money? How you grew up and were taught or learned, or not, about money will determine your financial success. But do not forget, *you can change and improve.*

> *"The philosophy of the rich versus the poor is this: The rich invest their money and spend what is left; the poor spend their money and invest what's left."* -- *Jim Rohn*

Thermostat excuses - Having thermostat excuses means your fears or excuses or how you rationalize (rational-lies) and make up reasons why you can't do something should be the first place to start. Take the foot off your brakes, find better content, and keep dropping your various dead weight excuses so you can increase your financial performance.

Thermostat settings and discipline - "Set the number, then move the needle." Establishing your *thermostat settings* means if you don't turn on your heater or A/C and set your house thermostat, the temperature will vary through the warm and cold cycles of a day and you won't get the benefits. Just like your home thermostat, each of us has financial thermostat settings. A financial *thermostat discipline* means you set a financial goal you want to work toward and then you take actions to move the needle to accomplish the goal. For example, this step-by-step process means you set your savings needle to save 5 percent of your paycheck each month with a goal to have $1,000.00 in the bank for emergencies. To achieve this result, you add 5 percent or more to your savings to move the savings needle from $0.00 to $1,000.00. Set realistic goals, then have the discipline (or set automatics deductions) to work to move the results needle toward your target goal. When you achieve each goal, you can then reset the goal or target to something different and change both the process and the results, as needed. We all have different thermostats of life and our business. Your business starts with priority #1.

1. **Service thermostat** - How many people does your business product or service intend to serve? There is only one Mona Lisa, so your service thermostat would be set to one, but there are millions of poor, so you could have a service thermostat set to a higher number. The larger number of people you help with your work or business, the greater your reward.

2. **Earning thermostat** - Whether one is working in a job or as an entrepreneur, where is your earning thermostat set? If you earn double what you're earning now, how would you feel about it? Triple it and how would you feel? Quadruple? Would you stop earning at double your income, or would you continue to find ways to earn more? I know a realtor that once earned more in six months than most did in a year. Then they went on vacation, until their money ran out. This constant yo-yo of their income/vacation life, going from feast to famine and back again, caused them stress.

3. **Giving thermostat** - How much are you giving of what you earn? I know of a millionaire that recently talked about buying a $5,000.00 purse, and religious Christians condemned her. What they do not know is that she gives over 30 percent of her income to orphanages. Recent studies show the Christian giving rate is down around the 5 percent or less; this is a stingy giving thermostat setting!

4. **Saving thermostat** - Once you have the above thermostats set, your saving thermostat settings prepares you for emergencies. *Pay yourself first* by saving first from your earnings.

5. **Spending thermostat** - After you've done all of the above, now you're on to the spending thermostat. In most people's lives, your spending matches what you earn, but sometimes spending gets out of control and you spend more than you make. This is where most individuals and families have difficulty and require a rethinking and setting a new financial discipline on what is the right number to set it to.

The issue I have seen is that some people have a low thermostat setting for their various areas of motivations. Motivations can or are self, parental, manager, friends or even professionally imposed, but the real question becomes:

What are or should be God's various thermostat settings for you?

Earning a profit: good money, bad money

Jewish tradition views a person's quest for profit and wealth to be inherently moral because money is a testament that you have pleased another human being. King Solomon, the world's wealthiest person, wrote about it the book of Proverbs.

> Prov 14:24 The *crown of the wise is their riches*, But the folly of fools is foolishness. [emphasis added]

The wise learn to attains riches. The quality of the content the wise person learns provides the foundation for the level of wealth that a person can potentially achieve. The more high quality content they learn, the more they increase their earning potential and become wealthy by serving others. Regarding money itself, God Himself wrote in Genesis that gold as a medium of exchange is good:

> Gen 2:12 And the *gold of that land is good;* the bdellium and the onyx stone are there. [emphasis added]

Gold, a metaphor for money and wealth, is good. Jesus got gold, frankincense and myrrh from the magi at His birth (These were standard gifts to honor kings in the ancient world: gold as a precious metal, frankincense as perfume or incense, and myrrh as anointing oil)[122]. It is OK to ask God to be prosperous, but God gives prosperity only to those that can handle and use it correctly. Money has no feelings, does not make a decision, determines who to follow, and is not a magnet to attract other

---

[122] biblicalarchaeology.org See *Why Did the Magi Bring Gold, Frankincense and Myrrh?*

money. *Money is a tool*, nothing more. Man's freedom and freewill determines whether it's used for good or bad.

> Prov 13:21 Adversity pursues sinners, But *the righteous will be rewarded with prosperity*. [emphasis added]

Doing good with your talents and service will bring you wealth and prosperity, whether a neurosurgeon or a plumber. Jesus points out His spiritual and physical approach to life.

> John 10:10 The thief comes only to steal and kill and destroy; I came that *they may have life, and have [Or, have abundance] it abundantly*. [emphasis added]

Jesus says that we "may have" life and have it abundantly; He did not say it with certainty, but the potential is there. If one pursues a good life, you serve others with your talent that is constructive, that builds others up.

Good Money. When someone is pleased with your efforts and work at serving them, then the money you have earned is always a good thing. Good money is decided when it becomes investments that improves other people's lives either by giving them pleasure (good food, good coffee, good entertainment, etc.) or relieving them of pain (medical surgery, etc.).

> Prov 10:22 It is the *blessing of the LORD that makes rich*, And He adds no sorrow to it. [emphasis added]

However, you can cross the line when you focus only on riches and serving your neighbor becomes an afterthought.

> Prov 11:28 He who *trusts in his riches will fall*, But the righteous will flourish like the green leaf. [emphasis added]

When one becomes successful there is potential that with their wealth they become self-righteous, but Jesus shows a way of keeping our feet on the ground and focused on good works and rewards that last for all eternity.

Luke 12:33-34 Sell your possessions and give to charity; make yourselves money belts which do not wear out, an *unfailing treasure in heaven*, where *no thief comes near nor moth destroys.* For *where your treasure is, there will your heart be also.* [emphasis added]

The word "treasure" means "the things laid up in a treasury, collected treasures." Treasure, like money, has no value other than what value man puts on it. When Jesus tells them to "sell your possessions" and "where no thief comes near nor moth destroys," He's warning them they "are not commanded to retain nothing for their own use (for Christ Himself had a purse out of which He gave alms); but to take care that fear of poverty does not interfere with benevolence."[123] Wealth on this earth has many enemies and allies, but that which is *earned and stored in heaven can never be touched and is safe from all.*

Bad money. Bad money results when selling a product or service for money, and it harms another person. The first time the "love of money" or greed has been discussed you find the very first example of it when God gives the tenth commandment.

Exod 20:17 You *shall not covet* your neighbor's house; you *shall not covet* your neighbor's wife or his male servant or his female servant or his ox or his donkey or *anything that belongs to your neighbor.* [emphasis added]

Greed and coveting are a heightened, unhealthy condition of desire. This commandment is the most difficult, while all of the others were about physical aspects in the physical world, this one is about monitoring and controlling one's thoughts.[124] When you have a thought, your first choice is whether to feed that thought, and your second choice is whether or not to take action on that thought. Feeding and controlling one's thoughts means you control the starting point of one's actions, for without a thought, no actions would occur. You find similar words in the NT.

---

123 *International Critical Commentary: Luke* by Driver, Plummer, Briggs, pg 328-329

124 chabad.org See *Thought Control* by Mordechai Wollenberg

1 Tim 3:3 not addicted to wine or pugnacious, but gentle, peaceable, *free from the love of money*. [emphasis added]

The phrase "free from the love of money" is also found here.

Heb 13:5 Make sure that your character is *free from the love of money*, being content with what you have; for He Himself has said, "I WILL NEVER DESERT YOU, NOR WILL I EVER FORSAKE YOU," [emphasis added]

The phrase "free from the love of money" (Greek ἀφιλάργυρος, aphilargyros) is the negative ἀ + φιλάργυρος which means "loving money, avarice." Play close attention to this verse! So the Amplified Bible says, "Let your character or moral disposition be free from the love of money [including greed, avarice, lust, and craving earthly possessions] and be satisfied with your present [circumstances and with what you have]; for He [God] Himself has said, I will not in any way fail you *nor* give you up *nor* leave you without support. [I will] not, [I will] not, [I will] not in any degree leave you helpless *nor* forsake *nor* let [you] down (relax My hold on you)! [Assuredly not!] [Josh 1:5]"

When in the same verse you see both the issue of *being free from the love of money* and *that God will not leave you nor forsake you*, it is a promise that should give everyone some economic comfort, "nor leave you without support."

It is when you take your trust focus off of God and onto money is where problems occur.

1 Tim 6:9-10 But those who want to *get rich* fall into temptation and a snare and many foolish and harmful desires which plunge men into ruin and destruction. For the *love of money is a root of all sorts of evil*, and *some by longing for it* have wandered away from the faith and *pierced themselves with many griefs*. [emphasis added]

The word "get rich" means "to be rich, to have abundance." The Amplified Bible says, "But those who crave to be rich fall into temptation and a snare and into many foolish (useless, godless) and hurtful desires that plunge men into ruin and destruction and miserable perishing." Notice, "crave to be rich" is where there is concern. The word "love" (Greek φιλαργυρία, philargyria) means "the love of money, avarice, greed, or covetousness." This Greek word is used only this one time in the NT, that makes it unique and that we should take notice of how it is used in this context.

A similar word is used to describe how the Pharisees attitude was toward money, too.

> Luke 16:14 Now the Pharisees, who were *lovers of money*, were listening to all these things and *were scoffing at Him.* [emphasis added]

This word for "love" (Greek φιλάργυρος philargyros) means "lovers of money, avaricious" and occurs twice, here and in 2 Tim 3:2. The word avaricious means "having or showing an extreme greed for wealth or material gain." The word "scoffing" means "to deride by turning up their nose, to sneer at, scoff at" (see also Luke 16:14; 23:35). To sneer at Jesus' words shows their attitude toward doing with was right in God's eyes, they had become religious secularists, living and acting just like the world, but with religious connotations.

These were Jewish religious denomination individuals, and just as easily could be a Christian today. Money does not choose sides, man does. Is being rich wrong? No. Is a profit bad? No. Is being greedy wrong? Yes. Money rightly used as a tool for growth and added value is good, or it is used to be greedy. Lovers of money, i.e. greed, can affect anyone or any organization.

The "Proverbs: Good and the Bad" table (more verses in Proverbs than are displayed) shows how Proverbs provides various contrasts around issues. In the inner two columns, both the good poor and good rich are the ones God blesses, no matter their station in life. It is when you move outside of God's plan, outside the table parens, where things go wrong. While the table shows just a few verses from the Bible, research the rest of the verses to get a complete picture of how God sees both the rich and poor. It boils down just one statement:

Proverbs: Good and the Bad

Bad Poor	Good Poor	Good Rich	Bad Rich
10:4		10:4	
10:15		10:15	
	13:7		13:7
17:5	17:5		
		18:11	
21:17			21:17
	22:2	22:2	
22:7			22:7
	28:6		28:6
	28:11		28:11

We either love God and use money or love money and use God.

And this thought is echoed in this verse.

> Jas 1:9-11 But the brother [i.e. church member] of *humble circumstances* is to *glory in his high position*; and the *rich man* is to *glory in his humiliation*, because like flowering [Literally: the flower of the grass] grass he will pass away. For the sun rises with a [Literally: the] scorching wind and withers the grass; and its flower falls off and the beauty of its appearance is destroyed; so too the *rich man* in the midst of his pursuits will fade away (Isa 40:6-7). [emphasis added]

Greed is at the heart of the bad poor and bad rich, love is at the heart of good poor and rich. It is when one chases after the glitter and "shiny objects" of money that gives rise to bad attitudes towards money and your neighbors. Just as we fight to do good, so we must fight to keep bad away.

Handling profit and wealth: living, giving, investing

As with all Christian responsibilities, first and foremost, you're to earn as much as you are capable of earning (See the parable of the talents above). After you have earned it, the next question is what is a Christian to do with their wealth?

> 2 Cor 9:7-8 Each one *must do just as he has purposed in his heart*, not grudgingly or under compulsion, for *God loves a cheerful giver*. And God is able to make all grace abound to you, so that *always having all sufficiency in everything, you may have an abundance for every good deed*; [emphasis added]

The mature and prosperous believer gives of their time, wealth, success, love, personality, and whatever their prosperity might be. Having more wealth requires more levels of responsibilities and more potential harm when it comes to giving. John Adams sent a letter to Thomas Jefferson on December 21, 1819 in which he posed the question:

> *"Will you tell me how to prevent riches from becoming the effects of temperance and industry? Will you tell me how to prevent riches from producing luxury? Will you tell me how to prevent luxury from producing effeminacy, intoxication, extravagance, Vice, and folly?"*[125]

When it come to giving: Others might quit working or feign not being able to work. People visit multiple churches and synagogues on the same day to reap the benefits of their charity: free stuff.

John D. Rockefeller, one the richest Americans during the late 1800s and early 1900s, similarly struggled like Adams: How to help others without harming or enabling them? One of his philanthropic recipients was an African-American college later becoming Spelman College. Rockefeller could have paid off all their debts, but didn't. Give too little, and he would not have helped at all, give too much, and people might stop working. Rockefeller chose the middle road to encourage earning their way towards their goals.[126] Today you provide matching funds with what an organization raises in donations.

Benjamin Franklin said of the poor.

> *"I am for doing good to the poor, but I think the best way of doing good to the poor, is not making them easy in poverty, but leading or driving them out of it. I observed that the more public provisions were made for the poor, the less they provided for themselves, and of course became poorer. And, on the contrary, the less was done for them, the more they did for themselves, and became richer."*

"Charity" implies that your heart motivates you, but the word "tzedakah" (Hebrew צֶדֶק , tsedeq) literally means "righteousness" —-*doing the right thing.* It's about someone who fulfills all his obligations, *whether they are in the mood or not.* As Jacob himself said to God.

> Gen 28:22 This stone, which I have set up as a pillar, will be God's house, and of *all that You give me I will surely give a tenth to You.* [emphasis added]

---

125 *The Adams-Jefferson Letters* Edited by Lester Cappon, pg 551

126 *Titan The Life of John D. Rockefeller* by Ron Chernow, pg 240-242

Recognizing that God is the source of all blessings means we give Him the recognition He deserves because we're stewards of all that He owns, which is everything. Cheerfully giving God the first 10 percent means other 90 percent we're to manage for Him. And yet the average American today gives less than three or four percent, if that.

> Prov 3:9 *Honor the LORD from your wealth*, And *from the first* of all your produce; [emphasis added]

However, from a Jewish perspective, a person of ordinary means who gives less than a tenth of his income to charity is considered a miser. When we fail to recognize God for His Blessings, we rob Him of His rightful recognition. What does He say to us about this?

> Mal 3:8-10 "Will a man *rob God?* Yet you are robbing Me! But you say, 'How have we robbed You?' In tithes and offerings. You are cursed with a curse, for *you are robbing Me*, the *whole nation of you!* Bring the *whole tithe* into the storehouse, so that there may be food in My house, and *test Me now in this*," says the LORD of hosts, "if I will not open for you the windows of heaven and *pour out for you a blessing until it overflows.*" [emphasis added]

One should always give his best for God, not only as individuals, but as a neighborhood, community, a business and more (See the below section on tithing for clarification of the above verse).

> Lev 3:16 The priest shall offer them up in smoke on the altar as food, an offering by fire for a soothing aroma; *all fat is the LORD'S.* [emphasis added]

God gave you the best, you, and by giving Him the best of what He as given you, He'll continue to give you His best.

God's prosperity process: Roots, shoots, fruits, and seeds

When it comes to a person's personal security, of primary importance is one's soul (spiritual, mental, emotional) and lastly physical health and prosperity. You get this sequence from what John wrote.

> 3 John 1:2 Beloved, I pray that *in all respects* you *may prosper* and *be in good health, just as your soul prospers.* [emphasis added]

The word "prosper" (Greek εὐοδόω euodoō) means "to prosper, be successful; of persons" and is present, passive, infinitive, meaning God will continuously make you prosper. But notice the sequence that John writes, your *soul (spiritual then mental health) needs to prosper first,* before your spiritual and physical areas becomes prosperous.

Roots, shoots, fruits, and seeds. Germination of a seed requires three things once it is planted: water, oxygen, and temperature. Oxygen levels in the ground rarely change. The temperature to grow a seed is within a range, i.e. spring, summer, and fall. But water is the absolute essential ingredient needed to *start a seed growing.* Damp soil, neither too much nor too little water, is needed to start the process within the seed.

First, germination of a seed starts with the application of water. Then the seed sends out its *roots* out to gather more good quality water and nourishment. The *quality and quantity of the nourishment determines the quality and quantity of the fruit,* but without the roots going out, each individual taking actions, there is no growth. Second, the root supplies the *shoot* and grows out of the seed and heads above ground level. Third, it produces its flower then through cross pollination it produces its *fruit.*

Our spiritual and mental roots must "go deep" into God's nourishing Word to become spiritually and mentally fruitful before we become physically fruitful and prosperous. T. D. Jakes writes, "God did not bury you; he planted you," with the intention of you blooming and growing to produce high quality fruit.

> 1 Pet 5:10 After you have *suffered for a little while,* the God of all grace, who called you to His eternal glory in Christ, *will Himself perfect, confirm, strengthen and establish you.* [emphasis added]

Two issues. First, plants go from flowers to fruits by cross-pollination, i.e. pollen from one plant must be transferred by wind, birds, or insects to other plants. *Plants are pollinated by multiple plants.* Any good works we do cross-pollinates with God in the midst of two or more people creating a bountiful and productive harvest of fruit for all involved. This creates a bountiful harvest, i.e. exponential blessings.

> John 15:5 I am the vine, you are the branches; he who abides in Me and I in him, *he bears much fruit*, for *apart from Me you can do nothing.* [emphasis added]

Lastly, *each piece of fruit has the potential to create more fruit,* but action is required: a *growing fruit must mature to produce seeds* which then must be planted and nourished to continue to receive more fruit. The fruit we receive are the blessings we receive. We take any blessings we receive, from God first and from others, and plant/share them with others and we need to nourish then share those blessings to be more fruitful with God causing the growth.

> 1 Cor 3:6 I planted, Apollos watered, but *God was causing the growth.*

Every believer's good work, whether freely given or paid for in your business, has the potential to create more good works. It requires *receiving first from God, then doing good works for someone else first before one can receive back.*

> Acts 20:35 In everything I showed you that by working hard in this manner you must help the weak and remember the words of the Lord Jesus, that He Himself said, *"It is more blessed to give than to receive."* [emphasis added]

And the more seeds/blessings you plant, i.e. the more people you serve, the more you receive, and that includes one of the smallest seeds (or the least talented person) in the world, the mustard seed.

> Matt 13:8 And others fell on the good soil and *yielded a crop, some a hundredfold, some sixty, and some thirty.* [emphasis added]

What is your yield of good works/blessings: 100X, 60X, even 30X? *Are these productive numbers from individuals with a poverty mindset? Does every person need to be equal with the production of their individual talents? Does God expect equality of outcomes?* These three questions are cold water to the face of any business: labor and management, business and customers. *Failure to properly nourish and prune a plant reduces the harvest yield, but no yield is ever equal!*

Said another way, "Trouble tests character. 'A good knight is best known in battle, and a Christian in the time of trouble and adversity.'"[127] A shallow root creates an unstable shoot and poor fruit, one that would not withstand the bad weather and testing that will come. Do you think God wants you to fall or fail? No, He doesn't. Keep sending your roots deeper and deeper into God's Word, prayer, and get well grounded.

As one's roots goes deeper, the shoots grow stronger, and then God prunes the less productive branches (bad habits, won't let go of a bad past, lack of forgiveness, etc.) for greater growth, then *productivity leads to prosperity.*

The deeper the roots, the stronger the shoots, the greater the fruits and seeds of good.

You can readily see that God used His wealth and took care of the Jews while they were "on the road" traveling in the desert.

Deu 8:16-18 "In the wilderness *He fed you manna* which your fathers did not know, that *He might humble you* and that *He might test you*, to *do good for you in the end.* Otherwise, you may say in your heart, 'My power and the strength of my hand made me this wealth.' But *you shall remember the LORD your God, for it is He who is giving you power to make wealth*, that He may confirm His covenant which He swore to your fathers, as it is this day. [emphasis added]

Man, government, or creditors can take away your wealth from you, but they can't take the source of your prosperity, God and His provision.

Prov 22:29 Do you see a man *skilled in his work*? He *will stand before kings;* He will not stand before obscure men. [emphasis added]

---

127 *The Expositor's Greek Testament*, Vol. 5, pg 205

What you have learned, what you have put in your head, is something no one can take from you and is portable and mobile. The more you learn, the more potential wealth you can earn because you can combine your knowledge and experience into performance in both higher paying jobs or earning more through your own business. We're to enjoy what we do and then enjoy what we earn, for it is a blessing from God.

> Eccl 5:18-20 Here is what I have seen to be good and fitting: to eat, to drink and *enjoy oneself in all one's labor* in which he toils under the sun during the few years of his life *which God has given him*; for this is his reward. Furthermore, as for every man to whom *God has given riches and wealth*, He has also *empowered him to eat from them and to receive his reward and rejoice in his labor*; this is the *gift of God*. For he will not often consider the years of his life, because God keeps him occupied with the gladness of his heart. [emphasis added]

Wealth brings on a whole new set and level of problems: More in number and larger in size. We must learn to grow into wealth.

> Prov 13:11 *Wealth obtained by fraud* dwindles, But the one who *gathers by labor* increases it. [emphasis added]

The Amplified Bible says of this verse, "Wealth [not earned but] won in haste *or* unjustly *or* from the production of things for vain *or* detrimental use [such riches] will dwindle away, but he who gathers little by little will increase [his riches]." True wealth building in reality is slow and steady, forget the shortcuts and "get rick quick" schemes, it's not worth it. The Complete Jewish Bible says of this verse, "Wealth gotten by worthless means dwindles away, but he who amasses it by hard work will increase it."

While it is essential that while you learn, become wise, and with your positive efforts and work become wealthy and prosperous, we have an example of Job where he denied trusting in his wealth, but trusted God.

> Job 31:24-28 If I have *put my confidence in gold*, And called *fine gold my trust*, If *I have gloated because my wealth was great*, And because *my hand had secured so much*; If I have looked at the sun when it shone Or the moon going in splendor, And my heart became secretly enticed,

> And my hand threw a kiss from my mouth, That too *would have been an iniquity calling for judgment,* For *I would have denied God above.* [emphasis added]

There's a saying about rich people, "He who dies with the most toys wins." But a new saying is, "He who dies with the most toys still dies!"

> Luke 16:13 "No servant can serve two masters; for either he will hate the one and love the other, or else he will be devoted to one and despise the other. You *cannot serve God and wealth.*" [emphasis added]

The word "wealth" means "treasure, riches (where it is personified and opposed to God)." The Amplified Bible says, "No servant is able to serve two masters; for either he will hate the one and love the other, or he will stand by and be devoted to the one and despise the other. You cannot serve God and mammon (riches, or anything in which you trust and on which you rely)." Where is your trust?

> Jas 4:13 Come now, you who say, "Today or tomorrow we will go to such and such a city, and spend a year there and *engage in business and make a profit.*" [emphasis added]

Wealth allows people an independence from God that can be dangerous for their spiritual state, and James wishes to convict people about this arrogant autonomy. "Today or tomorrow" and "such and such" shows their lack of involving God in their planning. The future tense ("we will") of all of the verbs, "go," "spend," "do business," and "profit" displays a confidence that these plans *will* be carried out. *James is not rebuking these merchants for their plans or even their desire to make a profit.* Their worldly self-confidence they exhibit galls James in the attitude reflected in a proud complacency that suggests a blatant desire to become rich. It is not their occupation, but their attitude, which has become secular.[128]

Andrew Carnegie, who wrote *Gospel of Wealth: And Other Timely Essays* in 1901, said, "As a rule, there is more general satisfaction, a truer life, and

---

128 *Exegetical Commentary on the New Testament:* James by Blomberg / Kamell, pg 206

more obtained from life in the humble cottages of the poor than in the palaces of the rich....that from the ranks of the poor so many strong, eminent, self-reliant men have always sprung and always must spring."[129]

Wealth and treasure

> *When wealth is lost, nothing is lost; when health is lost, something is lost; when character is lost, all is lost. –Billy Graham*

Wealth. God's chosen Abraham, Job, Solomon, and others were wealthy. Bible verses show that wealth is seen as evidence of God's blessing to individuals and to those that are associated with them.

> 1 Chron 29:12 *Both riches and honor come from You*, and You rule over all, and in Your hand is power and might; and it lies in Your hand to make great and to strengthen everyone. [emphasis added]

How does one attain wealth? There are Seven Factors of Wealth[130] that nearly all truly wealthy individuals *do* versus what some "wealthy" individuals *display*, these are the seven habits of wealthy individuals and families:

- Chose the right business or occupation.
- Proficiency in targeting market opportunities.
- Allocate time, energy, resources conducive to building wealth.
- Spend less than you make.
- Financial independence is far above displays of social status.
- Adult children are taught to be economically self-sufficient.
- Parents did not provide children economic outpatient care.

The authors of the *Millionaire Next Door* discovered that building wealth "takes discipline, sacrifice, and hard work."[131] Parents and *those they associated* with their kids *taught and instilled in their children the various aspects of good wealth building habits* to be prosperous. In contrast, some families never lift a finger

---

129 *Gospel of Wealth: And Other Timely Essays* by Andrew Carnegie, pg xi-xii

130 *The Millionaire Next Door* by Stanley and Danko, pg 3-4

131 *The Millionaire Next Door* by Stanley and Danko, pg 5

to prepare their children for life, such as one friend who told me his father's only financial advice was: Nothing! He learned everything about money on his own. The number one characteristic of successful business owners is: They all enjoy what they do and take pride in going it alone.[132]

Wealth is not an amount, and God tells us how to view wealth.

> 1 Tim 6:17-19 Instruct those *who are rich* in this present world not to be conceited or to fix their hope on the uncertainty of riches, but on *God, who richly supplies us with all things to enjoy.* Instruct them *to do good,* to be *rich in good works* [Or, deeds], to *be generous and ready to share,* storing up for themselves the treasure of a good foundation for the future, so that they may take hold of that which is life indeed. [emphasis added]

Treasure. Jesus gives the best example of how to look at treasures.

> Matt 6:19-21 "*Do not store up for yourselves treasures on earth,* where moth and rust destroy, and where thieves break in and steal. But *store up for yourselves treasures in heaven,* where neither moth nor rust destroys, and where *thieves* do not break in or steal; for where your treasure is, there your heart will be also. [emphasis added]

The word "treasure" means "the things laid up in a treasury, collected treasures." The definition of treasury is "a place or building where treasure is stored, a store or collection of valuable or delightful things." You collect, store, or display your property as a way of showing off to others versus putting your profits, versus treasures, to work helping others.

The word "thief" means "an embezzler, pilferer." If you store wealth, thieves will scheme to steal it. Investing one's treasure in others, joy, and rewards are multiplied when God rewards us for doing good with the wealth He has given you. A much better focus for treasure.

> Prov 2:1, 5 My son, if you will receive my words, And *treasure my commandments* within you, 5 Then you will discern the fear of the LORD And *discover the knowledge of God.* [emphasis added]

---

132 *The Millionaire Next Door* by Stanley and Danko, pg 240

The word "treasure" means to "to lay up, to store up; to hide with one's self (lay up in one's heart)." Hiding God's Word in your heart creates both earthly and eternal treasure, nothing finer than that, and eternal to boot.

Giving

Examine one's giving attitude, one should never expect to receive back from giving a gift, that becomes a business transaction, not giving.

> 2 Cor 9:7 Each one *must do just as he has purposed in his heart*, not grudgingly or under compulsion, for *God loves a cheerful giver.* [emphasis added]

One gives for God's praise, not man's. Giving and work are worship.

> 1 Cor 16:1-2 Now concerning the *collection for the saints*, as I directed the churches of Galatia, so do you also. On the *first day of every week each one of you is to put [Literally: put by himself] aside* and *save, as he may prosper*, so that no collections be made when I come. [emphasis added]

From your earnings (*never* go into debt to give), you're to give cheerfully, and not grudgingly or compelled (2 Corinthians 9:6-7) from your successes and profits so that others receive.

Giving is a concentric circle starting from those that are closest and most important to you, God first, and then moving outward from yourself and progresses to your family, friends, neighbors and beyond:

- God - You need to find His Causes that He wants you to give to.
- Family and Extended Family - Second line of giving.
- Friends - Those in proximity and you know their story.
- Community - Anywhere in your local community such as charitable organizations, churches, synagogues, non-profits, food banks, etc.
- State, country and bordering countries and everyone else.

The point of prioritizing giving is that you help those that are closest to you because you know their story better than those that are farther away.

Even the Jews in the OT were productive in gathering up manna, but in the end, those that were the most productive gathering the manna gave to those that were not as productive so that all would not suffer.

Exo 16:18 When they measured it with an omer, he who had *gathered much had no excess*, and he who had *gathered little had no lack*; every man gathered as [Literally: according to his eating] much as he should eat. [emphasis added]

In this situation, God provided enough for everyone, but it was an *individual choice, responsibility, and reward to give* to their Jewish neighbors, no different when it comes to an individual's responsibilities today. And God will recognize all of your gifts of time, treasure, and talents because every good thing you do that honors God is remembered and recognized by Him.

Tithes and Taxes

All businesses will pay taxes; startups and entrepreneurs are no different, and as such, it is why this subject is in this book for entrepreneurs. We are to pay taxes, but the real questions are: What should be the tax rate for every individual and business? What should be taxed? How are people taxed?

Jesus and all of the references in the NT are opposed to tithing, i.e. taxation (Matt 23:23; Luke 11:42; 18:12), the only other mention is in Heb 7:5-9 and is purely historical. Here is why.

The Jewish system of *tithing is taxation* for the *nation of Israel* (versus the Church being called the *Body of Christ*) and was used for the upkeep of the priests and Levites, those that were in charge of administering the law. Tithing has no meaning nowadays because there is no Temple with which the Jews would participate. Tithing was a *straight percentage, a flat tax,* for every person regardless of income and is true equality before the law. A graduated income taxation is redistribution of wealth, which is evil and destroys an economy. It is your Christian duty to pay taxes and equal taxation is essential for the economy and is based on the same percentage for all. A sales tax is the only fair tax because it neither favors nor punishes people. That is true equality. There is no skin in the game for those that pay no taxes.

The word "tithe" or taxes occurs 21 times in 18 verses. The first use of this word is here.

Lev 27:30-31 'Thus all the *tithe of the land*, of the seed of the land or of the fruit of the tree, is the LORD'S; it is holy to the LORD. 'If, therefore, a man wishes to redeem part of his tithe, he shall add to it one-fifth of it.

Tithing in the OT was for the *Jewish nation*, which is separate and different for the first century Jews under a *Roman nation* or rule (no different today with Jews being under an American tax system). The Jewish nation had a tax requirement that:

- a first 10 percent tithe for all Jewish citizens, both believers and unbelievers, for the maintenance of the Levites for their presentation of the Bible (Num 18:21, 24). *Tithing is not pertinent for today.*
- a second 10 percent tithe for all Jewish citizens, both believers and unbelievers, to support the cost of the Lord's sacrifices (Deut 14:22-24). *This is also not pertinent for today.*
- a third 10 percent every third year which Israel required the payment of a charity tithe for those who legitimately needed help (Deut 14:28-29, "in order that the LORD your God may bless you in all the work of your hand which you do."). This was a 10 percent income tax paid by all the people and was charity and is not socialism.

So every year there was a 20 percent tithe/tax, and it was only every third year there was an additional 10 percent tax rate for a top tax rate of 30 percent.

Tax rates. How does history stack up with God's tax rates? Andrew Mellon was the fourth wealthiest man in America during the early 1900s and President's Harding and Coolidge Secretary of Treasury during the 1920s. He outlined in his 1924 published book *Taxation: The People's Business* exactly the right tax rate the Bible points out and says it concisely:

> *The problem of the Government is to fix rates which will bring in a maximum amount of revenue to the Treasury and at the same time bear not too heavily on the taxpayer or on business enterprises. A sound tax policy must take into consideration three factors. It must produce sufficient revenue for the Government; it must lessen, so far as possible, the burden of taxation on those least able to bear it and it must also remove those influences which might retard the continued steady development of business and industry on which, in the last analysis, so much of our prosperity depends. Furthermore, a permanent tax*

> *system should be designed not merely for one or two years nor for the effect it may have on any given class of taxpayers, but should be worked out with regard to conditions over a long period and with a view to its ultimate effect on the prosperity of the country as a whole.*[133]

At the behest of Harding, Coolidge and Mellon, the top tax rate during WWI of 77 percent and was reduced to 25 percent to increase revenues to the Treasury. Coupled with the big reduction in the size and spending of the Federal government created the Roaring Twenties. This allowed the US to reduce the national debt by ¼, from $24 Billion to $18 Billion by the end of the decade. The Laffer Curve, named after Arthur Laffer, was coined during the Ford Administration and described, exactly as Mellon's experience, the approximate tax rate that would bring in the largest revenue and provide the greatest freedom for economic growth and prosperity. Yet centuries earlier, Alexander Hamilton had a similar idea.

> *They can have no temptation to abuse this power, because the motive of revenue will check its own extremes. Experience has shown that moderate duties are more productive than high ones. When they are low, a nation can trade abroad on better terms—its imports and exports will be larger—the duties will be regularly paid, and arising on a greater quantity of commodities, will yield more in the aggregate, than when they are so high as to operate either as a prohibition, or as an inducement to evade them by illicit practices.*[134]

A 20 percent maximum tithe/tax rate (to an "emergency" 30 percent), provides the greatest freedom for citizen's prosperity and greatest revenue for a government to function for the good of all citizens of a country.

Taxes. The word "tax" occurs 36 times, three are in the OT (Num 31:28, Eza 7:24, Neh 5:4), the rest in the NT. Most of the NT cases reference tax collectors (22x), a poll tax (4x), and the poll tax booth (3x). "Taxes" occurs only four times (Ezra 6:8; Luk 20:22; 23:2; Rom 13:6).

> Luke 20:22, 25 "Is it *lawful for us to pay taxes* to Caesar, or not?" And He said to them, "Then *render to Caesar* the things that are Caesar's, and to God the things that are God's."[emphasis added]

---

133 *Taxation: The People's Business* by Andrew Mellon, pg 9

134 Alexander Hamilton, Continentalist, no. 5, 18 Apr 1782

The word "render" (Greek ἀποδίδωμι apodidōmi) means "tribute, and other dues to the government" and is in the imperative mood, it is a command for us to pay justifiable taxes, not overburdening taxes.

> Rom 13:6 For because of this *you also pay taxes*, for rulers are servants of God, devoting themselves to this very thing. [emphasis added]

The word "taxes" (Greek φόρος phoros) means "tribute, especially the annual tax levied upon houses, lands, and persons" and is used five times in four verses in the NT, Luke 10:22; 23:2; Rom 13:6, 7 (2x).

Rome collected taxes (tribute) for the Roman emperor in addition to the numerous local Jewish taxes (See Tribute Penny[135]). When Jesus is asked in Matthew 22 about "paying tribute to Caesar," he says, "render to Caesar the things that are Caesar's; and to God the things that are God's." It was the combination of tax from Jewish leaders (Matt 23:13, 23; Luke 11:43, 46) and Roman requirements that one readily sees how the Jewish people were looking for relief (Matt 11:28-29). However, Gospel comments by Jesus in context, the desire for relief had more to do with the hostility, hypocrisy, and burdensome issues from Jewish leadership and less to do with Rome.

American Founding Father's tax quotes. Here are some quotes regarding taxes from our Founding Fathers after their study of human history and governments. Thomas Jefferson said, "To compel a man to furnish funds for the propagation of ideas he disbelieves and abhors is sinful and tyrannical." Benjamin Franklin is quoted as saying, "When the people find that they can vote themselves money, that will herald the end of the republic." Jefferson's first inaugural address he said, "A wise and frugal government…shall restrain men from injuring one another, shall leave them otherwise free to regulate their own pursuits of industry and improvement, and shall not take from the mouth of labor the bread it has earned. This is the sum of good government." James Madison, in a speech to the Virginia Ratifying Convention, June 16, 1788 wrote, "There are more instances of the abridgment of the freedom of the people *by gradual and silent encroachments* of those in power than by violent and sudden usurpations [emphasis added]." "The power to tax is the power to destroy," wrote John Marshall, memorably, for a unanimous Court in McCulloch v. Maryland.

---

135 jewishvirtuallibrary.org See *The Tribute Penny*

See the section Money Secrets - Effective Money Management Step in my book *How to Start a Business: Mac Version* on page 232 for effective money management.

Dead Last *is greater than* Did Not Finish *which trumps* Did Not Start!

12 Startups: struggling, suffering, or schooling?

Prov 1:7 The fear of the LORD is the beginning of knowledge; Fools despise wisdom and instruction.

Entrepreneurs who "go it alone" in most cases do struggle alone in their endeavor, but they don't have to nor should they. In reality, every entrepreneur goes through some of the same issues as any other startup; sometimes the problems are the same, just on a different scale. Jimmy and I are no exceptions, and like any other business, the number one issue encountered by all entrepreneurs: Marketing to find new customers. In one discussion, Jimmy talked about calling up customers to see if he can sell them what he had to offer. One of the most difficult parts of when a "business struggles" is understanding the relationships between the customer and business. The mental switch comes when a business understands "people don't like to be sold, but they love to buy."[136]

When customers buy, it is when the *customer is ready to buy,* not when the *business is ready to sell.* This comes front and center when businesses market "fishing net" versus "fishing hook" style and is best illustrated in the example when selling tires. If a customer buys tires that are expected last 40,000 miles, based on their driving habit of 20,000 a year, the customer should get a marketing piece about six months before their tires wear out at 40,000 miles (fishing hook), not every month after you bought them (fishing net).

In Jimmy's case, there was no "mileage" that he could measure to tap into when customer needed to buy his personal defense training, but he

---

136 *Little Red Book of Selling* by Jeffrey Gitomer

could use the illustration of a fire extinguisher in his marketing. You buy a fire extinguisher *before you encounter a fire* so you're prepared, not after. And since most crimes are never planned for by the victim, it is best to be prepared and get the training before it happens. So Jimmy needs his marketing to reflect this perspective.

Joke. Sam telephones Abe and says, "Oy vey, Abe. Am I in trouble? My best customer has just gone bankrupt, and I have lost $1,000,000, so I am going to close my store."

"Although you're my main competitor," says Abe, "I'm still sorry to hear that, Sam. So who is he?"

"Nice try Abe," replies Sam. "Do you think I'm meshugga, insane, crazy? You think I'm going to tell you the name of my best customer?!"

While this is a great joke, it does give light to the fact that businesses have periods of both up and down and sometimes they have to close down. Whether from internal issues that we can control or external issues that we can not control, issues *will arise* for every startup and business. Guaranteed.

But the simple fact is that having business ups and downs is a normal fact of life, but in some cases, it's downright sinfully scary. In fact, James J. Hill, the CEO of the Great Northern Railroad and the only railroad that did not declare bankruptcy because of his business acumen, has a quote that fits just right in this section:

> *The wealth of the country, its capital, its credit, must be saved from the predatory poor as well as the predatory rich, but above all from the predatory politician.—James J. Hill (1838-1916), CEO of the Great Northern Railroad.*

Hill bought the bankrupted Minnesota railroad that had been run into the ground by the government-subsidized Northern Pacific (NP) railroad, which was recklessly built. Hill's decisions to use higher quality rails and ties, lower topographical grade routes (finding the cost-saving "Lost Marias Pass" over the Continental Divide), his win/win vision with his rail customers, and superior strategic business decisions allowed him ultimately to beat his government-subsidized competitors with a more effective and efficient railroad transportation system for his customers.[137]

Hill's motto, "We have got to *prosper with you, or we have got to be poor with you*," was a significant part of his overall customer and business strategy. He provided free seed grain; imported sheep, cattle, and hogs; and helped

137 *James J. Hill* by Michael P. Malone, pg 131

create "model farms" to educate his farmer customer base on the latest developments in agricultural science. He also knew that monopolistic price gouging of his customers would equate to killing the goose that lays the golden egg. Thus, he believed in having a community of interest.[138] The equality was of opportunity, not of outcome, but creating opportunities together as a community.

Hill's quote above shows that no one lacks in potential to do bad or to commit a sin, at any point in one's life. Whether one is poor, rich, politician, business, government, or a customer, everyone has a chance, every day, to commit wrongdoing. Sin creeps in when you deviate from loving your neighbor and *become predatory*, as Hill says. Jesus outlines these Jewish leadership predatory sin issues in the below verses.

> Matt 23:23-24 Woe to you, scribes and Pharisees, hypocrites! For you tithe mint and dill and cumin, and *have neglected the weightier provisions of the law: justice and mercy and faithfulness*; but these are the things you *should have done without neglecting the others.* You blind guides, who *strain out a gnat and swallow a camel!* [emphasis added]

The word "neglected" means "to send away, to omit, neglect." The word "weightier" means "weighty, i.e. of great moment, the weightier precepts of the law." To give a comparison, it's like some of our legislators today writing laws that do not address nor tackle the major issues their constituents are going through. The Jewish leaders did things (include any of our current leaders, Christian or otherwise) to be seen of men and they looked for their reward for what they did—in the lust of human applause and approbation.

A struggle is training to learn and grow, not to suffer

Grow! The definition of "struggle" means to "strive to achieve or attain something in the face of difficulty or resistance." The word "suffer" means to "experience or be subjected to (something bad or unpleasant)." *To struggle or strive for something is not exactly the same as suffering.* To grow is not the same as suffering. When working to better oneself, in nearly all the cases the struggle is worth the effort, but it is not suffering. The pain of the struggle

---

138 *James J. Hill* by Michael P. Malone, pg 198

is far less than the pain of suffering, the main point is to see and seize the opportunities to rise above the situation. It's to have opportunity eyes.

When you're physically out of shape, a workout will involve pain, work, effort, straining, and stretching to get healthy. With weightlifting you start just above what you can lift and then over time increase repetitions and add weight. Working out is one thing, competing is another. Competing means to qualify for the competition at a certain level. Spiritual weightlifting in God's language is tribulation.

> Rom 5:3-5 And not only this, but we [Or, let us also exult] also exult in our tribulations, knowing that *tribulation brings about perseverance*; and perseverance, proven character; and proven character, hope; and *hope does not disappoint*, because the love of God has been poured out within our hearts through the Holy Spirit who was given to us. [emphasis added]

"No pain, no gain" is God's weight training, and He does test us.

When you read Job's story, he could not have done anything different with his life. He did everything right. Job's workouts were good, but in his case, he was being tested to see if his motives were right.

> Job 1:1, 5-6 There was a man in the land of Uz, whose name was Job, and that man *was blameless, upright, fearing God, and turning away from evil.* And it came about, when the days of feasting had completed their cycle, that Job would send and consecrate them, rising up early in the morning and *offering burnt offerings according to the number of them all;* for Job said, "Perhaps *my sons have sinned and cursed God in their hearts.*" Thus *Job did continually.* [emphasis added]

In a nutshell, Job was a Godly man, righteous and wealthy. Satan's argument in God's court with Job is this: If one man, who was created lower than the angels, rejects God because of adversity, then Satan's argument, God is unfair, wins. But truth be told, Satan lost in God's court because no matter what Satan threw at Job, Job did not reject God. He may have doubted, got angry, or questioned God, but in the end, Job still embraced God, and he was rewarded double what he had before.

Preventing most calamities is being careful, but is never a guarantee that you won't come under attack somewhere or sometime. Preventing bad starts with focusing on doing good, if you don't know what is good, ask.

> Jam 1:5 But *if any of you lacks wisdom,* let him *ask of God,* who *gives to all generously and without reproach,* and *it will be given* to him. [emphasis added]

The word "ask" (Greek αἰτέω aiteō) is in the present tense, active voice, and imperative mood. We're *commanded to continually and actively ask for wisdom from God who will gladly give it to us!* Oh, what tons of blessings come from this verse. The Amplified Bible, Classic Edition says, "If any of you is deficient in wisdom, let him ask of the *giving God [Who gives] to everyone liberally and ungrudgingly, without reproaching or faultfinding,* and it will be given him" (emphasis added). Based on the above Bible verse, God wants you to do good, and be prosperous and to have success. He tells you in that verse what you need to do.

> Matt 7:7 *Ask* [Or, Keep asking], and it will be given to you; *seek* [Or, keep seeking], and you will find; *knock* [Or, keep knocking], and it will be opened to you. [emphasis added]

Keep on asking, seeking, and knocking (ASK), and God will provide. And God has already told everyone where they can find the answers.

> Luke 16:29 "But Abraham said, *'They have Moses and the Prophets; let them hear them.'* "But he said, 'No, father Abraham, but if someone goes to them from the dead, they will repent!' "But he said to him, *'If they do not listen to Moses and the Prophets, they will not be persuaded even if someone rises from the dead.'"* [emphasis added]

The Jews had (and Christians and non-believers have) the answers in front of them: In God's Word, the Bible!

Disbelief or unbelief is a terrible thing. Disbelief is defined as "inability or refusal to accept that something is true or real." At some point, one has to face reality. Unbelief is defined as "lack of religious belief; an absence of faith." God has given us His Word to guide us through our lives and no matter *what experience one has*, Truth will be backed up by God's Word and rejecting what He has said is rejecting Him at His Word, thus rejecting Truth.

To prevent bad means one has to know what is good is, and it starts with filling and learning with your mind good thoughts and working on creating new, good habits.

> Rom 12:1 Therefore I urge you, brethren, by the mercies of God, to present your bodies a living and holy sacrifice, acceptable to God, which is your spiritual service of worship. And *do not be conformed* to this world, but be *transformed by the renewing of your mind*, so that you may *prove what the will of God is*, that *which is good and acceptable and perfect.* [emphasis added]

By renewing one's mind with goodness, righteousness, justice, and love is what keeps one from "going bad" in life and with your relationships with God and your neighbor and ultimately your business.

Don't "grieve" or "quench" the Spirit

At the point of salvation, we are all baptized by the Holy Spirit and become personally and spiritually connected with the Trinity (1 Cor 12:13). This spiritual connection means that we have a relationship, and as with all relationships, there can be ups and downs. When you're up with the Spirit, you want to remain up, but when you're down, you want to know why and how to get back up.

There are familiar comments within the Christian community about "grieving" and "quenching" the Holy Spirit in our lives. We hinder His efforts to make a difference in being productive for God.

> Eph 4:30 *Do not grieve the Holy Spirit of God*, by [Literally: in] whom you were sealed for the day of redemption. [emphasis added]

The word "grieve" (Greek λυπέω lypeō) means "to grieve, offend." The Amplified Bible says of this verse, "And do not grieve the Holy Spirit of God [do not offend or vex or sadden Him], by Whom you were sealed (marked, branded as God's own, secured) for the day of redemption (of final deliverance through Christ from evil and the consequences of sin).

We're next not suppose to "quench" the Spirit.

1 Thes 5:19 Do not quench the Spirit;

The word "quench" (Greek σβέννυμι sbennymi) means "metaphorically to quench, i.e. to suppress, stifle divine influence."

Both the words grieve and quench in the Greek are present, active, imperative, meaning both of these words are commands that we are to refrain continually from offending or stifling the Holy Spirit in our lives.

I proposed to a friend about starting a God Master Mind group. This group of Christian entrepreneurs would tap into God's mind, the Bible and the Holy Spirit and "when two or three are gathered in My Name" to help us pursue His business goals for our lives. After the meeting, I was preparing to send out an email to everyone and praying about it. While praying, I was struck with the thought, a "God ping" or "God download," about grieving and quenching the Holy Spirit.

It was not my normal, selfish thought about how I stifle the Holy Spirit with my thoughts and actions. The stifling was not about me.

The God ping was: how do I *grieve and quench the Holy Spirit in others?*

Shock! Like cold water to my face.

Most think of ourselves first, but how many think of hindering the Holy Spirit in others doing their work for God? Do we think we know better how God will use others? Notice the wording in the above verses, it does not say *who* grieves or quenches the Holy Spirit. But it commands *all of us* not to stifle the Holy Spirit, including when the Holy Spirit is operating in others in their lives.

When you grieve or quench the Holy Spirit in others, you work at making others and their lives less relevant to God. It means that we *devalue, cheapen, discount,* or even think who they are, what they think, or what they do as *valueless to God.* We have decided for God. How many have "taken" from our fellow Christians, with no thought of returning the favor. How many have "cheated" or "diminished" or even "oppressed" our fellow Christians in their endeavor to please God?

Rom 8:14 All who are being led by the Spirit of God, these are the sons of God.

How to correct your life starts first with confessing your sins to God, and He will forgive you.

> 1 John 1:9 *If we confess* our sins, He is faithful and righteous to *forgive us our sins* and to *cleanse us from all unrighteousness.* [emphasis added]

"Forgive us our sins" means all *known sins,* "all unrighteousness" means all *unknown sins,* so that if we confess, God will clear our sin slate clean each time we use this verse. We confess, He forgives.

Next, after using 1 John 1:9, it's a matter of daily meditating on His Word to change your mind and to improve it (Rom 12:1-2, "but be transformed by the renewing of your mind, so that you may prove what the will of God is").

Struggling versus suffering: Pain both good and bad

We will all struggle and suffer through problems, and there are three different ways of looking at one's pain.

- *Suffering for Blessing* - God is testing you directly (like Job) or indirectly (like Job's friends). When you pass, you'll be blessed and promoted. Notice that Job had his blessings doubled.
- *Struggling* - you've done nothing wrong, but you are working at becoming better and improving yourself and those around you. Not everything we do is a sin, sometimes it's just plain being human and living.
- *Suffering for Punishment* - you've done something wrong.
    - Law of *Personal Choice* and responsibility.
        - Negative or wrong *thinking* = self-imposed misery.
        - Negative or wrong *motivation* = self-imposed misery.
        - Negative or wrong *decisions* = self-induced misery.
        - Negative or deliberately *wrong actions* = self-induced misery.
        - Impulsive wrong actions = self-indulged misery.
    - Law of *Divine Discipline* - God's discipline and timing is perfect, do not intervene or revel or celebrate in His punishment of others or it will come back to you (Prov 24:17-19).

Expect/guard for stumbling blocks, false teachers

There are 14 verses in the NASB that contain the phrase "stumbling block," six in the OT and eight in the NT, here is the first occurrence.

> Lev 19:14 'You *shall not curse* a deaf man, nor *place a stumbling block before the blind*, but you shall revere your God; I am the LORD. [emphasis added]

And this verse regarding stumbling blocks.

> Matt 16:23 But He turned and said to Peter, "Get behind Me, Satan! *You are a stumbling block to Me;* for you are not setting your mind on God's [the things of God] interests, but man's." [emphasis added]

The word or phrase "stumbling block" (Greek σκάνδαλον skandalon) occurs 27 in 13 verses and means "any person or thing by which one is ('entrapped') drawn into error or sin." It's where we get our word "scandal" from. It occurs *three times* in the next verse alone.

> Matt 18:7 "*Woe to the world* because of its *stumbling blocks!* For *it is inevitable that stumbling blocks come;* but *woe to that man through whom* the *stumbling block* comes! [emphasis added]

The word "inevitable" means "necessity is laid upon me, the Amplified Bible says, "Woe to the world for such temptations to sin and influences to do wrong. It is necessary that temptations come, but woe to the person whose account or by whom the temptation comes!" Don't participate in evil doing, you're accountable for your actions.

> Rom 14:13 Therefore let us *not judge one another* anymore, but rather determine this—*not to put an obstacle or a stumbling block in a brother's way*. [emphasis added]

The word "obstacle" means "to furnish one an occasion for sinning." Someone entices, markets, convinces, or cons that what they're saying will help you. What is your responsibility?

> 1 Pet 5:8 Be of sober spirit, *be on the alert. Your adversary, the devil, prowls around like a roaring lion,* seeking someone to devour. [emphasis added]

Guard yourself, i.e. being trained in spiritual, moral, and physical self-defense and have an attitude of being prepared against stumbling blocks and against the devil, both for your life and your business. Guard your family, community and your nation. Lastly, the issue surrounding one's liberty and freedom to do good as God wants gives one the opportunity to improve and grow oneself and one's business, but ensure that one's *might does not make right.*

> 1 Cor 8:9 But take care that *this liberty [right] of yours* does not somehow become a *stumbling block to the weak.* [emphasis added]

The Amplified Bible says, "Only be careful that this power of choice (this permission and liberty to do as you please) which is yours, does not [somehow] become a hinderance (cause of stumbling) to the weak *or* over scrupulous [giving them an impulse to sin]." Do not allow your liberty to infringe on other people's lives, rights, and responsibilities.

Evil loses profit. Paul cast out an evil spirit in a woman that others were profiting from, Paul immediately created a loss of profit for their evil businesses.

> Act 16:19 But when her masters saw that *their hope of profit was gone [Literally: gone out]*, they seized Paul and Silas and *dragged them into the marketplace before the authorities*, [emphasis added]

Expect that evil competitors will take you to court, you may even go to prison for doing what is right and good, because they want to perpetuate their evil attitude of greed in business or organization.

> Matt 23:13 "But woe to you, scribes and Pharisees, hypocrites, because *you shut off the kingdom of heaven from [Literally: in front of] people* [Gr anthropoi]; for *you do not enter in yourselves, nor do you allow those who are entering to go in.* [emphasis added]

The blind leading the blind. Not only will these evil people not enter, but they will drag others toward their evil path, too.

13 Various struggles are not sins, but …

1 Tim 4:16 Pay close attention to yourself and to your teaching; persevere in these things, for as you do this you will ensure salvation both for yourself and for those who hear you.

In the military, those that are in the Special Operations Forces (SOF) are considered the best of the best and are highly esteemed by the rest of the military. Meeting Jimmy was no different, nothing but respect, esteem, and admiration for his skills and service. But as with anyone who is at the top of the game in their game, outside of their game, everyone can struggle in a new environment. A new arena, new problems, new challenges, we all will struggle with a new job or business environment until we master it. Whether it be a simple new task or a whole new job, it takes time to learn the ropes. The quicker we learn, the quicker we're productive.

Both Jimmy and I started our businesses by starting. Take an idea, outline some steps, and take action on it. I started writing my first book by starting writing; Jimmy took his SEAL experience and began training people in professional security. We persevere through the various struggles and obstacles to achieving our God-given goals.

In the NT, the word "persevere" (Greek ἐπιμένω epimenō) is in the NT 18 times and is translated as: tarry, continue, abide, abide in, abide still versus the word "suffer" is in the NT 32 times. The word "persevere" means "continue in a course of action even in the face of difficulty or with little or no prospect of success." The word "suffer" means "experience or be subjected to (something bad or unpleasant)."

To *struggle* is what you put yourself through, to *suffer* is what others put you through, struggle is positive, suffer is negative. It's important that we keep the right perspective of the pain we're going through.

Failure, weakness, and strengths are not sins

As a Christian and an entrepreneur in a business environment and market there are four areas of one's life that need to be understood, they are weakness, failure, strength, and sin. When it comes to each of these, the key issue is that not all struggles are sins.

Failure is not Sin. In business, you can fail to make a sale, and it is not a sin. Your product or service can fail; it is not a sin. In business, you'll always have failures in getting things done, you missed an appointment, you've failed to finish a project, etc. There is no sin in failure. How should one look at failure:

FAIL = First Attempt In Learning!

Simple–success comes through the path of many failures. It could be one major failure, like New Coke, where the corporate offices received over four times the daily number of phone calls complaining about it. Or a series of failures, like Edison's 10,000+ attempts to create a light bulb or Dyson's 5,126 attempts to invent a bagless vacuum cleaner. Winston Churchill said this, "Success is not final, failure is not fatal: it is the courage to continue that counts." Failure doesn't last; quitting does.

Weakness is not Sin. A weakness can be many different things to different people. You can be physically, mentally, emotionally, even morally weak, but having a weakness or two does not make you a sinful person, it says you're human. Very few people can do everything well. That means that if someone is weak in one area, those that are strong in their weakness needs to come along side and help in their weakness. We all need each other because of our various weaknesses.

Not all pain is sin. When you are weak, you need to strengthen yourself. In military circles there's a saying, "Pain is weakness leaving the body." When you are doing mental, spiritual, emotional, or physical learning or training, whether for an encounter with an enemy in the military or training oneself to be better in a specific area of one's life, there is inevitably some pain from the work that is involved. There's pain in making mistakes, pain involved with repetition to get it right, pain with doing it wrong, and even pain when it is applied in a real world situation versus doing something in training or a classroom. Jesus wants us to work at His Ministry, so weakness and pain are a pair that will be inevitable to your journey. Embrace the suck and wear it as a badge of honor.

> 2 Cor 12:7 Because of the surpassing greatness of the revelations, for this reason, to keep me from exalting myself, *there was given me a thorn in the flesh, a messenger of Satan to torment [Literally: beat] me—to keep me from exalting myself!* [emphasis added]

Paul had pain. God wants to lift us up by giving us permission to use 100 percent of our talents and skill sets, but He *does not* want us to get arrogant, egotistical, covetous, or selfish about them either. Either God handles it to prevent that or we take responsibility to prevent it by focusing on serving others.

Strength is not Sin. Each having our individual strengths is not sinning. Those that are weak in your strength might consider you arrogant, but in and of itself having a strength is not a sin. Since everyone has various strengths, we're to use our strengths to help others in their weaknesses. Competition is not sinning. Strength of force or violence, as used in law enforcement or the military, is not sinning when used justly.

But sin sprouts from them and unbelief

Weakness, strength, or failure in the human pot of experience, none of these are or become sin, either individually or together. Even *having a thought* of a weakness, a strength, or a failure in and of itself is not a sin, it is only when one feeds the thought and then takes an action on that thought to do something negative that it turns into sin. For example, anger is not sin.

> Eph 4:26 *BE ANGRY, AND yet DO NOT SIN;* do not let the sun go down on your anger, [emphasis added]

There are seven sins the Lord hates.

> Prov 6:16-19 There are six things which the LORD hates, Yes, *seven which are an abomination* to [Literally: of His soul] Him: Haughty eyes, a lying tongue, And hands that shed innocent blood, A heart that devises wicked plans, Feet that run rapidly to evil, A false witness who utters lies, And *one who spreads [Literally: sends out] strife among brothers.* [emphasis added]

But God tells us in this next verse what goes to the heart of the matter for God to look down on these abominations.

> Prov 26:22, 25 The *words of a whisperer* are like dainty morsels, And they go down into the innermost [Literally: chambers of the belly] parts of the body. When he [Literally: his voice is gracious] speaks graciously, do not believe him, *For there are seven abominations in his heart.* [emphasis added]

So the gossiper has all seven abominations in their heart. Jewish rabbis says that *when you murder*, you kill a person once, but *when you gossip*, you kill many times over. Your words are like a leaf-filled bag dumped on a windy day; you can't bring the blown leaves, or your words, back once they are out. Negative words spoken by others kill, or murder, a person's spirit, and death of one's spirit comes not by a thousand cuts, but a few words repeated over and over again and turn into thousands of words.

And of course, there's the ever-present human trait.

> Prov 16:18 *Pride goes before destruction*, And a haughty spirit before stumbling. [emphasis added]

In the religious world sin is very often the topic of discussion among many people. The problem is based on the discussion above; it's finding the right focus of both what is sin as well as what is just plain being human.

> Jas 1:14-15 But each *one is tempted* when he is *carried away and enticed by his own lust.* Then *when lust has conceived, it gives birth to sin*; and when sin is accomplished, it brings forth death. [emphasis added]

The word "sin" means "that which is done wrong, committed or resultant sin, an offense, a violation of the divine law in thought or in act." Sin is succumbing to one's thoughts and taking action on one's weakness, strength, or failure and once sin enters into one's mind it hinders the revelation of truth. There are:

- *Sins of commission* are an active part doing bad to others. For example, the robbers assaulting a man in the story of the Good Samaritan (Luke 10:25-37). Another, someone is evicted and you take the evicted persons things (it's NOT your property, you didn't earn it, so that's stealing!) and use the excuse "finders keepers" to take it home with you. Or, you expect and take more than is required to make amends for a mistake someone else makes.

- *Sins of omission* mean you do not take action. The priest and the Levite in the Good Samaritan story who failed to help the beaten man. In a business setting, you'd fail to admit to others that there is a problem with your product in the hopes that the problem and your customer will just go away. In an emergency or criminal setting, one does not assist the person in need, such as a person being evicted, you do not help, such as providing some temporary shelter for the individual or their things.

Whether in thought, word or deed, sin happens. The Bible says about sinning.

> 1 John 1:8 If we say that *we have no sin*, we are deceiving ourselves and the truth is not in us. [emphasis added]

Ah, if we have no sin that means we're sinless, we did not sin yesterday, today, or in the future. And seeing it from the other side.

> 1 John 1:10 If we say that *we have not sinned*, we make Him a liar and His word is not in us. [emphasis added]

We never sinned in our lives? Denial! Not quite, from the day we're born the opportunity is always there.

> Luke 22:31-32 Simon, Simon, behold, *Satan has demanded permission* to sift you like wheat; but I have prayed for you, that your *faith may not fail;* and you, when once you have turned again, *strengthen your brothers.* [emphasis added]

The word "fail" here means "to fail, i.e. to leave off, cease, stop," this definition is not our english definition of "be unsuccessful in achieving one's goal." The Amplified Bible, Classic Edition states, "Simon, Simon (Peter), listen! Satan [a] has asked excessively that [all of] you be given up to him [out of the power and keeping of God], that he might sift [all of] you like grain, But I have prayed especially for you [Peter], that your [own] faith may not fail; and when you yourself have turned again, strengthen and establish your brethren." Jesus says:

> *"I working against Satan, and [was] successful. … that thy faith may not (utterly) fail or die (Luke 16:9), though it prove weak or inadequate for the moment. Job's faith underwent eclipse. He did not curse God, but for the time he lost faith in the reality of a Divine government in human affairs. So Peter never ceased to love Jesus, but he was overpowered by fear and the instinct of self-preservation."*[139]

The above definition of "fail" is different from the next verses.

> 2 Cor 13:5-6 *Test yourselves* to see if you are in the faith; examine yourselves! Or do you not recognize this about yourselves, that Jesus Christ is in you—unless indeed you fail [Literally: are unapproved] the test? But I trust that you will realize that we ourselves [Literally: are not unapproved] *do not fail the test.* [emphasis added]

Here the word "test" (Greek πειράζω peirazō) means "to try, make a trial of, test" and is in the present, imperative, meaning we're commanded to test continually to see if we're "in the faith." It's either on or off, not how much. Why do you think God says we're to "meditate day and night" on His word (Josh 1:8)? So that we don't give our human lusts an opportunity to motivate us to sin.

The word "fail" here means "which does not prove itself to be as it ought." The Amplified Bible says, "Examine *and* test *and* evaluate your own selves to see whether you are holding to your faith *and* showing the proper fruits of it. Test *and* prove yourselves [not Christ]. Do you not yourselves realize *and* know [thoroughly by an ever-increasing experience] that Jesus Christ is in you—unless you are [counterfeits] disapproved on trial and rejected? But I hope you will recognize and know that we are not disapproved on trial *and* rejected." Notice that Paul says there are Christian counterfeits, outwardly doing what other Christians do, but inwardly are still an unbeliever or carnal believer with carnal motivations.

---

139 *The Expositors Greek New Testament*, Vol 1, pg 628

We're to test to see if we've "disconnected" from operating under the motivations of the Holy Spirit and the Bible versus operating under our secular motivation.

From unbelief to doubt to belief

The word "unbelief" occurs ten times in the NASB. The Jews leaving Egypt had unbelief regarding God's promises (Num 14:11) to them, even after all of His miracles and hardness of their heart (Heb 3:7-19). Jesus was restricted by towns from doing miracles in them because of their unbelief (Mark 6:4-6; 9:22-29). Unbelief will appear to be extremely heinous because it is the parent of every other iniquity; unbelief not only begets, but fosters sin; unbelief disables a person for the performance of any good work.

Having *doubt* means you're open to the evidence, and because you have faith, God can and will work with that. *Unbelief* is the absence of faith after seeing the evidence of truth. Doubt is faith that is just above zero; unbelief is zero faith in the face of just above zero evidence and facts.

> *Christ never failed to distinguish between doubt and unbelief. Doubt is can't believe. Unbelief is won't believe. Doubt is honesty. Unbelief is obstinacy. Doubt is looking for light. Unbelief is content with darkness. –Henry Drummond*

It is the *object of faith*, namely Jesus Christ and His plan and purpose for your life and business, that fosters every virtue that counts, not the worthiness or amount of the person with faith. There is no merit in believing; the merit lies in the object of faith. To conquer doubt and unbelief (cf. Rom 11:30, 32; Heb 4:6, 11) is to love and hope, it means to take positive actions to overcome negative feelings. It is only when we enter into His rest through belief that we can move forward (Heb 4:1-13).

> Prov 3:3-4 Do not let kindness and truth leave you; *Bind them around your neck, Write them* on the tablet of your heart. So you *will find favor and good repute,* In the sight of God and man. [emphasis added]

By knowing and meditating on God's word it becomes a part of who we are. Because it becomes a part of us, we look at ourselves and our neighbor differently.

Rom 13:10 Love does no wrong to a neighbor; therefore *love is the fulfillment of the law.* (emphasis added)

In other words.

Love is the fulfillment of the law

When God is love, and we love God, ourselves, and others, there is less and less chance for us to sin! Love your customers as you love your business, you do good in God's eyes and do not sin.

The yoke to rob or con others: Prov 13:22

The word "rob" means "take property unlawfully from (a person or place) by force or threat of force." To "con" someone is to "persuade (someone) to do or believe something, typically by use of a deception." The word "deception" means "cause (someone) to believe something that is not true, typically in order to gain some personal advantage." Any time force or deception is used to take or get from anyone else, you've robbed them, and it applies equally when you rob God or man. The act does not negate the fact of who was the victim.

There are two issues–and only two–that have always endangered the public peace. … Slavery is a violation, by law, of liberty. The protective tariff is a violation, by law, of property.[140]

The basis for all economic activity in business is wealth, but let's see how wealth is accumulated by both righteous and evil businesses.

Prov 13:22 A good man *leaves an inheritance* to his *children's children,* And the *wealth of the sinner is stored up for the righteous.* [emphasis added]

Notice the phrase "children's children" in the above verse. That means a father blesses his children so that his grandchildren receive generational blessings. If people truly believed that all their needs would be satisfied as a

140 *The Law*, by Frederic Bastiat, pg 11-12

result of God's mercy and providence, then they would have no need to rob God or man. But they would also not hesitate to share their time, treasure, and and talent wealth with others, i.e. in the higher calling of paying someone for their labor. It is a denial of trust or unbelief in God. It is a rejection of God's merit as the provider of the needs of man and a poor assumption that their wealth is the result solely of their work or ability.

Rob or con God? Matt 21:12-13

Jesus has two "throw the bums out" Temple incidents (John 2:12-25 at the beginning of His ministry, Matt 21:12-13 at the end).[141] In John 2, Jesus enters Jerusalem during Passover. People were preparing for the Passover season by meticulously inspecting and cleaning their homes of any kind of yeast or substance that could cause fermentation. In the Temple, something seriously dirty was going on. Jesus found that *immoral thinking had followed through with immoral actions.* He found in the Temple:

- An extortion racket of money changing (service price for exchanging Roman for Temple coins).
- Another extortion racket of money laundering (sale of "blessed" animals for sacrifice at exorbitant prices) the Jewish people could ill afford the high Temple prices.
- His Temple dirty and stinking to high heaven because of all of the thousands of all sorts of animals that were in His Temple.

Having visited the Temple throughout his life and observing what He saw, no wonder Jesus was angry at what had happened to His House (Psal 69:9, "For the zeal of thine house hath eaten me up"; Mal 3:3b, "He will purify the sons of Levi and refine them like gold and silver, so that they may present to the LORD offerings in righteousness."). Exchanging Roman for Temple money, a legitimate business, had crossed the line when they charged exorbitant prices, sometimes as much as half the value of the money paid for this service.

Passover sacrifices need animals without blemish or imperfection. Jews coming from abroad may have brought their own animals, the priests would inevitably find "something wrong" and sell them a "pre-approved and blessed animal." While their home brought animals may have had a high intrinsic value birthing and raising the animals themselves and an extrinsic value of $0.15, the priests sold them an animal for as high as $15.00. Thus

141 raystedman.org See Ray C. Stedman's *The Temple Cleanser*

the Temple's "tyranny and monopoly tended to make the Temple worship hateful to the people."[142] With as many as two million people in the city, this was a tremendous and highly profitable racket for the priests. The clincher is how dirty the Temple had become handling all of the tens of thousands of animals with all the smells and noises of those many animals and people.

Notice, Jesus does not destroy property, steal the money, or release the birds to go free from the Temple.

> Mat 21:12-13 And Jesus entered the temple and drove out all those who were *buying and selling in the temple*, and overturned the tables of the *money changers* and the seats of those who were *selling doves*. And He *said to them, "It is written, 'MY HOUSE SHALL BE CALLED A HOUSE OF PRAYER'; but you are making it a *ROBBERS' DEN* [Literally: cave]." [emphasis added]

The priests were the "government" for the Jews (see the "Taxes and Tithes" section above) and were no longer satisfied with their "limited government income" from Jewish tithes (taxes). They abandoned a free market and the legitimate taxes paid to them, they now had "gone into business" to make money from their positions.

For a church or synagogue to operate and be *financially responsible like a business* is honorable. Clergy can be in business for themselves, but a church or synagogue is not to *become a business* using it's position as a "broker of God" or as a "rent seeker," as we see in the above example of Jesus "cleaning the Temple." In Matt 23:2-5 the scribes and Pharisees seat themselves in places of authority and "all that they tell you, do and observe, but *do not do according to their deeds; for they say things and do not do them. They tie up heavy burdens and lay them on men's shoulders, but they themselves are unwilling to move them with so much as a finger* [emphasis added]." Those in charge made things harder and costly for their people, Jesus makes a "strong statement pointing to the subtle ways of evading strict rules invented by the scribes"[143] and offers the Jewish people a less burdensome, not a "free of responsibility," way to live.

---

142 *The Expositors Greek New Testament*, Vol 1, pg 707

143 *The Expositors Greek New Testament*, Vol 1, pg 279

> Matt 11:28 *Come to Me, all who are weary and heavy-laden [*Or *who work to exhaustion], and I will give you rest. Take My yoke* upon you and *learn from Me,* for I am gentle and humble in heart, and *YOU WILL FIND REST FOR YOUR SOULS.* "For My yoke is easy [comfortable or pleasant] and My burden is light. [emphasis added]

Jesus means He will lighten their exhaustive burdens designed by their corrupt leaders. They added works and He was fighting their carnal urge to make irrelevant God's grace. Even Peter tells them putting this heavier, self-righteous, works related yoke was wrong for people, even their Jewish history shows it was wrong.

> Act 15:10 "Now therefore *why do you put God to the test* by *placing upon the neck of the disciples a yoke* which *neither our fathers nor we have been able to bear?* [emphasis added]

Notice Jesus does not say, "Take no yoke," meaning having no responsibilities at all toward God, yourself, and others. He was saying He'd significantly reduce their man-imposed burdens of laws and regulations, there was no mention of Him making it zero, as in anarchy, i.e. no laws.

The Jewish religious leaders were Israel's government, and they created *law and regulation creep.* The Jewish leaders could have changed their minds and lessened the people's burdens, but they "themselves are unwilling to move them with so much as a finger" (Matt 23:4).

Jesus elevates *servanthood* and condemns *status* seeking individuals because the leaders had multiplied the number of ways in which man may *offend God,* but failed in helping man *please God.* Everything the Jewish leaders did was calculated to produce the praise of others, they "orchestrate all their deeds for attention." Their phylacteries, called *tefillin* outlined in the Torah (Exod 13:1-16, Deut 6:4-9, 11:13-21) were most likely worn by Jesus (Mattt 9:20, 14:36). But the Jewish religious leaders "added to" what God had said and became more concerned with their status, titles, and their "power dressings" in the community than reducing their community's burdens.[144] Think overburdening laws, regulations, and taxation.

---

144 *Exegetical Commentary on the New Testament* by Grant R. Osborne, pg 836-839

Mar 2:27 Jesus said to them, "The Sabbath was made for man, and not man for the Sabbath.

When any government, association, churches, synagogues, or businesses have the power to oversee an individual's or a society's behaviors, it may go to their head. John Acton[145] (Lord Acton, 1834-1902) said, "Power tends to corrupt, and absolute power corrupts absolutely. Great men are almost always bad men." Abraham Lincoln gives additional credence to this idea saying, "Nearly all men can stand adversity, but if you want to test a man's character, give him power." This applies to anyone that uses their power or might to manipulate and rob others.

Mal 3:8 "Will a man *rob God*? Yet *you are robbing Me!* But you say, 'How have we robbed You?' In *tithes and offerings*." [emphasis added]

Tithes are Jewish taxes and *offerings are spiritual giving*, God made a distinction in these two words. The nation of Israel and other nations need taxes to administer how a local economy will work. Laws that are written to punish some and reward others is a sin because it uses man's view of right and wrong versus God's views of equal justice for everyone. Jewish tithes are taxes and *the amounts to be collected* are to be used to fund only those necessary parts that provide and maintain order for the whole nation, not for the benefit of select individuals or group. Does man rob God? Yes. People fail to pay taxes and those that have a fiduciary responsibilities with the collected taxes use the money for wrong reasons.

God outlined His tax principle using Israel's example of the *top combined tax rate* (ex. federal, state, local, etc.) is 20 percent while an emergency could put it as high as 30 percent for a short period of time. Any amount over the 20 percent shackles people's efforts to improve their lives, and those that use their government and organizational positions to improve their lives do so at the people's expense. As Milton Friedman has stated, "We have a system that increasingly taxes work and subsidizes non-work."

Higher taxes above God's amount means taking away the people's God-given incentives, choices, opportunities, rewards, and blessings for their labor.

145 acton.org See *Acton Institute* for the study of religion and liberty

The question from this information asks: If 20 percent should be the highest level of taxes, what would 20 percent split three ways between local, state, and federal tax rates look like? That's about seven percent each.

Rob or con man? Lev 19:13

You see people rob and deceive their neighbor on a regular basis; they are disconnected whole or in part from their neighborly responsibilities.

> Lev 19:13 'You *shall not oppress* your neighbor, *nor rob him.* The wages of a hired man are not to remain with you all night until morning. [emphasis added]

The word "oppress" means "to defraud, anyone, to extort from him by fraud and violence." The Amplified Bible says, "You shall not defraud or oppress your neighbor or rob him: the wages of a hired servant shall not remain with you all night until morning." Why would it say this? Sometimes there is a daily need of the worker to pay for things they are in need. The english word "defraud" means "illegally obtain money from (someone) by deception." The word "deceive" means "cause (someone) to believe something that is not true, typically in order to gain some personal advantage." The word "extort" means "obtain (something) by force, threats, or other unfair means." The word "mislead" means "cause (someone) to have a wrong idea or impression about someone or something."

Robbing man comes in many forms besides just criminal acts of robbery, forgery, speeding or assault.

> *I have never understood why it is "greed" to want to keep the money you have earned but not greed to want to take somebody else's money. Thomas Sowell*

A *customer/vendor robs* businesses when a business gives out food samples and customers take them when they have no intention of buying the product. People "buy" a product (dress, equipment, etc.), use it, then "return" it for a full refund rather than rent it. When a customer has been "wronged," they bully a business to give them more. Or, you take up a business or sales person's valuable time to gain information, then go online to "get it cheaper." They had *no intention* of buying the product or service or buying it from the person that served them. Theft and robbery occur when you take *any resources* that *you won't or don't use or never intend to pay for.* Simply put, it's called *fraud, waste, and abuse of God's and your neighbor's resources.*

A *business robs* others by "locking in" customers to their product and service so that the customer has little to no choice but to keep using their business. A business robs others when it does not fulfill it's obligations. Is it right to punish a customer when they've done nothing wrong to you as a business? You mean you can't improve your marketing and business to stay competitive with the market? Simply put, it's called *fraud, waste, and abuse of God's and your neighbor's resources.*

> Prov 22:22 Do *not rob the poor* because he is poor, Or *crush the afflicted* at the gate; [emphasis added]

To "rob" means to "despoil anyone by fraud of injustice." To "crush" someone is to "break into pieces; to trample (with the feet) especially in the administration of justice." The Amplified Bible says, "Rob not the poor [being tempted by their helplessness], neither oppress the afflicted at the gate [where the city court is held]. [Ex 23:6; Job 31:16, 21]." How many of us see those that are less fortunate not give them a second look? No encouraging words? Given them a job to earn what you give them and give them some dignity? Paid them for their idea or efforts? Or, because of your status in your area you do not return the favor you received from them.

When others see the less fortunate and see an opportunity to take advantage of them, they make the poor's situation worse.

> Isa 10:2 So as to *deprive the needy of justice,* And *rob the poor of My people of their rights,* So that *widows may be their spoil,* And that *they may plunder the orphans.* [emphasis added]

The english definition of "deprive" is: "deny (a person or place) the possession or use of something." The rich deprive the poor of their efforts (labor, ideas, property, etc.) or the poor deprive the rich (poor productive labor, stealing time, ideas, property, etc.). The Amplified Bible says of this verse, "To turn aside the needy from justice and to make plunder of the rightful claims of the poor of My people, that widows may be their spoil, and that they may make the fatherless their prey!" The Complete Jewish Bible says of this verse, "to deprive the impoverished of justice and rob my people's poor of their rights, looting widows and preying on orphans!"

The same applies with ANYONE paying someone that works for you.

> James 5:4 Behold, *the pay of the laborers* who mowed your fields, and *which has been withheld by you*, cries out against you; and the outcry of those who did the harvesting has reached the ears of the Lord of Sabaoth. [emphasis added]

Be discerning of those wrongly desiring to be in leadership positions.

> 2 Pet 2:1-3 But *false prophets* also arose among the people, just as there *will also be false teachers* among you, who *will secretly introduce destructive heresies*, even denying the Master who bought them, *bringing swift destruction upon themselves.* Many will follow their sensuality, and *because of them the way of the truth will be maligned*; and *in their greed they will exploit you* with false words; their judgment from long ago is not idle, and their destruction is not asleep. [emphasis added]

The word "greed" means "greedy desire to have more, covetousness, avarice." Notice the word covetousness in the definition, same as the Tenth Commandment in the OT, Ex. 20:17 "You shall not covet … anything that belongs to your neighbor." It has the connotation of, "I want what you have and I intend to get it." It's seeking to possess unlawfully or immorally someone else's property, no matter who the property belongs to.

The word "exploit" means "to deal in; to use a thing or person for gain; [A.V. make merchandise of]." The Amplified Bible say of verse three, "And in their covetousness (lust, greed) they will exploit you with false (cunning) arguments. From of old the sentence [of condemnation] for them has not been idle: their destruction (eternal misery) has not been asleep." It is the same word used twice in Jas 4:13 for "business" and "profit," but in Jas 4:13 it means "to go a trading, to travel for business, to traffic, trade."

Greed and selfishness have no boundaries or amounts.

Both the spiritual (church, synagogue) and physical setting (business) we're to be on the lookout for those individuals that bring in controversies and bad ideas or habits that will have a negative effects.

> Jas 1:9-11 But the brother [i.e. church member] of *humble circumstances* is to glory in his high position; and the *rich man* is to glory in his humiliation, because like flowering [Literally: the flower of the grass] grass he will pass away. For the sun rises with a [Literally: the] scorching wind and withers the grass; and its flower falls off and the beauty of its appearance is destroyed; so too the *rich man* in the midst of his pursuits will fade away (Isa 40:6-7). [emphasis added]

Whether one is poor or one is rich, remember that you are under the authority of God and His watchful eyes.

14 Survive, recover, and learn from life

1 John 1:9 If we confess our sins, He is faithful and righteous to forgive us our sins and to cleanse us from all unrighteousness.

The day I took Jimmy's personal defense training I won't forget. I was waiting outside his building for my turn, and when it was my turn, he came and covered my head with a black hood. Because I could not see a thing, he leads me into his building, down a short hall and into the training room. My heart was pounding; I was breathing hard (really on the verge of sucking wind). I was ready. For what. I don't know. I was oblivious to what might happen next.

I would love to tell you what exactly what I went through, but if I told you, I'd have to…well, not really. But I wouldn't want you to miss his training experience. As a Master trainer, Jimmy trains all types of people. He trains so others can better *handle unknowns, which is your best confidence builder,* and just like these unknowns, life is God's training ground for each of us.

While Jimmy, I, other military service members, first responders, medical professionals, and others have trained to make life and death decisions, most businesses may not require that level of concern. In fact, most decisions we make we can recover from, given time, and the hope that we learn from our mistakes so we don't do it again. That's why God forgives us and expects us to forgive others. He allows for a second, third, or more chances to get things right. When we do wrong, we need to make amends, and then to move forward. As individuals, we expect the same of our neighbors as we do with ourselves. As Jesus says in Matt 6:12, "And forgive us our debts, as we also have forgiven our debtors." Neighbors forgive neighbors, neighbors serve neighbors. That is equality.

Joke. It's lunchtime, and punctual 70-year-old Moshe always walks into Minky's Diner for his daily bowl of matzo ball soup. Waiters always know he is coming in and always have his table and his soup ready for him.

Moshe sits down at his usual table and smiles at his regular waiter Steve. Almost immediately, a bowl of soup is placed in front of Moshe. But as Steve is walking away, Moshe quickly calls him back to his table. "Please taste this soup," Moshe says to Steve.

"Why?" asks Steve. It's the same soup as you always have."

"Please taste the soup already," Moshe says again to Steve.

"But there's nothing wrong with your soup," says Steve.

"For the third time, Steve, I ask you, please taste the soup," says Moshe.

"Alright…if you insist," says Steve, looking around the table. "But where's the spoon?"

"Ah hah," says Moshe raising his finger and a big smile on his face.

All things work together. When we're in a bad situation, most times it's our fault, we caused the problem, and we're living with the consequences of our thoughts, decisions, and actions. But sometimes things are out of our control and bad things do happen to good people.

> Rom 8:28 And we know that God causes *all things to work together for good* to those who love God, to those who are called according to His purpose. [emphasis added]

While all things work together for good, not all things that happen are good. We bring things on ourselves, others put things on us, but there is a third way. You may not be able to get out your situation right now. God has you right where He wants you, for a reason; He wants you to change.

Growth means learning a lesson, a new path to take, or instilling a new habit

How quickly do you learn the lesson? Change your path? Or instill that new habit? God wants us to grow, and it *depends on your willingness to make permanent changes to your life* for the better. Most of your answers are in God's Word. For Moses, though, his change took 40 years in the desert.

Moses in the desert - Sufferings turn into blessings

In Exodus 2:11-12 it says of Moses, "he struck down the Egyptian and hid him in the sand." Pharaoh wanted Moses killed, so Moses fled to Midian (Exod 2:15) and stayed there for 40 years. Why did Moses stay 40 years and not 10, 29, or 15 in the desert?

Moses didn't go back to the Jews until 40 years had past because there are things that are out of your and my control and God is watching out for us and turns all bad into good. God tells Moses (Exod 4:19), "Go back to Egypt, for all the men who were seeking your life are dead."

Moses could not go back because it was *not the right time to go back*, in the meantime, the Jews suffered an additional 40 years. Are you a Moses? Or are you a Jew that is waiting for a Moses to lead you to the Promised Land? It may or may not be your fault you're not where you want to be, but keep on keeping on. God's timing is everything.

At the right time, God says to Moses to "circle the wagons" of the Jews from Egypt, and take them where? To the desert! So who were the Jews going to listen to about how to live in the desert? Moses, who now could *share 40 years of living in the desert* with the hundreds of thousands of Jews who were following him into the desert! That is a lot of people to train in new habits.

Lessons Learned:

- Moses was learning *how to live in the desert* in Midian, learning about flora and fauna, providing for his family in a desert environment.
- How long would it have taken for Moses to learn what he needed to know (medicinal plants, what to eat, and not to eat, etc.). We don't know, but *to be proficient with the knowledge* with it would have taken years.
- God gives, takes, or even allows detours and backward steps (curses and other negatives) and uses all of them for His glory. *Spending time and effort improving our talents and skills is profitable for our growth and His glory.*
- God takes trials and tribulations and *turns them into blessings* when we trust in Him for the path we take.

You find the same idea in Deut 23:5, "the Lord your God turned the curse into a blessing for you because the Lord your God loves you." Neh 13:2 records this example for others to learn, "However, our God turned the curse into a blessing."

Joseph in jail - God's in your life, His timing is perfect

Joseph, the one with the coat of many colors, was sold into slavery to traders by his brothers. But the Lord was with Joseph (Gen 39:2-3, 21-23;) and "caused all that he did to prosper" (Not all "injustices" against the Jews were not met with violence?). The traders took Joseph down to Egypt where Potiphar, an officer, and head of the kitchen of Pharaoh, bought him. Joseph was successful there (Gen 39:2-3) and Potiphar made Joseph his personal attendant, putting him in charge of the entire household.

Joseph was well-built and handsome (Gen 39:6) and after some time Potiphar's wife tried to seduce him (Gen 39:7). She approached Joseph day after day, and he refused her each time, citing loyalty to Potiphar and to God (Gen 39:8-9). One day, Joseph came into the house to work, Potiphar's wife grabbed his coat, and he ran away. She then pretended that Joseph had tried to seduce her and slandered him first to her servants and then to her husband (Gen 39:11-18). Potiphar was furious and sent Joseph to a jail for the king's prisoners.

Long story short, Joseph helped the butler get out of jail, and Joseph asked him to remember him before Potiphar (Gen 40:14). The butler didn't, even though Joseph wanted it to happen, because God's timing was not ready. *Joseph was in jail for two years* (Gen 41:1) for having done nothing wrong. Then the Pharaoh had a dream, and the butler reminded him about Joseph. The Pharaoh heard his dream interpretation and then gave Joseph the rank of *second in command* and to administer and gather the seven years of grain to prepare for the seven years of drought.

Lessons Learned:

- you might be going through difficult times, did nothing wrong to end up in your situation, *always do good and do not seek revenge* so that God will still be with you.
- God is just, and He may be *preparing your way* for better things or to help others. Any bad decisions you make during this troubling time might cause God's plans for you to go awry.
- God uses various *setbacks,* not for our *slaughter* to take us out, but for our *setups* for greater good, so don't quit just yet.

Job's HOPE, faith of a mustard seed

In some instances, you're doing everything right and events that are beyond your control happen to you. All you sometimes have is hope, and if things look hopeless, then you're not looking in the right place. HOPE = Hold On Pain Ends.

Job was just such a man and his family. In Job 1:1, 5, it says, Job "was blameless, upright, fearing God and turning away from evil" and watching his family and offered "burnt offerings according to the number of them all" that "perhaps my sons have sinned and cursed God in their hearts. Thus Job did continually."

Job lived and worked and did good. And God blessed Job because of it. But testing was to begin, but not just for Job as we will see.

In Job 1:6-22 the first attack by Satan and in Job 2:1-10 is the second and final attack. Thus begins Jobs commentary on his life and how he lived and how Job's friends saw his life. We'll handle the business side and focus on Job's results: How to see Job gives one example as to what it takes to recover. In the last chapter, Job gives what he learned, after much discussion over the previous chapters with his friends. Chapter 42 is the culmination of all of the discussions Job had with his friends.

Lessons Learned:

- *God is in complete control,* and everyone's life is accountable to God, and to each other.
- Job acknowledges trusting in God (Job 13: 15, "Though He slay me, I will hope in Him") and in God's will (Job 42:6, "Therefore I retract, and I repent in dust and ashes").
- Job did nothing wrong; *God was testing him* (See Exod 16:4, "that I may test them, whether or not they will walk in My instruction [law]).
- Job's friends are a different matter; *they judged Job* with various arguments supporting their judgment of his calamity.
- Job's *friends were being tested on how they responded* to Job's calamity (Job 42:7, "because you have not spoken of Me what is right as My servant Job has."
- Job lost his family and business life, and he rightfully and agreeably questioned why God would do what He was doing to him, *Job never lost sight of who God is.*
- Job in the *physical realm* was at the lowest point in life as someone who lost everything including one's health. In the *spiritual realm,* he was at the highest he could attain from God's perspective, Job 42:8, "My Servant Job will pray for you." While Job's position was *physically low and bankrupt*, he was *spiritually high and wealthy*, Job's friends position were the opposite, physically high and spiritually low.

- Job's spiritual high position required him to *pray for his enemies*, even in his current physical situation (See Paul's "thorn" 2 Cor 12:7).
- Job *prayed for his enemies* God blessed him once again. Job 42:10, "And the *Lord restored the fortunes of Job when he prayed for his friends*, and the Lord increased all that Job had twofold [emphasis added]". God prospered Job for passing His test, and *Job's restoration took years to occur.*
- Job's friends "reinvested" in Job's success, Job 42:11, "And *each one gave him one piece of money*, and *each a ring of gold* [emphasis added]".
- Never judge someone's calamity. Be the Good Samaritan (Luke 10:29-37) and help others out, regardless of who they are or what they are going through (Acts 10:1, 4, 22, 31, 34-35).

Having the faith of a mustard seed. Entering into a very difficult part of our life, I was motivationally empty. Flat, running on fumes from my motivational and emotional tank. I was eking along, like when you see a car running out of gas, lurching forward with each last gasp of getting the last bit of gas into the engine. That was where my wife's and my life were in 2009-12. But it was not until I attended a Christian men's weekend retreat in the fall of 2014 that I got some clarity concerning this earlier "dark period." A doctor diagnosed my very good friend Mike's wife with breast cancer and he told me that Saturday. Praying for Mike, his wife, and their five-year-old little girl the Monday after the retreat I had a "God ping" while specifically praying for them. It was only then that I fully understood, looking back and having "come through" this time, what it means to have the "faith of a mustard seed."

When physically, mentally, emotionally, or spiritually "all seems lost" or is overwhelming, picture in your mind holding one, lone mustard seed between your thumb and finger. That one small seed may represent the total of your faith at this very moment or period in life. Hold on, don't let go. Hold On Pain Ends = HOPE.

It's easy to be "faithful" when things are going well, the testing of our faith comes in times of struggle or trouble. In all areas of our lives, God uses our experiences to bring light and understanding and remind us of Scripture. No different than being tested in math, english, or gym in school. Hold onto that one mustard seed of faith until you pass this God test. Job's experience above showed that not only was he being tested, but so were his friends. Job passed his test, his friends did not. Pass your test so God will promote you just as He did with Job after he passed.

Prodigal Son - We suffer until we learn Luk 15:11-32

In the story of the Prodigal Son in Luke 15:11-32, here's a son who "had it all" living at home with his father.

Lessons Learned:

- asked for a share of his father's estate (v. 12).
- squandered it with bad living (v. 13-14).
- a famine hit and no one felt sorry for him, ended up feeding pigs, the lowest of the low for a Jew (v. 15-16).
- the son *became aware* and then "*came to his senses*" and realized his sinful ways, to *God first and his father second,* and planned and determined what he would do (v. 17-18).
- he reasoned (thought through his situation); he *changed his mind* (repented); then most importantly *changed direction* about his life's path; *did not call home* for help (no prayers or letters sent); but *took action steps* to head home and *demonstrated to God and all around him* his changed attitude and actions (v. 19).
- his father, who *never went after his wayward son,* was waiting and watching for his return (notice that this is a perfect illustration of God and wayward man). Man *wanders away* (Prov 15:29) from God, *then he changes direction and turns back*, God never moves (v. 20).
- the son said, "Father, I have *sinned against heaven (God first) and in your sight (man second)*" (v. 21).
- the son repented, but *his father never intimated or acknowledged* that he forgave his son, told him of all of the wealth he lost, or demanded him to do something more for his forgiveness. The *father went straight into celebrating the return of his son*, much like our Father in Heaven does with us when we return. *Riches are replaceable, relationships matter more* (v. 22-24).
- the prodigal father *so wanted to help his son,* but did not want to enable him by funding his bad habits and poor choices. Once his son had changed his path, he showered him with love and blessings.
- it's all about our Heavenly *relationship,* never about the *riches.*

God wants us back in that relationship with Him! Jesus was telling the Jews they were the prodigal son; they were squandering their spiritual inheritance with the world (See Matt 21:33-45, especially verse 45). If they just were to return to God and resume their relationship with Him. If you don't know, ask God for direction and knowledge, then apply it to your life and the marketplace.

> Jam 1:5 But *if any of you lacks wisdom,* let him *ask of God,* who *gives to all generously and without reproach,* and it *will be given* to him. [emphasis added]

Ask!

15 Bibliography and resources

Rev 22:9 But he said to me, "Do not do that. I am a fellow servant of yours and of your brethren the prophets and of those who heed the words of this book; worship God."

When it comes to being an entrepreneur and running a business, it touches a number of different subjects: relationships, economics, money, systems, process, people, rewards, personalities, good, right, wrong, bad, heaven, and hell. The Bible is the starting point, because there never will be just one book that can handle all of the subjects a business needs. Much like learning from the Bible about the soul, there is not much medical content in the Bible regarding the brain. and one has to consult with medical text books to find more details. Same with books about startups and entrepreneurs and the subject of entrepreneurship.

Bonuses, books and documents

Head over the website the HWJDB.com and check out the bonus chapters and materials that are available to those that have purchased this book. Here is the info to connect, updates will occur, so check back:

URL: http://wp.me/P5KgZE-4P
Password is: hwjdb150305

Just as the Bible points out the good, the bad, and the Truth, so each resource below will do the same. You as an individual must pick and choose which resource you will readily apply toward your life as it is your responsibility to do as God leads you. You don't throw out the Bible because it tells you both truth and lies, but what is important is being able to discern between what are lies and what is the truth.

1. The Bible.
2. *The Theory of Moral Sentiments*, by Adam Smith.
3. *The DNA of Relationships*, by Dr. Gary Smalley.
4. *Crucial Conversations: Tools for Talking When Stakes are High* by Patterson, Grenny, McMillan, and Switzler.
5. *Servant Leader*, by Ken Blanchard.
6. *The One Thing*, by Gary Keller.
7. *Half Time*, by Bob Buford.
8. *So What Do YOU Do: Discovering the Genius Next Door with One Simple Question* by Joel Comm
9. *The Art of Work*, by Jeff Goins
10. *Lead like Jesus*, by Ken Blanchard.
11. *First Steps to Wealth*, by Dani Johnson.
12. *The Law*, by Frederic Bastiat.
13. *I, Pencil*, by Leonard E. Read.
14. *Thou Shall Prosper*, by Rabbi Lapin.
15. *Instinct: The Power to Unleash Your Inborn Drive* by T. D. Jakes.
16. *Start with Why*, by Simon Sinek.
17. *Economics in One Lesson*, by Henry Hazlitt.
18. The Declaration of Independence.
19. *The Road to Serfdom*, by F.A. Hayek.
20. *The Secret: What Great Leaders Know -- And Do* by Mark Miller and Ken Blanchard.
21. Constitution of the United States.
22. The Federalist Papers.
23. *The One Minute Entrepreneur*, by Ken Blanchard and Don Hutson.
24. *The E-Myth Revisited*, by Michael E. Geber.
25. *Profit First*, by Mike Michalowicz
26. *Basic Economics*, by Thomas Sowell.
27. *Return on Relationships*, by Kathryn Rose and Ted Rubin
28. *The Wealth of Nations*, by Adam Smith.
29. *How Capitalism Saved America*, by Thomas DiLorenzo.

30. *EntreLeadership: 20 Years of Practical Business Wisdom from the Trenches*, by Dave Ramsey.

31. *Jesus, Entrepreneur: Using Ancient Wisdom to Launch and Live Your Dreams*, by Laurie Beth Jones.

32. *The Missing Piece in Leadership*, by Doug Krug.

33. *Business By The Book: Complete Guide of Biblical Principles for the Workplace*, by Larry Burkett.

34. *Business for the Common Good: A Christian Vision for the Marketplace*, by Wong and Rae.

35. *How to Run Your Business by The Book: A Biblical Blueprint to Bless Your Business*, by John C. Maxwell.

36. *The Missional Entrepreneur: Principles and Practices for Business as Mission*, by Mark Russell.

37. *The Generosity Factor: Discover the Joy of Giving Your Time, Talent, and Treasure*, by Ken Blanchard and S. Truett Cathy

38. *How to Start a Business: Mac Version*, by Kevin Cullis

39. *Why Business Matters to God: (And What Still Needs to Be Fixed)*, by Jeff Van Duzer.

40. *Work Matters: Connecting Sunday Worship to Monday Work*, by Tom Nelson.

41. *The Slight Edge*, by Jeff Olson.

42. *Work Matters: Lessons from Scripture* by R. Paul Stevens

43. *Jesus and Money*, by Ben Witherington.

44. *The Business Bible: 10 New Commandments for Bringing Spirituality & Ethical Values into the Workplace*, by Rabbi Wayne Dosick PhD

45. *Triumphant Democracy*, by Andrew Carnegie.

46. *Your Work Matters to God*, by Doug Sherman and William Hendricks.

47. *Business Secrets from the Bible*, by Rabbi Lapin.

48. *Business for the Glory of God: The Bible's Teaching on the Moral Goodness of Business*, by Wayne Grudem.

49. *The Mystery of Capital*, by De Soto.

50. *The Conservative Mind: From Burke to Santayana*, by Russell Kirk.

51. *The Fighter Pilot Who Changed the Art of War*, by Robert Coram, Boyd.

52. *Business as Mission: A Comprehensive Guide to Theory and Practice*, by C. Neal Johnson.

53. *Who Owns this Icehouse*, by Clifton Taulbert and Gary Schoeniger.

54. *On Liberty*, by John Stuart Mill.

55. *Patriot's History of the United States*, by Larry Schweitkart.

56. *How Full Is Your Bucket?* by Tom Rath, Donald Clifton.

57. *There's No Such Thing As Business Ethics*, by John C. Maxwell.

58. *The Millionaire Next Door*, by Thomas J. Stanley.

59. *Leadership Unbound: A Primer for Leaders and Entrepreneurs*, by Lawrence Corbett and Jerre Stead.

60. *Doing Business by the Good Book*, by David Steward.

61. *Six Thinking Hats*, by Edward De Bono.

62. *Marketing like Jesus*, by Darren Shearer.

63. *There's No Such Thing as "Business" Ethics: There's Only One Rule for Making Decisions*, by John C. Maxwell.

64. *The Most Effective Organization in the U.S.: Leadership Secrets of the Salvation Army*, by Robert A. Watson/Ben Brown.

65. *How to Lead by The Book: Proverbs, Parables, and Principles to Tackle Your Toughest Business Challenges*, by Dave Anderson.

66. *Power of Full Engagement*, by Jim Loehr and Tony Schwartz.

67. *Free to Choose*, by Milton Friedman.

68. *Rich Dad, Poor Dad*, by Robert Kiyosaki

69. *Toxic Charity: How Churches and Charities Hurt Those They Help, And How to Reverse It*, by Robert D. Lupton.

70. *Common Sense Economics*, by James Gwartney, Richard L. Stroup, and Dwight R. Lee.

71. *The Carpenter: A Story About the Greatest Success Strategies of All*, by Jon Gordon, Foreword by Ken Blanchard.

72. *Economics In Christian Perspective*, by Victor V. Claar and Robin J. Klay.

73. *Foundations of Economics: A Christian View*, by Shawn Ritenour.

74. *Are All Economists Basically Immoral?*, by Paul Heyne.

75. *Introduction to Economic Reasoning*, by David Gordon.

Web Sites

- Institute for Faith, Work, and Economics (tifwe.org).
- Corporate Chaplains of America (chaplain.org)
- Prager University (prageruniversity.com)
- The Center for Faith and Work The Center for Faith & Work closes the gap between Sunday and Monday (centerforfaithandwork.com).
- Larry Burkett (crown.org) founded his company in 1976 and covers both money and business.
- International Fellowship of Christian Businessmen (ifcb.org) is a non-denominational, non-political group of businessmen and professionals.
- The Lausanne Movement's distinct calling is to connect influencers and ideas for global mission (lausanne.org).
- C12 is a group (c12group.com) for established business owners.
- Dave Ramsey (daveramsey.com) covers financial areas such as investing, real estate, insurance, health insurance, and tax services.
- Business As Mission (businessasmission.com).
- CBMC International (cbmcint.com) CBMC International is an interdenominational, evangelical Christian organization comprised of national associations around the world.
- Chuck Colson Center for Christian Worldview (colsoncenter.org).
- Faith Driven Business (faithdrivenbusiness.com).
- National Association of Christian Women Entrepreneurs (nacwe.org).
- Christian Business Academy (christianbusinessacademy.com).
- Giants for God (giantsforgod.com).
- Entrepreneurial Leaders Organization (entrepreneurialleaders.com).
- Biblical Business Training (b-b-t.org).

About the author and book

About this book. This book was written in Apple's Pages application and printed by CreateSpace, an Amazon.com Company. The book cover was designed by Michael Schultz. The back cover painting is an illustration of what the marketplace would have looked like around and after the time of Jesus, and the sixth century AD. A cardo[146] (also cardo maximus) was a

---

146 wikipedia.org See *Cardo*

north-south oriented street in Roman cities, military camps, and coloniae. The cardo, from the Greek word "heart," was an integral component of city planning, was lined with shops and vendors and served as a hub of economic life.

The color scheme of the veil in the Temple during Solomon's time was symbolic. Blue represented the *heavens*, while red or crimson represented the *earth*. Purple, a combination of the two colors, represents a meeting of the heavens and the earth. Since this book is about the meeting of both the spiritual and the physical, the color purple is used to denote this emphasis.

About this author. The combination of both a business and a computer process perspectives makes Cullis unique in how to save and make money. *How to Start a Business: Mac Version* is his first book and this new book covers the basics for doing business the way God intended it and Jesus worked it. Matthew Bennett wrote the book *Maternal Journal* after the idea struck him having lunch with an OB/GYN doctor. The doctor's problem? He was having difficulty getting first time mothers to write down their health issues. Bennett wrote his book having no kids, was not married, and is not a doctor. He showed that as long as you produce quality content, anyone can write and sell a good book. Hence, the reason Cullis wrote this book.

He can be reached at kevin.cullis@gmail.com or visit his website HWJDB.com for more information and free resources. You can also connect and follow him on LinkedIn: linkedin.com/in/kcullis.

Please contact the author for volume purchases starting at 5 copies:

- 10–20 units: 10% savings + shipping
- 21–30 units: 20% savings + shipping
- 31 or more: 30% savings + free domestic shipping

Ecc 3:12-13 I know that there is nothing better for them than to rejoice and *to do good in one's lifetime;* moreover, that every man who eats and drinks *sees good in all his labor—it is the gift of God.* [emphasis added]

Made in the USA
San Bernardino, CA
18 May 2016